# Learning the Language of Faith

EDITED BY JOHN SULLIVAN

**Matthew James Publishing Ltd**

First published in Great Britain 2010 by:
Matthew James Publishing Ltd,
19 Wellington Close,
Chelmsford,
Essex CM1 2EE
www.matthew-james.co.uk

ISBN 978-1-898366-94-2

Chapter 3, 'Begin with the Heart' was originally published in Daniel O'Leary, *Begin with the Heart*, Columba Press (Dublin, 2008) and appears here with the kind permission of the publisher.

Chapter 11, 'Connection without Control' was originally published in *Christian Higher Education*, Volume 6, Number 2 (March-April 2007) and appears with the kind permission of the Editor.

Chapter 12, 'Religious speech in the public square' was first published in *Political Theology*, Volume 10, Number 1 (January 2009) and appears with kind permission of the Editor.

Cover design by Gill England
Printed and bound in Great Britain by MPG Biddles, Norfolk

# Contents

# Contributors

**John Sullivan** has been Professor of Christian Education, Liverpool Hope University since March 2002. In addition to his postgraduate certificate in education, he has a BA in History & Politics, advanced diplomas in Theology and in the History & Philosophy of Education, a MLitt in Religious Studies and a PhD in Catholic philosophy of education. With 20 years' professional experience in schools as teacher and senior manager, he has also been a Chief Inspector in a London Local Education Authority, with oversight of 100 schools and colleges and an educational management consultant, working with many different educational institutions and groups. For five years he directed a Master's programme in Catholic School Leadership while at St Mary's University College, Twickenham, winning an award from the USA National Catholic Educational Association in 2001 for "an outstanding contribution to Catholic teacher formation and development." His books include *Catholic Schools in Contention* (2000), *Catholic Education: Distinctive and Inclusive* (2001), *The Idea of a Christian University* (2005), *Dancing on the Edge: Chaplaincy, Church & Higher Education* (2007), and *Communicating Faith* (2010). John has had more than 70 chapters and articles published on aspects of religion and education. He now teaches and supervises doctoral research in Christian education and leadership, Catholic Studies and in the interconnections between theology and education, as well as teaching an MA course on Religion and Politics. He is frequently invited as keynote speaker at local, national and international conferences on aspects of mission into practice in Christian education. John continues to contribute to parish 'education for discipleship' programmes. John has been married to Jean for 38 years; they have four children and three grandchildren.

**David Evans** is parish priest of St Teresa's, Charlbury, Oxfordshire, in the Catholic archdiocese of Birmingham. He was educated at Cotton College, North Staffordshire and the Venerable English College, Rome. He taught philosophy at Oscott College, the seminary of the Birmingham diocese, from 1983 - 2001. He is a member of the British Society for the History of Philosophy and is currently completing a doctoral degree (exploring pastoral philosophy) at Liverpool Hope University.

**Joe Fleming** is a consultant in religious education. He has spent 36 years in a variety of roles within Catholic Education, with 25 years as a teacher in Catholic schools. He has been Lecturer in Religious Education at Australian Catholic University and Manager of Religious Education at the Catholic Education Office in Melbourne. In 2002 he was awarded a scholarship to attend the Bat Kol Institute in Jerusalem to explore the Jewish understanding of the Torah. In 2006 he was the Cardinal Basil Hume Visiting Scholar at the Margaret Beaufort Institute at Cambridge University. He has a BA, MEd in religious education and a PhD. He has a wide range of publications (articles, chapters and books) in religious education. He is currently a member of the International Consulting Faculty of Cloverdale College, Indiana and a member of the planning committee for the Australian Association of Religious Education.

**Kevin Kelly**, a moral theologian, now retired, has served as parish priest and taught in colleges and universities. He was for several years Parish Priest at St Basil & All Saints, Shared RC/C of E Church, Hough Green Widnes. He is a former lecturer in Moral Theology, Heythrop College, University of London. He has a DD from Fribourg University, Switzerland, an LCL from Gregorian University, Rome, and an Honorary DD from Liverpool Hope University. His books include *New Directions in Moral Theology,* (1992), *Divorce and Second Marriage: Facing the Challenge* (1997), *New Directions in Sexual Ethics*, (1998), *From a Parish Base,* (1999). He has a special interest in ecumenical dialogue and HIV/AIDS. Kevin is a Member of Association of Teachers of Moral Theology and the Catholic Theological Association of Great Britain.

**Pat Lynch** has worked as a Lay Minister in her parish for 24 years. She is currently engaged in research for a degree at Liverpool Hope University on the topic of Lay Ministry in the Roma Catholic Church in England and Wales in the 21st century. She has experience in building parish community, faith formation, justice and peace and local ecumenism. Her earlier studies were in medical and dental science. Married in 1960, she has four children and seven grandchildren. After taking part in the first Lay Ministry Course in the UK (at Upholland Northern Institute) in 1986, she later graduated from Loyola University, New Orleans, as a Master of Pastoral Studies (MPS) in 2005.

**Daniel O'Leary** is a priest in the Diocese of Leeds, with 28 years experience in parish ministry, in Yorkshire and in the U.S.A. He is Episcopal Vicar for Christian Formation in Diocese of Leeds. He also has 15 years experience as a theology lecturer at St Mary's University College, London, during five of which he served as Head of Department in Religious Studies and Religious Education. He studied at All Hallows College, Dublin; Lancaster University (MA); Oakland College, California (MA). He has had 13 books published (in USA, Ireland and the UK), including the best-seller, *Travelling Light* and *Already Within*. He is a regular columnist for *The Tablet* and *The Furrow*. His most recent book is *Begin with the Heart* (2008).

**Terry Phillips** is Dean of Arts & Humanities, Liverpool Hope University. Before becoming Dean, Dr Phillips was Head of the Department of English and then Head of the School of Humanities. She holds a BA in English from the University of London and a PhD from the University of Liverpool. Her main research interests are in First World War Literature and twentieth and twentieth-first century Irish Literature. She has published several chapters and articles in these areas.

**Peter Shepherd,** now retired, has been Headteacher of two Church of England secondary schools, and continues to serve the church and its schools in a variety of capacities, including as inspector and consultant. He studied at the Universities of Reading (BA in History), London (BD in Theology), Lancaster (MA in Education Management), Brighton (MPhil, with a dissertation on Christian-Hindu Dialogue) and at the Open University (PhD with thesis on church schools). He is editor of the *Journal of the Association of Anglican Secondary School Heads*, and Reviews Editor for *Journal of Education and Christian Belief*. He serves as a consultant for a Church of England Spirituality & Values project and also for Liverpool Hope University's Centre for Christian Education. He is author of *Values for church schools* (1998). His research interests include Christian Education, values, spirituality, Religious Education, faith school issues.

**Ian Terry** has a BA in Philosophy & Theology from University of Durham, an MA in Religion & Education from St Mary's University College, Twickenham, and a teaching qualification from St John's College, York. His PhD (University of Surrey) was on the distinctiveness of Anglican schools. He has taught in Anglican Secondary Schools in Lesotho, Southern

Africa, Guernsey and Surrey, and has been Head of Religious Studies and Chaplain. He has also worked as an Anglican Priest in Parishes in Buckinghamshire, Norfolk and Surrey and as part-time Prison Chaplain in Bisley, Surrey. From 1994 he has been an inspector of Anglican schools. Ian was Director of Education for the Anglican Diocese of Hereford from 2002 – 2008, since when he has served as school chaplain and once again as a parish priest. Ian and his wife, Lucinda, have four teenage children.

# *Chapter 1*

## INTRODUCTION

*JOHN SULLIVAN*

When we consider whether to read or even perhaps to buy a book we want to know the answer to several questions: What is it about? Who is it for? How is it different? When taken together these three questions help us to find out what sort of work a particular book is. Let me attempt to address these questions very directly.

This book is about faith and about learning. It takes into account the diverse settings in which we learn the language of faith. Faith is usually expressed in terms that are deeply personal, intimate, concrete, subjective, informal and particular. However, there are occasions when we need to adopt a more critical, detached, abstract, objective, formal and general approach to faith language. Here both types of faith language are deployed. This is because many of us play different roles with regard to faith at different times in our lives and even several roles in the same time period. We can be simultaneously sons or daughters, mothers or fathers, teachers and students, parishioners and citizens, friends and neighbours, employees or employers. So this book is about the role of home and parish in the task of faith formation. It is also about school and university, as settings where learning moves into a different mode and register from our more immediate roots. The opportunities and constraints for learning the language of faith here offer an important contrast with the foundational experiences from which they must necessarily build. Beyond this, this book takes into account that our faith should connect to the public world, at once plural, secular and yet multi-religious, where the human and the heavenly kingdoms jostle and collide, restrain and reinforce each other. This public world goes beyond, even while it must include, the political sphere; it must also embrace the world of culture and our global connectedness. As examples of this wider remit, this book also touches upon literature and perspectives from Europe and Australia.

The book is primarily intended to be useful for people engaged in sharing and teaching faith. These include parents, priests, catechists, lay ministers, chaplains and those working in schools and universities. Many of the readers held in view will be serving within the church and see their contribution as part of the church's mission. Some will be doing so more explicitly, more frequently and perhaps more formally than others for whom their connection with learning the language of faith is more implicit, intermittent and informal. Diocesan officers, advisors and inspectors, school governors, members of religious orders, it is hoped, will derive some benefit from this book, as well as those with family, teaching or parish roles. Although most of this book builds on experience of the Roman Catholic context, it also draws upon insights from our Anglican community in the UK and it directs attention to the ecumenical imperative as a constitutive dimension of communicating Christian faith. Thus it is offered to our fellow Christians as a contribution to the ongoing wider dialogue among the denominations about how we can better serve the gospel together in study, worship and joint action.

This book has three special features. First, the book speaks in a two-fold register. While being underpinned by scholarship, it is not afraid to use devotional language. Rarely are these two types of speaking combined. This is not a detached work, indifferent as to whether people come to know and love God; it is passionate. At the same time, it is not reluctant to engage in demanding and critical argument when appropriate. Faith must be resilient as well as sincere, robust in the face of critique, able to withstand and respond constructively to difficult questions that are prompted by life's challenges and willing to address concerns and criticisms that arise both from within and from beyond the church. Thus some chapters speak directly from personal experience or as reports 'from the field.' Here the register is intimate, individual and easily accessible. Others engage with appropriate background academic literature as they reflect on some aspect of the task of learning the language of faith or as they analyse the factors that play a part in this, either inhibiting or enhancing our facility to use faith language to steer us through life. Here the register is more objective, analytical and complex. Both registers are required and both are deployed in this book, in some chapters only the first one of them, in some chapters only the second, and in yet others they are blended in varying measures and combinations.

Second, it brings together consideration of a wide range of agencies that are engaged in the handing on of faith (for example, families, parishes, schools) and several contexts where the language of faith is expressed, explained, critiqued, deployed and applied (for example, universities, literature, the political arena, in church documents, in our own society and in other countries). Rarely is such breadth of coverage attempted in works about faith. Yet, if faith is for the whole person and if it is meant to be life-long, then it is appropriate to take into account the range of contexts where it is communicated and shared, where it is modelled and applied, where it is supported and challenged. Faith is to be connected; therefore the interconnectedness of the agencies and contexts where it breathes, is enlivened or stifled, encouraged or suppressed, needs to be brought out. If we are to learn from the experience of the faithful, then it matters that there is honest exchange between parents, clergy, parishioners, teachers, lecturers, politicians, writers, theologians and church authorities.

Third, while this book will refer to such key building blocks and resources for faith development as the Bible and liturgy, its focus is not on the content to be taught, important, indeed vital as that is. This is *not* an outline of doctrine, nor a theological treatise; it does not seek to replace such a crucial compendium as *The Catechism of the Catholic Church* or other expositions of church teaching. It turns our attention instead to *learning*, although inevitably along the way, and in various chapters, teaching also is explored. Learning the language of faith does depend on formal and official sources given to us by the church. But if learning beyond the superficial is to take place, and if faith that is truly owned responsibly, and lived out creatively is to flourish, these official sources need to build upon, relate to, cast light on and connect with the real, ordinary, day-to-day lives and normal experiences of people. Only in this way will the outer word and the inner word from God come into harmony and be fruitful as lives touch and light up lives. Only in this way will the sense of the faithful, the *sensus fidelium*, come to play its proper part, alongside - and in a healthy dialogue between - sacred scripture, tradition, the work of theologians and the office of the magisterium, within a teaching and learning church.

In this chapter there are four parts. First I speak of the respective role of the Holy Spirit and of human persons. Second, various aspects of faith and of learning are brought into view. Third, I pick out key elements in learning the language of faith. Finally, the overall structure of the book is described and a summary is provided of what readers will encounter in each chapter.

## 1. THE HOLY SPIRIT AND HUMAN INFLUENCE

For hundreds of years Christian faith was transmitted without benefit of schools, universities or seminaries. With only the most rudimentary parish structures, before catechisms were drawn up, and while most people could neither read nor write, somehow the language and practice of faith has been learned and has been passed on. Under pressure of persecution and in the midst of war, terror, torture, disease and death, as well in the face of indifference and rejection, new Christians have been formed, tested, and grown to maturity as disciples. From the very beginning Christians argued about what should be included in sacred scripture, about the central elements of doctrine, about how worship should be celebrated and about how authority should be exercised. Despite constant temptation, backsliding, scandal and sinful shortcoming, displayed by Christians at every level of learning and status within the church, and throughout every century of its history, somehow the faith did not die. Thus, faith was learned and flourished not because of the provision of what might seem to be the necessary supporting structures and institutions, resources and curriculum, nor because Christians enjoyed agreement, safety, stability, or a congenial environment. How was this possible?

Before, during and after all the work of the church, whether by this we refer to the reading of sacred scripture, the passing on of tradition, the work of theologians, the judgements of the magisterium, the exercise of reason, the practice of preaching, the faithful engagement in prayer, the care for the poor, the part played by retreats, pilgrimages and spiritual directors, by shrines and relics, by icons and religious art in all its forms – underlying all this we believe is the Holy Spirit in operation. The Spirit of God elicits and encourages, challenges and comforts, strengthens and blesses, inspires and illuminates, heals and sustains the faithful, so that they do not go under in the face of disappointment and difficulty, of darkness, despair or defeat. We believe that we are held in the loving arms of God, that God reaches out to us from across eternity, to embrace us and that our responses are prompted by God's Spirit, rather than simply by our own efforts, that in trying to explain our faith in our limited and inadequate, stuttering and stammering attempts, the spirit of God is working both from within us and through all those we meet. Prior, then, to every act of evangelisation and catechesis, of preaching, and teaching, of prayer and service, God is already at work, arousing us from our slumbers, directing our attention, stimulating our efforts, picking us up when we fall and loving us throughout, regardless of our apparent success or failure.

Once we have properly conceded to God's Holy Spirit the primacy, in time and importance, of initiative, of action and of efficacy, then we can acknowledge the importance of personal influence, of lives touching lives, of example showing us the way. When those who are for us significant others – whether these be family or friends, or people we have come to trust and respect, who we feel care for us, but who also care about what is true and good – when such people seem to live by and from faith, we feel its pull, its attraction, its power. We feel invited to follow. If their faith, whether clearly articulated or not, seems embodied in a life, exemplified in their actions, integral to the kind of person that they are, we feel moved to participate in such a life. John Henry Newman emphasised the role of personal influence in helping us to learn the language of faith: "Persons influence us, voices melt us, looks subdue us, deeds inflame us."[1] He refers to the "moral power which a single individual [who practices what he preaches] may acquire in the course of years."[2] And, of course, over the centuries the saints have been the most effective ambassadors for the credibility and the appeal of Christian faith, the most influential mediators of God's loving presence and God's invitation to share the divine life.[3] As Ormond Rush says, "It is above all in the witness of lives transformed by grace that the reality of divine salvation is realized and manifested."[4]

In recent years emulating the saints – or indeed, any other person - has not been high on the agenda in Christian learning. The notion that we might model ourselves on the life of someone else has come to seem undesirable, even unworthy. Of course, "imitation can be, among other things, a sign of flattery, mockery, humility, worship, or dependency."[5] In becoming authentically our own person, in exercising independence of mind, in freely deciding our lifestyle, in building our own self, it is often assumed that the more original, creative and autonomous we are, the more truly we display maturity. This is partly down to the picture of what we understand a proper person to be that is operating beneath the surface of our minds.

Since the Enlightenment humanity has been called upon to throw off its shackles and no shackles are felt to be more confining than those being advocated by religious authorities. In this light, notions of surrender and obedience seem demeaning of our dignity. In this light, we are not called to be copies but originals. To be anything less would be to be a forgery. Resistance to the notion that imitation might play a positive part in our path towards maturity and flourishing is also to some degree a response to the pace of change. "Although learning by example may have worked well in more stable societies, learners in today's world need to be able to 'think for themselves.'"[6]

Of course, previously in our history people believed that following the right way, the way we were made to live, was the only way to flourish, since to ignore the maker's instructions and live 'against the grain' would lead to painful encounters with splinters and indeed ultimately to self-destruction if we persisted in such a life. It was more important to be right than to be original or innovative. Learning by apprenticeship, by observation and obedience, by imitation and instruction under the guidance of a master has been the predominant mode of learning until recently. Instead of thinking that deriving a judgement from another immediately threw into question not only its authenticity as your judgement but also its soundness as a judgement, because judgements should be first-hand, not dependent on others, it was once believed that "imitation was compatible with sound judgement, but also that imitation was compatible with human freedom."[7]

## 2. LEARNING AND FAITH

While it may be tempting to think of learning as something confined to formal institutions set up for the express purpose of promoting this, such as schools, colleges and universities, we very soon find we have to acknowledge that in fact learning occurs anywhere and everywhere, sometimes deliberately, often accidentally, occasionally unconsciously – and without reference to specific timetables or schedules. Learning is life-long; it can be actively sought and it can be passively undergone; it can be unintended, unmonitored, not evaluated; it takes place beyond anyone's control, and it can turn out differently from what we or others expected. It can happen in any circumstances, though some settings are surely more conducive to ordered and systematic learning and disciplined reflection than others. It can focus on the cognitive or the aesthetic, the kinaesthetic or the corporeal; it may be more concerned with the will or with the spirit. It may be individual and it may be communal. Faith-learning will be both: the route to heaven is not a solo expedition but a journey we travel hand in hand with other members of the walking wounded who comprise the church, the body of Christ. The creed is ours, not mine; the scriptures are ours, not mine; the sacraments are ours, not mine. Yet, at the same time, despite its strongly communal nature, Christian faith is also mysteriously individual and unique to each person. No one can believe instead of another; they cannot do someone else's believing for them.

Rush summarises the theologian Karl Rahner as saying that "every believer creates a concrete catechism, which is necessarily a selection of beliefs for this or that concrete situation in daily life."[8] This is because, at any particular moment of life, we have limited horizons; we can see some things but others are beyond us, inaccessible at this time. Our location both enables us to see and yet also prevents us from seeing all that might be seen if we were differently located. "The multiple elements that determine one's horizon of understanding include one's personality, language, culture, moment in history, family upbringing, education, gender, religious tradition, personal life history, perceived social status, perceived economic status."[9] These are what make up who we are; they influence the filters through which we sift and weigh experience; these are also the ways through which we need to be reached, for they are parts of a life that needs to be converted in every dimension.

People arrive at learning via many different routes and deploying diverse styles and strategies of approach.[10] There often seems a very loose connection between the efforts of some to teach and the learning that occurs; it can seem as if the first does not automatically lead to the second and that the second does not obviously follow the first. This is not so much a counsel of despair for teachers but simply recognition of the capacity of people, of all ages, to learn in ways that transcend the intentions that teachers have for them and that can never be confined to those plans. Learning is inherently unpredictable and therefore often dramatic, with a multiplicity of factors at work enhancing or inhibiting the chance of success. It is even a complex task to identify what 'success' entails and to discern if and when it is achieved in the interactive process of teaching and learning.

Apart from all the normal developmental tasks and stages of childhood, when we expect a huge amount of learning to take place, there continues to be a life-curriculum with enormous demands for continuing learning for the rest of our days. The psychologist Robert Kegan unpacks key elements from this life-curriculum, as it relates to parents and partners, employees and bosses, citizens and leaders, in his book *In Over Our Heads*.[11] Kegan brings out the multi-layered mental and emotional demands of modern life, showing the learning at the heart of coping with complex tasks and often conflicting sets of expectations. Identity and integrity in character, intimacy in relationships and duty to bring up children responsibly that follows when such intimacy leads to parenthood, effectiveness, reliability and credibility in the workplace, dealing with difference in personal relationships and in society more generally, finding the right company for our flourishing – all receive attention in the life-curriculum analysed by Kegan. He brings together, in a most illuminating way, literature that is rarely treated together: that on the tasks of adolescence, of marriage, of work (as employee and employer), of adult education, of being a member of society in a post-modern culture.

We should expect learning the language of faith to be a lifelong task; there is no question of being adequately prepared or equipped by the end of formal schooling. This is not on account of any inadequacy on the part of teachers, nor a sign of recalcitrance on the part of learners. Learning is, as Kegan demonstrates, required for the whole of life and since faith is for the whole of life, in all of its dimensions, and at every stage of our existence, it too must be life-long; after all, we are invited to share God's life for eternity; we need a whole life to become ever less unready to accept such an invitation.

In learning the language of faith the same kind of diversity will surface as appears in other kinds of learning. There will be both moments of contemplation and time for action. Learning is a way of seeing the world and of responding in the light of such seeing. Some aspects of learning the language of faith will appear very similar to learning about other matters. At the same time, some features will take on special importance. Learning the language of faith requires not only the capacity to receive but also the capacity and the willingness to hand to others what one has received. It cannot be preserved for oneself alone; such faith withers without connection to the vine from which it feeds, but it also atrophies when it is not in turn feeding back into the vine from which others draw sustenance. Faith is one of those goods that can only be retained if given away.[12] Part of learning to be faithful entails developing the capacity to belong, to participate, to share this faith with others. Disciples gradually become familiar with, acclimatised to, practised at dwelling in a world envisaged as God's creation and as a journey of sharing God's life and love. Faith-learning might be compared to being in the water of grace and progressing erratically from paddling to swimming, immersed in a reality (God's world) that encompasses one, surpassing one's possession, imagination, perspective or even aspiration, a reality in which one can see that others too, like oneself, are also swimming, with varying degrees of buoyancy and progress, of direction and drift, of choking and drowning. If all learning requires risk-taking – and we are tempted to avoid the pain of vulnerability – then faith-learning requires the greatest risk-taking of all, the surrender of our very selves, handed over to Christ as Saviour, trusting that we be transformed into his likeness, so that we become other Christs. Along the way, during the learning, there will be times when we wrestle with Christ and other times when we welcome letting go into him. The learning will sometimes be experienced as policing our desires when they become wayward and when we need discipline; at other times our faith-learning will be experienced as play, as sheer delight, especially as we let go and let God take over. We will find our real and full self activated when our loves are rightly oriented and in tune with God's kingdom.

## 3. KEY ELEMENTS IN LEARNING THE LANGUAGE OF FAITH

At this point I offer three pointers for what is needed if learning the language of faith is to be adequate. First, it must reflect each of the essential dimensions of discipleship, and I suggest that there are five key dimensions. Second, learning the language of faith means getting to know the church and getting to know the church requires multiple approaches to be taken into account; here I pick out ten ways of coming to know the church. Third, the four constitutive 'languages' of faith all need to be engaged. I will briefly summarise each of these four 'languages'.

The moral theologian Timothy O'Connell says that discipleship is made up of five dimensions.[13] These are relationship, understanding, commitment, behaviour and affiliation. First, disciples of Christ do not merely carry out his orders in some disembodied fashion as programmed robots or machines; rather they follow someone they know and with whom they have a relationship. Second, this relationship rests upon some grasp, however inadequate to its object, of the person of Christ and what he stood and stands for; in turn the relationship helps to make the knowledge that contributes to this understanding both more accessible and 'live'. Third, the will is engaged in such way that the knowledge is put to work and the relationship sustained over time: this is commitment. Fourth, the priorities adopted and the pattern of actions undertaken take their shape from and they are oriented by the preceding relationship, understanding and commitment; certain acts will be prescribed as either necessary or advisory; others will be either discouraged or even forbidden. Fifth, the life of discipleship will be arrived at, conducted, maintained and understood only in the context of a believing, practicing and worshipping faith community, rather than in isolation and solitariness. Of course, some parts of discipleship and of Christian learning will take place as an individual activity, but in the end they find their significance and ultimate meaning only in the context of the church.

There are many ways of coming to know the church. In no particular order they might be listed as including at least the following ten features. First, there is reading sacred scripture. Second, this should be accompanied by private prayer. Third, community worship draws upon both of these and sets them in a broader setting. Fourth, the hearing – and heeding - of sermons connects the word of scripture with the Word of life and seeks to encourage us to realize these words in our lives. Fifth, participating in the sacraments is another way to allow ourselves to be incorporated into the divine life for the healing of self and the world. Sixth, we take the word out from the worship and into our daily decisions in the world, hoping it will help us to be discerning, creative, loving and brave. Seventh, we share in the responsibilities and opportunities of church life, enjoying its benefits and bearing its burdens. Eighth, we mix and celebrate with other members of the church, strengthening our sense of belonging, ownership, participation and responsibility. Ninth, we carry out acts of service to those in need; without this the gospel fails to be incarnated, to have 'skin', to exercise any deep purchase on our lives; it remains only superficially – and cheaply - assimilated. Tenth, we study the church's teaching, engage with its intellectual traditions, relate these insights to other knowledge we have and, in the process, become aware of its multiple and manifold self - expressions in other times and places. Within the limitations of one book not all of these can be dealt with properly but many of them are considered, even if inadequately, in several of the chapters in Part Two.

Four main languages jointly constitute what we might describe, using different metaphors, as the architecture, the habitat or the economy of Christian faith. First, there is the proclamation of and about Jesus the Christ, the message of the Gospel. Traditionally this teaching has been called the *kerygma*. There is a message to convey, a message that needs to be explained; surrounding the message the church has built up a set of doctrines, to preserve it from misunderstanding, to ward off distortions, in order to serve God's purposes in seeking to offer us salvation. Then, second, there is the construction of community or fellowship. The official term here is *koinonia*. Not only as social beings, but as members of the Body of Christ, we belong to one another. We need each other to journey towards God. The life of grace flows freely back and forth between all participants in this communion, overriding all other ties, loyalties and allegiances. Third, there is the celebration of worship or liturgy. This is *leiturgia*. More is said about this in chapter 7. To complete this structure of Christian faith, fourth, there is the offering of service to those in need, which itself is a form of worship, this time of the image of God in the needy person. Such service has been called *diakonia*. Jesus highlighted its importance in the example he gave in washing the feet of his disciples. These four languages of faith relate to four aspects of formation for Christians. There is a story and set of concepts to learn, a way of thinking to assimilate and indwell; there is a way of belonging within a community; there is a way of worshipping; and there is a way of behaving, the way of self-sacrificial love for others, especially the suffering or those in want. All are necessary. None are complete on their own. Each reinforces the others.

## 4. STRUCTURE AND OUTLINE OF THE BOOK

This book is divided into four parts. Part One, Foundations, comprised of two chapters, explores key principles that govern how we might understand and set about the task of helping others learn the language of faith. Part Two, Home and Parish, in four chapters, immerses us in those two basic starting points from which most people encounter the language of faith for the first time, the family setting and the local church building and community. Part Three, School and University, with four chapters, takes us away from the more informal ambiance of home and parish, where learning is often a by-product of other activities, and into organisations that have the promotion of learning as their primary responsibility. Two chapters are devoted to the school context and two to the university. The conditions, challenges and opportunities for learning the language of faith here differ significantly from those that surface in Part One. Part Four, Expanding Horizons, takes us even further away from our starting points. One chapter considers what is at stake when we move into the public square, where there is political deliberation and debate about how we should build a society where all can flourish. What place can faith language play here? Another chapter enters into the world of literature, a realm that can form our imagination and deepen our understanding of self and others. How does faith language operate in this world? The final two chapters in Part Four take us outside the UK context, with one analysing an ecclesial document about the prospects for faith in Europe and the other offering a point of comparison from the perspective of the Australian Catholic Church.

## PART ONE: FOUNDATIONS

In 'Education and Evangelisation', which forms Chapter 2 of this book, I claim that, while some might see these two activities as contrasting and as radically different from one another, they can be shown to exhibit several important similarities and they overlap to a considerable extent, more than is often acknowledged. Two objections to this claim are considered, one from a position external to Christian faith, one from within a Catholic perspective. Though these counter-positions are taken seriously, it is argued that they do not invalidate my central claim. Ten similarities between education and evangelisation are proposed. A better understanding of the similarities between education and evangelisation is likely to enhance dialogue between Christian and secular educators on the one hand, and, on the other hand, it should contribute to a deeper appreciation of some of the factors that facilitate authentic learning within the church.

In Chapter 3, 'Begin with the Heart', Daniel O'Leary addresses the priority of relationship over concerns for rationality, comprehensiveness and formality. Here a view of communicating faith emerges that has a joyful lightness of touch, one that is simultaneously life-giving, liberating, loving, experiential, imaginative and positive. O'Leary offers four thresholds into receiving the love of God: (i) theology, (ii) evangelization, (iii) liturgy and (iv) language. When O'Leary deploys 'equipment' from the church's treasury, as part of the process of communicating faith, this is always in service of, but never dominating the person(s) it is for. Transcending the tendency to divide reality into sacred and profane, he holds before us a God who is already present in all dimensions of life, waiting to be found and received. In this chapter, O'Leary offers a lyrical example of how to combine theological insight with a sense of how beauty and grace permeate creation. He builds bridges between the human and the divine in a holistic and incarnational vision of evangelization; in so doing, he demonstrates how theology, language, liturgy and life can be interwoven in communicating faith effectively as good news.

## PART TWO: HOME AND PARISH

As an example of the outworking of the vision given by O'Leary, in Chapter 4, 'Faith in the Family' I try to recollect – despite the notorious unreliability of memory – the ways I first encountered the language and entered into the life of faith in childhood and adolescence, bringing out some of the interaction between home and church. From the perspective of a parent I reflect on the rhythms and routines of family life and show how these can be perceived as providing the human soil for the workings of grace. In commenting on different kinds of talk in the home, serious and playful, I hope to show how patterns of behaviour in family life have the potential to open us up to the grammar of prayer. Talk in the family can function as soil for the seed of prayer. This is shown by reference to the kinds of conversation that emerge from games, stories, meals, sharing memories, asking questions and coming to decisions. The final part of Chapter 4 comments on other features of the life of a family, bringing out their challenge and potential for inducting people into the language and life of faith.

Having worked in a joint Catholic and Anglican parish that takes seriously the ecumenical imperative emphasised in Pope John Paul II's 1995 encyclical *Ut Unum Sint*, Kevin Kelly, in Chapter 5, shares insights from this unusual pastoral context, bringing out its promise and thereby encouraging others to engage similarly. In his chapter 'Communicating Faith Ecumenically' parish life, ecumenical theology and deep pastoral commitment are interwoven in sensitive, creative and courageous ways. Receptive learning - mutually, and humbly yet joyfully receiving, celebrating and learning from the gifts each church offers - is shown as a wonderful way for a parish to grow towards the gospel and can provide an essential prerequisite for Christians as they jointly prepare to communicate their faith to outsiders. Reflecting on lessons from lengthy pastoral experience, and pointing the way towards mutually appreciative receptive learning through ecumenical collaboration, he shows how persons of faith can allow their experience to challenge their preconceptions, and the value of being open to others, confidently trusting God's presence within oneself, in one's own tradition, but also in that of others who differ in important respects. Kelly models the centrality, in the task of communicating faith ecumenically, of conversation, backed by prayer and worship and underpinned by careful study.

In Chapter 6, 'Lay Ministry', Pat Lynch analyses faith, orients this to the Kingdom of God and stresses the co-responsibility of all the baptized for sharing the faith, for building up the church and for promoting the Kingdom. She reports on some of the many ways that lay people exercise ministry, sometimes overlapping with and in support of those who are ordained, sometimes separately. Hindering and helping factors for communicating faith here are identified: communication systems within the church, the power of the parish priest and the history of lay-ordained relations tend to present obstacles to be overcome; while the shortage of priests, universal education and elements within contemporary culture are shown as offering opportunities for addressing hindrances to lay ministry. Lynch calls the laity to share in the prophetic office on behalf of the Kingdom of God. The task of communicating faith for them requires receiving the Christian message from the past and reinterpreting it for today. She considers communication *ad intra*, within the parish, and *ad extra*, as the parishioners face outwards to their locality and beyond. Living out a baptismal vocation should lead to co-responsibility and active participation in the church and lifelong learning about the implications of being a disciple. She is alert to the operation of power in group dynamics, as should be the case with all communicators of faith. Lynch explores aspects of being church at the local level and suggests contributions that lay ministry can make that emerge from and are endorsed by the community. In her vision, there is a reciprocal relationship required between, on the one hand, personal gifts (and commitment) and, on the other hand, authorization from the church.

Chapter 7, 'The Church as a Learning Community', explores essential features of and foundational conditions for learning in general and then for learning the language of faith in the context of the church, arguing that the church herself needs to apply in her own modes of teaching the lessons we have learned about what helps and what hinders learning. After this initial analysis, I focus on key elements in learning about matters of faith, first, as the church hands on the living tradition, especially via the liturgy and via sacred scripture, second, as she addresses the ecumenical imperative - now acknowledged to be an integral dimension of being a Christian – of learning from and sharing with other Christians, and third, in the dialogue with culture that is essential to her missionary role. Finally, I return to some central communicative virtues at the heart of learning about faith. Trust, freedom, letting go, humility and charity serve as keys that enable us to receive and to benefit from what life gifts us with.

## PART THREE: SCHOOL AND UNIVERSITY

Having led Church of England secondary schools for 25 years, Peter Shepherd is well placed to reflect on some of the arguments and challenges facing people in similar situations. In Chapter 8, 'Communicating faith in church schools,' he forthrightly addresses a set of sensitive – and frequently fudged – questions and issues about the nature and purpose of church schools within a nationally funded education system. He explores possible tensions between the task of communicating faith and what are considered to be acceptable educational goals by the society that funds them. Who are church schools for? Should they be open to all or do they make sense only for children of the particular faith or Christian denomination that sponsors the school? Shepherd provides a rationale for church schools and for the task of communicating faith in them. In defence of the notion of Christian education but deploying a different trajectory of approach from the one I followed in Chapter 2, he argues that evangelism and education can be compatible. Pupils should be encouraged to be open to other perspectives; indoctrination is rejected; the aspiration to neutrality is shown to be neither possible nor desirable.

In Chapter 9, 'The work of a diocese in supporting schools', Ian Terry, experienced in depth and breadth as an Anglican pastor, teacher and chaplain, draws here on his work as a director of diocesan educational provision (for schools, further education and youth work), a role that requires close cooperation between the Church of England, on the one hand, and, on the other, the state and local secular authorities. He stresses the importance of a collaborative approach, one that calls for considerable patience, political realism and willingness to compromise, combined with a vision inspired by the Gospel and a determination to commit energy, talent and resources over the long term to serve society through forms of education that witness to the Kingdom without imposing this on others. In the ongoing practical negotiations and decisions made at diocesan level, institution by institution, one sees diverse and creative efforts at inculturating the Good News, embedding it in policies, staff appointments, guidance, always seeking ways to combine Christian 'salt' (or distinctiveness) with a generous inclusivity. If the language of faith is to be learned in ways suitable for both the informal settings of home and parish and the more formal settings of school (and beyond) there need to be effective links between the church and the school. Terry brings out key features of the collaboration required in supporting schools.

In 'Joining Conversations on Christian Higher Education', Chapter 10, I open up some of the communication challenges facing Christian educators in the university sector, as they take into account their own colleagues and students, norms prevailing in the academy, the needs of church communities and the expectations of the societies to which they belong. Then I survey some issues that have emerged as neuralgic in recent conversations about Christian higher education, with a special focus on the notion of living tradition, the role of theology, and how we might understand religion in relation to the secular. In the final part of this chapter I briefly indicate some of the communicative virtues required to carry out the kind of conversations needed in any university, not least in the Christian university.

Chapter 11, 'Connection without Control: theology and the university curriculum' addresses three questions. First, why should theologians promote interconnectedness in the Christian university? Second, why might this endeavour be problematical? Finally, how might this be attempted, while avoiding the dangers? An invitational style is proposed rather than one that seeks control. In the end, faith cannot be imposed or compelled, but its all-encompassing 'reach' or application is something to which witness should be given. Yet, from the perspective of the person concerned with communicating a faith tradition in the university, it is important to show that, whatever internal integrity and coherence a faith tradition may have, it cannot be contained within one discipline, disconnected from the issues raised in other disciplines; nor can it be isolated from other ways of knowing, thinking, deciding and valuing. Dialogue between disciplines must be promoted if learning is to engage the whole person and to serve the common good. Theology has an important part to play, both giving and receiving, but the tone of voice adopted and the style of the interventions of theologians will deeply influence how their attempt to reach out and facilitate debates about interconnectedness will be received. I seek to indicate some of the ways that theology faculty might engage with their colleagues, warning that theology cannot dictate without damaging the educational process or the cooperative culture in the university. Thus, theology can be a source of connection, but without control.

## PART FOUR: EXPANDING HORIZONS

In Chapter 12, 'Religious speech in the public square,' I examine the reasons often given for restricting religious language to the private domain. Despite acknowledging their force, I argue that suppressing religious speech in public conversations is inherently dangerous, suggesting that such a policy undermines mutual trust and confidence, is corrosive of individual integrity and that such marginalisation of religious language deprives social discussions of vital resources. Finally I propose a set of qualities and virtues that should underpin the way that religious languages and perspectives are deployed in public so that fears about this can be overcome in service of a more harmonious and enriched level of exchange in the public sphere.

Exploring the bearing of literature on the communication of faith, Terry Phillips, in Chapter 13, 'Literature and the Expression of Religious Ideas,' demonstrates how, across the past five centuries, changing interpretations of the role of literature have influenced the way that religious ideas have been communicated in writing. By reference to texts exemplifying different emphases with regard to religious faith from the sixteenth to the twentieth century, Phillips exposes some of the assumptions at work in such literature, either explicitly or operating beneath the surface, ending this part of her chapter by considering postmodernism and the problem of 'truth'. Then she provides a more detailed reading of David Jones's *In Parenthesis* as an example of how, without being didactic, the expression of personal experience can contribute to the communication of religious ideas.

David Evans, in Chapter 14, 'The Gospel Brings Hope to Europe' provides an overview of and commentary on a papal document that exhorts the church in that continent to continue to proclaim the gospel. Given that one of the means by which faith is learned is via authoritative guidance from church leaders, it is fitting that a chapter in this book is devoted to an analysis of an example such a medium. *Ecclesia in Europa* brings into dialogue, sometimes uncomfortable dialogue, what is entailed by accepting the gospel, a joyful and transforming relationship with Christ, and the voice of contemporary Europe, uncertain and forgetful about, even resistant to, Christian tradition. In his examination of the papal document Evans helps the reader to appreciate the need for a constructive encounter between, on the one hand, the invitation to share the life of God in a gospel of hope, and, on the other, those features of recent and contemporary European culture that give cause for concern and that appear to undermine faith and hope. After deftly interweaving the themes of hope and despair and appraising how humanity and transcendence are treated by Pope John Paul II, Evans briefly discusses how the Pope's project for Europe might be carried further. Evans assesses the way text and context interact and mutually illuminate each other in the task of communicating faith. The church is the bearer of a universal message, addressed to all humankind. But she always must necessarily speak in particular terminology and bear in mind particular challenges (and opportunities) if her communication of the message is to be heard and to have a chance to settle in (and move) the hearts of specific receivers of this word. The particularity of both language and features of life addressed always leave room for deeper insight, further development and wider application. *Sub specie aeternitate* all formulations fall short in some way of doing justice to the Kingdom and no context, however deeply penetrated, can draw out all the implications of the Gospel. None of us have a God's-eye view of the working out of salvation history and neither do we fully live out the limited vision we manage to attain. It behoves the person who seeks to share in the church's mission, therefore, to pay careful attention to the guidance texts she produces, as ways to expand our perspective and to deepen our appreciation of the church's thinking about God's will for, and ways of working among, humankind, even while being ready to make humble suggestions about how such guidance might need further development in some ways.

The issues facing religious educators in different parts of the globe unsurprisingly display many similarities. Through technologically advanced media for communication, financial interconnectedness and the economic dominance of multi-national companies, travellers find much that is familiar if they move from Manchester to Melbourne, from Dallas to Delhi, from Dublin to Dortmund or from Sydney to San Francisco. Thus the challenge to faith education posed by Fleming in Chapter 15, 'Stories of an Australian Journeying Community' will be recognizable to people thousands of miles away. He alerts readers to changing trends within the wider context of Australian society, drawing upon analyses from researchers and church authorities, before presenting examples of stories that illustrate the complex interaction between context, sense of identity, issues of concern to people and ways to tap into these in faith communication. In an ultimately hopeful account, Fleming presents some of the experiences of those engaged in communicating faith in his country. The examples provided are down-to-earth and small-scale, yet they are also fruitful and suggestive prompts for us of how to identify, welcome and encourage signs of the Kingdom. He provides a positive reading, even in the midst of parallel evidence of institutional decline for the church, seeing signs of new hope for the shaping and sharing of faith. Sharp-eyed realism about shortcomings and sources of alienation are combined in his chapter with warm-hearted acknowledgement of much basic goodness in people and recognition of the working of the Spirit of God when deep and imaginative connections are made between tradition and people's present experiences. It is important that faith educators do more than lament losses; they must be alert to and welcoming of new opportunities, along the lines suggested in Fleming's chapter. The Good News needs cheerful givers, conscious of God's presence, not people depressed by the passing of previous patterns of engagement.

At the end of the book a set of questions is provided. These are intended to prompt personal reflection and to facilitate group discussion. The questions highlight issues that emerge from the various chapters and they encourage readers to process the material here, to apply it to their own particular circumstances and contexts, to share their aspirations and concerns and to learn from one another's experience of the grace of God at work in our lives and the diverse ways we recognize and respond to such grace.

## Notes

1 J.H. Newman, *An Essay in Aid of a Grammar of Assent*, introduced by Nicholas Lash (London: University of Notre Dame Press, 1979), p.89. In *University Sermons*, introduced by D. M. McKinnon and J. D. Holmes, (London: SPCK, 1970), Newman devotes a whole sermon to personal influence; see especially p.93.

2 Newman, *University Sermons*, p.94.

3 For the powerful influence on the saints on the Christian imagination, see Aviad Kleinberg, *Flesh Made Word* (Cambridge, Mass: The Belknap Press, for Harvard University Press, 2008).

4 Ormond Rush, *The Eyes of Faith* (Washington, DC: Catholic University of America Press, 2009), p.54.

5 Bryan R. Warnick, *Imitation and Education* (Albany, NY: State University of New York Press, 2008), p.11.

6 Ibid.

7 Ibid., p.16.

8 Rush, op. cit., p.222.

9 Ibid., p.71.

10 See Robert J. Sternberg, *Thinking Styles* (Cambridge: Cambridge University Press, 1997). For a fine examination of the match required between contrasting preferred learning styles and adult religious education, see Yvonne Craig, *Learning for Life* (London: Mowbray, 1994).

11 Robert Kegan, *In Over Our Heads* (Cambridge, Mass: Harvard University Press, 1994).

12 See Augustine, (edited by R.P.H Green) *On Christian Teaching* (Oxford: Oxford University Press, 1997), p.8.

13 Timothy O'Connell, *Making Disciples* (New York: Crossroad, 1998), p.142.

# Part One:
# Foundations

# Chapter 2

## EDUCATION AND EVANGELISATION

*John Sullivan*

Education and evangelisation can easily be considered to be two quite separate, perhaps even completely contrasting activities. I intend to suggest that, from at least some points of view, they show some important similarities. I will claim that, far from being necessarily radically different, they are overlapping and in many respects highly compatible. It is misleading and a false reading to treat them as completely distinct, in the sense that, to do one of these is thereby *not* to do the other. I do not deny that they *can* be treated as totally separate, and perhaps opposed activities; indeed they often *have* been so perceived, interpreted and conducted. This chapter articulates, from the perspective of a Catholic educator, a way of seeing these two activities as ultimately contributing to God's work in ways that harmonise and are complementary. Sometimes it will be apparent that there are awkward tensions between the operations involved in evangelisation and those integral to education. However, I believe that such tensions can be seen, from a higher viewpoint, as moments within a larger process that brings to convergence and to fruition the efforts to educate and to evangelise. Education without evangelisation is incomplete, however valid and valuable. Evangelisation without education is also incomplete, however valid and essential. This view echoes that of Nicholas Lash, who regularly reminds us that Christianity is a life-long educational project, a school of prayer and of wisdom. As he says in his chapter in *Receptive Ecumenism and the Call to Catholic Learning*, 'We are a people charged unceasingly to seek some understanding of how obedience to the Gospel is to be expressed and realized in the cultural, scientific, economic, and political circumstances of our time' – a task that necessarily entails linking evangelisation to education.[1]

I hope to show that education and evangelisation are potential allies, in harmony with each other, suggesting that education serves evangelisation. This might seem obvious but a recent controversy, reported in the English

Catholic weekly journal *The Tablet*, and stimulated by an interview given by the Bishop of Lancaster, Patrick O'Donoghue, suggests that in some quarters at least there is suspicion within the church about the corrosive effects of education on the faithful.[2] While non-Christians may not hold evangelisation as something of value or to be promoted, I hope my argument might reassure them that evangelisation is not necessarily inimical to features of what they consider true education.[3]

## 1. TWO OBJECTIONS

Those outside of a religious faith position might well object to my claim that education and evangelisation have many similarities. Such an objection might go something like this. Education is about liberating the person from his or her present and particular cultural location and human inheritance. It is about equipping them to make their own decisions about worldview, lifestyle and affiliation. It is about developing critical thinking skills. It should provide each person with an inbuilt crap detector, a capacity to question and to distrust, inexorably, all authorities, religious, social, political, cultural, (including, of course, their own). It should make people open-minded, always ready to treat truth as provisional at best and ready to jettison such provisional 'truths' in light of new evidence. It must avoid, at all costs, closing down questions, doubts and issues, or implying in any way that some issues are beyond discussion, that they have already been decided in any irreversible way. Rather than embedding people in particular positions and affiliations, education should develop an appreciation of diversity and a capacity to enter with ease into multiple perspectives. It should give people the confidence to be creative in their selection from the cultures around them, and it should privilege individual ownership, authenticity, originality, innovation over communal belonging and its associated disciplines (and the benefits claimed for such communal belonging). It should maximise tolerance of and respect for alternative lifestyles in service of greater freedom for all. While promoting individuality, self-expression and a strong sense of self-worth, it should, at the same time, induce a proper caution and humility about our grasp of any truth, if such a truth is tenable within the relativity of cultures and the flux of time.

If education is conceived of in this way, then evangelisation can appear as a threat. Evangelisation may come across as seeking a premature commitment. It may seem too confident in the truth it advocates. It may appear too judgemental about those who do not accept this truth. It may seem to want to embed people in particularity, in particular practices and communities, in such a way as to trap them, to disable them from a more appropriate universality. It may ask for a surrender of self that is demeaning of human dignity. It may attribute much too much importance to authority (biblical, ecclesial), thereby undermining individual freedom and inviting oppression. It may so prioritise fidelity to tradition that it fails to address contemporary needs and renders itself irrelevant. It may pay insufficient attention to the diversity of views (and situations) and to objections to its teaching, leading to narrow vision, tribalism, sheep-like acceptance, complacency, self-righteous attitudes, condemnation of those who differ and exclusive practices that do not promote human flourishing.[4]

While all this *can*, sadly, be true in some, perhaps in many, cases, it certainly does not have to be so. It is possible to try to evangelise without slipping into coercion, threats, harassment, psychological bullying, manipulation and invading freedom; one can propose a faith perspective in ways that are respectful, transparent, honest and gentle, just as one can do so without these qualities.[5] Neither education nor evangelisation has lived up to the best they can be. It *can* be the case that education and evangelisation come across as radically different activities, deeply opposed, in spirit and in practice, to one another. Yet, as I set out to illustrate below, education and evangelisation can be mutually reinforcing rather than incompatible, and mutually beneficial rather than hostile to one another.

From within a faith perspective a different possible objection might arise in response to any attempt to suggest close partnership between education and evangelisation. It has become customary in Catholic literature about religious education to delineate a fairly sharp differentiation between evangelisation, catechesis and religious education.[6] Without going into detail I summarise how these terms have been used and then I explain why I think they have been too sharply differentiated.

Evangelisation has been taken to be an attempt to convey the Gospel to those who do not know it. It is proclamation of the message of Jesus and about Jesus. It seeks conversion, acceptance and discipleship. It is widely accepted that proclamation of the Gospel requires inculturation, a process of taking into account the cultures, thought-forms, priorities, leading metaphors, practices and ways of life of the people being addressed. In evangelisation people are called out of their previous way of life and evangelists want people to come to know, to love and to accept as their saviour Jesus the Christ, so that their lives can be transformed by following him as the way, the truth and the life. By its nature, the kind of conversion and commitment sought by evangelists requires a rejection of alternative ways of life and it overrides all other affiliations. One's first identity becomes being a child of God, with all that this entails. I cannot here adequately take into account the broadening interpretation of evangelisation that has taken place, where this term is used not only to refer to proclamation of the gospel, but also to bearing Christian witness more generally, and also to refer to involvement for justice in the world and the liberation of people from unjust practices; it has even been taken to include inter-religious dialogue.[7] Although there are some benefits from extending the term evangelisation to such activities, there are drawbacks too from such blurring.[8]

Catechesis is the sharing of and dialogue about faith between believers, in an attempt to deepen and reinforce this faith so that it becomes mature, more lively, more enthusiastic, better informed, more coherent. Catechesis assumes one is already within a community of faith and has (at least) some rudimentary understanding of this and that one belongs willingly. It assumes evangelisation has taken place, the initial confrontation with the Gospel; it builds on this and seeks to extend one's engagement with the ramifications that flow from discipleship and ecclesial membership. It is an activity for insiders.

Religious education is open to a greater variety of meanings and purposes that have been attributed to it. It tends to focus on literacy about religion, information, concepts; it does not depend on prior commitment; it does not (necessarily) assume membership of any particular faith. Its goal is to promote understanding about religious matters: the stories, scriptures, beliefs, practices, traditions and customs associated with a religion, or, more often in recent years, religions in the plural.[9] While it may not bypass the affective, its focus is cognitive, and while it considers religious communities, it holds in view the individual learner, not the requirements of the religious community or communities. Religious education is concerned to promote informed and intelligent thinking about a religion rather than fidelity to it, though some religious educators in some settings, for example, in faith schools, may also hope that religious education contributes to the processes whereby faith is developed, deepened and deployed.

There is validity in these distinctions. One needs to be clear about whom one is addressing, and alert as to what is and what is not legitimate to attempt in any particular setting (for example, the space of a compulsory school classroom is of a significantly different order from the space of a voluntary retreat). Both those engaged primarily in education and those in evangelisation must be mindful of their mandate and sensitive to the differing perspectives, expectations and needs of those who invite them, employ them, trust them, or put their children in their presence. They have to know what is the basis of the relationship they are to have with the 'to be evangelised' or the 'to be educated'. This is important ethically, lest they abuse their position; it is important epistemologically, because the type and source of knowledge being sought and conveyed might differ in significant ways for participants, depending on which of these three activities is being conducted; and because both education and evangelisation have in common that they are concerned with knowledge (whether the emphasis is on critical and independent knowledge or on faithful and communal knowledge) and with ethics as part of promoting human flourishing, then the type of relationship underlying the communication and exchange has pedagogical importance.

Having granted all this, I have never been completely convinced by this differentiation which has been the prevailing orthodoxy in many Catholic circles for nearly 35 years. There are many factors that influence how both education and evangelisation are received, factors relating to the context, always a triple context at least, involving the wider culture, the institutional setting and the individual context (stage of maturity, motivation, readiness for learning, and so on). These factors can make a huge difference to the way that the same content is received and they can deeply affect how efforts to evangelise or educate are perceived, regardless of whether ostensibly it is evangelisation, catechesis or religious education that is taking place. Furthermore, the personal style of communication and the pedagogy employed by the educator or evangelist again can make all the difference, as can the type of relationship established between teacher and learners and promoted between and among learners. Thus, regardless of the intentions of the person leading the activity (and regardless of the expectations of those employing them) the same activity can be received by one person as evangelisation, by another as catechesis and by another as religious education. The learning outcomes of both classroom and church activities are unpredictable, often invisible, ambiguous, sometimes dramatically effective and evident, often surprising, sometimes depressingly absent. Such learning outcomes are always interrelated in immensely complex ways with the purposes and expectations of participants, their personal conditions and wider contexts, and the range of technologies and resources, together with the diverse pedagogies and approaches adopted. At their worst, attempts at both education and evangelisation can be depressing, demeaning, oppressive, dispiriting and damaging. However at their best, both can provide the "magic moments" described by Derek Attridge recently in *Times Higher Education*:

> "magic moments" is not a bad description of the incalculable, unpredict-able, unforceable opening out to unexpected horizons that, taking student and teacher by surprise, can happen in the classroom.[10]

to which, one could add, wherever evangelisation, as well as education takes place.

Thus, the differentiations are useful categories, pressing us to be careful about the kind of activity we are engaged in, but they must not restrict our readiness to be surprised by the apparent lack of match that so often seems to occur between plans, performance and reception in education and evangelisation.

## 2. SIMILARITIES BETWEEN EDUCATION AND EVANGELISATION

Ten similarities between these two processes are suggested here. The first of these relates to key features of education and evangelisation: they are concerned with the whole person, aim for major change and are lifelong. The second likens similarities between education and evangelisation to similarities between the sacraments. The third proposes that the efficacy in both processes is not all down to us; that God is present and active in both. The fourth focuses on the more abundant life that is envisaged by educators and evangelists. The fifth relates to the necessity of connecting, though not slavishly, with culture, if education and evangelisation are to be fruitful. The sixth shows appreciation for the interaction of many factors operating in education and evangelisation. The seventh suggests that two types of love are prerequisite for education and evangelisation. The eighth draws attention to the role of dialogue and the dialectic between distance and closeness in both processes under scrutiny here. The ninth alerts us to how the quality of the inner life of educators and evangelists is crucial. The tenth underlines the importance of the tone of voice adopted and how this is related to careful listening.

1. Education, in any culture, is about how the capacities of human nature are developed, oriented, ordered and integrated in service of what one believes is most important about human beings, the kind of society we want to live in and what we believe to be the good life. These capacities include energy, emotions, intelligence, memory, will and conscience. The best kinds of education have in view the whole person, not just a part of him or her. So too, evangelisation aims to bring the whole person to Christ so that people can share in God's life and be renewed and transformed in every part of their being. Neither education nor evangelisation aim for minor or temporary changes in learners and disciples; ambitiously, they hold in view the whole person and consider that their endeavours are lifelong in duration.

2. A second similarity between education and evangelisation emerges in the light of reflection on sacraments. In sacramental theology Christians believe that God is 'doing' a similar thing in each of the sacraments, even if there is a difference in the focus of our attention as to which aspect of God's work is operative at any particular moment. Thus, Christians want to say that God's creative, redemptive, revelatory, liberating, forgiving, healing, inspiring, feeding, strengthening, consoling work is conveyed in all sacraments, rather than attribute feeding to one, forgiving to another, healing to another, and so forth. I suggest education and evangelisation are similar in the way that sacraments are similar. It might help us, in terms of focus and analysis, to break down these two sets of activities, education and evangelisation, into features that differ in some respects; this indeed might help us appreciate better how such activities operate, like knowing the workings of parts of the engine of the car we drive, or like knowing the internal workings of the piano we play. It is necessary and useful to pay very close attention to the detail of how education, teaching and learning, works and it is necessary and useful to pay close attention to how we seek

to mediate, recognize and accept into our lives God's grace in particular ways in the sacraments, for example, through the use of water, oil, candle, bread and wine, clothing, holy scripture, touch, prayer and so forth. We also, however, need to look out for what lifts and integrates these 'details' into more lofty and enduring goals that make sense of and give purpose to our endeavours. Thus particular activities comprise and contribute to education more generally; similarly, particular acts comprise and contribute to the sacramental perspective more generally.

3. From a faith perspective, when we engage in either education or evangelisation, in both cases we are participating in God's work, a work that precedes our proclamation. In the light of faith, we believe that God is already present and his Word is active before we ever enter the scene, eliciting growth, development and response before we plan to give a sermon or to teach a lesson. Further than this, believers claim, God is not only active *prior* to our involvement, but God is also active *alongside* our efforts, operating in ways unknown to us in the minds and hearts of would-be disciples and potential students, as well as those of us who are educators and evangelists. God continues to be present and active, inscrutably for us, long after we have left the scene.

4. In both education and evangelisation we are invited by our teachers and preachers to share in what they consider is the more abundant life. This more abundant life will be conceived of in different ways, with varying degrees of 'thickness'; it will have multiple dimensions; there will be ramifications for the way we think, feel, choose and act. Who we are, why we are and who we might be – these are questions central to both education and evangelisation.

5. Education and evangelisation, if they are to be internalised and effective, depend on a conscious connection being made (in both processes) between the culture that surrounds us and our inner life. It is highly likely that the culture we are immersed in will influence our imagination and sensitivity, our hopes and fears, our assumptions and habits, our relationships and expectations of others, our priorities and choices.[11] If one is not aware of how one's inner self is partly framed and constituted by the culture that surrounds us, something essential to both education and to evangelisation is missing. For self-knowledge and discernment about the sources of influence

on one are usually considered important for both the processes under review in this paper. The wise educator and the wise evangelist will encourage reflection on changing material conditions that shape the way we live, for example changes in food, household equipment, in entertainment and holidays, in communication and transport. Douglas and Rhonda Jacobsen[12] mention - as examples of significant changes - how the electric light bulb transformed the natural rhythm of life for all of us, how cars and paved roads turned people into commuters and how new forms of entertainment changed the context for engagement in religion. It goes against the grain of an incarnational theology to downplay how these affect our mindset.

Educators and evangelists need to be rooted in culture and local needs in order to be relevant and to get a hearing. However they also need to be able to transcend culture, in the case of liberal education, in order to be able to liberate people from the present and particular, or, in the case of evangelisation, in order to be adequately Christian and prepare people for God's Kingdom. The capacity to transcend culture, however, is strictly limited and the effort to do so should have the qualification 'so far as is possible', given that we cannot step outside our culture, for this would be to step outside of our very selves; but we should, nevertheless, be as discerning as possible about our culture and its assumptions, priorities, projects, entanglements and so forth, so that we can envisage possibilities for human flourishing beyond its current ways of thinking and acting. Educators and evangelists need specificity and particularity and sympathy with people's predicaments in the here and now, if they are to connect. They also need to have in view a bigger picture, so that they can help people move on from local and immediate concerns in the longer term. From a Christian perspective, some aspects of a culture provide access to Christianity, while other aspects of a culture are resistant to it. In turn, from a secular educator's perspective, some aspects of a culture can be embraced while others are life-diminishing and to be guarded against and resisted. Discernment is needed from both perspectives. Thus, both educators and evangelists should manage the delicate balancing act of being simultaneously at home, familiar and hospitable with those they seek to reach and yet also a stranger, unsettled and disturbing. They must combine realism about where people are with the idealism and vision to conceive of where they are not now but could be in light of education or evangelisation. In short, educators and evangelists must be bifocal and bilocated: they should strive to be here and see from here, while maintaining the capacity to be somewhere else and see from there.

6. In both education and evangelisation one can discern the operating and interaction of a very similar range of factors. These factors will influence how the work of the educator and the evangelist is interpreted by those on the receiving end, how it is accommodated or kept at bay, how it is accepted or rejected, how it is filtered or modified, how it is internalised and developed further. These factors include the cognitive ability of the learner or disciple, as well as that of the educator or evangelist, the degree of affection and warmth and affirmation and encouragement offered and received, the part played by example, the timeliness and clarity (or not) of explanations provided, the exercise and interaction of discipline and freedom, the power of motivation, the presence of challenge, the invitation and donation (or refusal) of commitment, plus the provision of safe places for exploration.

7. William May refers to two aspects of parental love, both of which are necessary and each of which can be overdone, to the detriment of children. He calls these accepting love and transforming love. Accepting love takes the child as she is, in a laissez-faire kind of way; it is not judgemental; neither is it interventionist. It is tolerant and it lets be. Transforming love wants to turn the child into the best she can be. It nurtures high ambitions for what the child can achieve and be like. It is demanding and it does not leave alone. "Accepting love, without transforming love, slides into indulgence and finally neglect. Transforming love, without accepting love, badgers and finally rejects."[13] In my view, both these kinds of love apply to both education and evangelisation.

8. Two other features that education and evangelisation have in common I draw from Aidan Nichols' book *The Realm*. The first of these is the importance, for both, of dialogue. Nichols puts it thus:

> Dialogue is a means to mission and condition for mission. It is a *means* to mission inasmuch as the exposure of the two parties in dialogue to the full range of each other's convictions offers an opportunity for the grace of God to convince the conscience of the other of Christian or Catholic truth – just as it offers the possibility of suasion from that truth. It [dialogue] is a *condition* of mission in that only a thorough grasp of the ideas and values

of the other can enable the missionary to locate those aspects of divine revelation which speak most acutely to the other's needs.[14]

Although Nichols is here referring to the role of dialogue in relation to mission, and therefore to evangelisation, rather than to education, clearly dialogue is a feature of education, if education includes the task of building bridges between people who start from different places and who inhabit different worlds, which I take to be at the heart of the educational endeavour.

The second common feature which Nichols prompts us to note is the need for attention to the dialectic between distance and closeness that operates in education but also in evangelising or mission work. Nichols puts it like this (in relation to mission):

> If the protagonists of mission come exclusively from *within* the culture, they won't be able to see it with sufficient objective distance to judge what its christening requires. If on the other hand they come exclusively from *outside* the culture, they won't have the inner sympathy for it and the depth or simplicity of identification with its members which is prerequisite for winning others.[15].

The same kind of dialectic between outside and inside pertains in education: the educators must display both distance and closeness. They cannot act as 'buddies' or peers in relation to their students; this leaves too far behind the world, tradition or discipline they represent and for which they serve as trusted elders; this is to get too close. On the other hand, unless they show a willingness to establish positive, caring and affirming relationships with learners they reduce the chances of their work being effective. An unspoken, underlying assumption of learners in any context might be: "we don't care what you know until we know that you care."

9. One cannot bring alive for others something that is not living in oneself. In both education and evangelisation in the end one communicates oneself; this is what will come across – for good or for ill. One will reveal a way of being, a way of life, embodied in how one lives, how one speaks, how one acts, how one relates, how one thinks, how one believes – and how all these hang together. Educators and evangelists, while entitled to privacy, nevertheless have to be ready to share themselves, to be vulnerable, to give themselves away to others. Without this, what they pass on is likely to be

distorted, even though we know that we fail to do justice to what we pass on because we are fallible, imperfect, often ignorant, limited, ourselves only partly educated and partly converted. Thus both the educator and the evangelist must nurture the sources of their teaching in themselves. Although updating and becoming better informed is part of this, more is implied. Being in the truth is not about accumulating more information; it is about appreciating, indwelling and realising (making real in one's life) what one already knows. Before they can animate – something they do for others in relation to some truth - they must realise (in the sense I have just given) what they wish to convey by embodying it in their own lives. Their being will speak more cogently here than their words.

10. The character of educators and evangelists and their intentions towards those they address will, however, be revealed by what they say, or, perhaps, more precisely, by *how* they speak. Here the tone of voice is crucial as this is often what opens the door or closes it for hearers. This is a theme that receives prolonged and penetrating treatment in George Dennis O'Brien's book *Finding the Voice of the Church*.[16] I take two connected points from O'Brien: the first is about getting the tone of voice right; the second is about how this often depends on a prior deep listening. O'Brien compares the voice of an actor in a play with the voice of those who represent the church.

> If the actor speaks in the wrong voice as lover, villain, hero, or clown, the play is ruined. So with the Christian voice ... spoken in the wrong voice – dictatorial, didactic, distant, or demeaning – the message fails. ... [A] presumptive tone, an over-assurance of attitude ... fails as the vehicle of faith. ... Speaking the faith in the wrong voice obscures the Church. ... A messenger in the wrong voice will distort the message beyond recognition.[17]

Teachers know that this as true for them as it is for preachers. Getting the tone of voice right is a difficult and complex task and it must be admitted one that is not wholly in the control of the speaker, since there are many variables at work influencing how what we say and how we say it is received. Nevertheless without careful prior listening to those we hope to reach out to, in education and in evangelisation, we are likely to get the voice wrong in some way. O'Brien puts it like this:

> No one is finally outside the Church and no Christian is fully inside – at least "inside" as a personal assured achievement and possession. Christians

are never wholly inside the truth; others are never wholly outside the truth. The conclusion is that Christian preaching to the outside has to begin with deep *listening*. ... The key to preaching the Gospel is not first defined by how one *speaks* but how one *listens*.[18]

O'Brien quotes from Ratzinger a beautiful reflection on listening:

> To listen means to know and acknowledge another and to allow him to step into the realm of one's own "I." It is a readiness to assimilate his words, and therein his being, into one's own reality as well as to assimilate oneself to him in corresponding fashion. Thus, after the act of listening, I am another man, my own being is enriched and deepened because it is united with the being of the other and, through him, with the being of the world.[19]

To put this in terms not used by O'Brien (nor by Ratzinger): what we need is not a bigger megaphone but a better hearing aid.

*** *** ***

In the end both education and evangelisation face three certain and inexorable realities. First, there is sin, however we define it, and plenty of it, flourishing in the world. No matter how idealistic an educator or an evangelist may be, to deny or to ignore sin is simply to live in unreality. However, second, even more abounding, there is grace, grace that will help us to overcome our worst selves and to collaborate with God in building and becoming a new creation. Third, we are given free will, the capacity, admittedly frequently weakened and damaged and obscured, but never totally obliterated, to choose, to change direction, to start again, to turn around.

In the face of these three realities, both education and evangelisation might be seen as kinds of capacity-building, capacity-building of minds, bodies and hearts, to live in the real world, God's world. Of both education and evangelisation one can claim that they clear the decks, remove debris, lift away obstacles, open ears, focus attention and stimulate imagination - so that we see differently. Both seek to excite the heart. However, the real work in both is done by God and responded to by learners who are disciples and by disciples who are learners.

## NOTES

1 Nicholas Lash, 'The Church – A School of Wisdom' in *Receptive Ecumenism and the Call to Catholic Learning*, edited by Paul Murray (Oxford: Oxford University Press, 2008), p.72.

2 Elena Curti, 'Bishop blames education for Church's decline' *The Tablet,* 8th November 2008, p.40. Nicholas Lash, 'Log in the Church's eye' *The Tablet*, 15th November 2008, p.12. Patrick O'Donoghue, 'Learning to be faithful' *The Tablet*, 22nd November 2008, p.12.

3 For a recent book linking Christian education and evangelism, see Norma Cook Everist (ed) *Education as Evangelism* (Minneapolis: Fortress Press, 2007).

4 For other, anti-religious complaints, see Douglas and Rhonda Jacobsen (eds) *The American University in a Postsecular Age* (New York: Oxford University Press, 2008), pp.7 & 10.

5 Francis Arinze, quoted in Suzanne Howard Carpenter, *New Hope for Catholic Higher Education* (Bloomington, Indiana/Milton Keynes: AuthorHouse, 2006), p.5.

6 For two excellent analyses, see chapters by Michael Warren ('Catechesis and [or] Religious Education: Another look') and Kieran Scott ('To Teach Religion or Not to Teach Religion: Is That the Dilemma?') in *Religious Education as Practical Theology* edited by Bert Roebben & Michael Warren ( Leuven: Peeters, 2001).

7 Desbruslais, as summarised by Christa Pontgratz-Lippitt, 'Lessons in survival from a Styrian hill' *The Tablet* 14th June 2008, p.S3.

8 On evangelisation, see Clare Watkins (et al) *Going Forth* (von Hügel Institute –Centre for the Study of Faith in Society, St Edmund's College, Cambridge, and Margaret Beaufort Institute of Theology, Cambridge, 2006); Philip Knights & Andrea Murray, *Evangelisation in England and Wales* (London: Catholic Bishops' Conference of England and Wales, 2002).

9 For a stimulating overview of some of the challenges posed by religious illiteracy, see Stephen Prothero, *Religious Literacy,* (New York: HarperCollins, 2007).

10 Derek Attridge, 'We've lost those magic moments' *Times Higher Education* 1st May, 2008, p.38.

11 On culture, see John Trapani, 'The Air We Breathe' in *Maritain and the Many Ways of Knowing* edited by Douglas Ollivant (American Maritain Association 2002), pp.182 – 188; Charles Taylor, *Modern Social Imaginaries* (Durham and London: Duke University Press, 2004) & Charles Taylor, *A Secular Age* (Cambridge, Mass: Harvard University Press, 2007).

12 Jacobson, op. cit., p.5

13 May, quoted by Patrick Deneen, *Democratic Faith* (Princeton: Princeton University Press, 2005), p.293.

14 Aidan Nichols, *The Realm* (Oxford: Family Publications, 2008), pp.24 – 25.

15 Ibid., p.29.

16 George Dennis O'Brien, *Finding the Voice of the Church* (Notre Dame, IN: University of Notre Dame Press, 2007).

17 Ibid., pp.xiv, 4, 5, 85.

18 Ibid., pp.77, 190.

19 Ibid., p.196.

# *Chapter 3*

## BEGIN WITH THE HEART
### EVANGELISING AS HUMANISING

*DANIEL O'LEARY*

Supposing, after a conversation with one of the men or women in his life, Jesus was asked about the precise nature of what went on between them – was it adult education or formation, evangelisation or pre-evangelisation, catechesis or pre-catechesis, how amazed he would be. Would he not say 'Oh, gimme a break! We were just having a heart-to-heart. Lovely woman. She made me feel better. We've arranged to meet again.' More at home with church-speak, there is a kind of simplicity that confuses us.

When it comes to a many-faceted term such as 'evangelisation' have we complicated things too much for people? Does friendship and intimacy with the Risen Christ not transcend all such mental divisions and distinctions? To be sure, all of these well-defined delineations and emphases have their place. They sometimes clarify things. But for ordinary souls and hearts, is there a simpler way of talking about loving God or Jesus? Where 'heart speaks to heart' the head does not always need to dominate. Real love has its own way of self-expression. Maybe its time to recover the language of love

After nearly half a century trying to teach, preach, evangelise and catechise, I sometimes wonder whether we get lost, too easily, in the persistent search for rational clarity; whether we confuse religious knowledge (and religious behaviour) with a heart-felt sense of belonging to God; whether we lose sight of falling in love with God in pursuit of a more doctrinally explicit creed of beliefs. Is there a great danger of missing the stunning message of the Incarnation, and its implications for our humanity, through insisting too much on a prescribed progression through pre-arranged hoops and sequential stages of initiation. Evangelisation will always be grounded in the simplicity and profundity of the human heart.

Or, we may ask whether too much emphasis can be placed on an overly 'evangelical-type' of Jesus-worship, a 'crusade for Jesus' kind of commitment that seems to be strangely silent about a surrender of our hearts to God our Saviour, and to the practical building up of the Kingdom of 'a God of all names'? There is a growing fundamentalism within Christianity that is popular and powerful. I suggest that evangelisation can also be seen as a way of liberating people from such fundamentalism into the glorious, human freedom of being children of God.

Put another way, what actually is the experience of a relationship with the person of Jesus? Is it not more than the adoration and worship of him, the knowledge about him, the creeds of the churches? Has it not more to do with the following of him, acquiring the mind and vision of him, sharing the passion of his overflowing heart and of his wounded body, and doing what he asked us to do?' Surely it can be no other than living and believing the sacramental vision of our transformed humanity in Christ, and consequently, our new empowerment to change the world so beloved of his Father?

In 2006 the Jesuits celebrated major anniversaries of their three founders. Michael Holman, currently their Provincial Superior, has written about the way they evangelised. Having commented on the limited success of many recent attempts to evangelise, he suggests that we learn something from the approach of these pioneering men.[1] They held that the secularism of their time was such 'that it could not be met by argument, only by an experience of Christ. Theirs was a personal approach that began with a conversation. It was never a matter of imposing Christ but of recommending him, proposing him as attractive because, first and foremost, he was supremely attractive to them. They managed to do what we find it hard to do: they evangelised the whole person, spiritu, corde, practice - in the spirit, from the heart, practically'.

There are many well-meaning but misleading emphases in our current approaches to evangelisation that obscure the powerful simplicity of the message of Jesus – a message that has to do with the purifying and completing of our humanity, with lives given over entirely to Christ. As we enter another year, perennially committed to spreading the Word and building the Kingdom, is there a place for some spring-cleaning to clear away unnecessary and distracting verbiage?

There is a story about Vince Lombardi, the famous American football coach. His team had plummeted from the top of the league. The previous season they had dazzled the country with the magic and sophistication of their passing strategies, their scoring techniques, their winning ways. This year they had lost the plot completely. He called them together and settled them down. 'We need to dismantle all the unnecessary clutter of yesterday.' he said to them. 'Here are the basics. This thing in my hand is called a football. And these are your legs and arms. Now our aim is to get that ball, using your legs and arms, in spite of those who will try to stop us, from one end of the field to the other'.

## TWO THEOLOGIES

For those who wish to embark on such an exercise of simplification, of clarifying the central aims of our various ministries, of trying to focus again on the heart of the mission and vision of Jesus, there are many starting-points. For now, out of many possibilities, I single out four dimensions of such work, offering a few free-flowing reflections on each – theology, evangelisation, liturgy, and language. I will be trying to show that these aspects of our faith, and for that matter, all the dimensions of Catholic education and catechesis, are not ends in themselves (important as this outcome may be in other more cerebral contexts) but thresholds into the unique Christian revelation that we are loved intensely by a God who became human so as to convince us of that life-changing truth.

Unpopular and inaccessible as many aspects of theology may be – and mainly because they mostly leave our needy lives untouched – it is important to remember that all our efforts to grow closer to God through prayer and the sacraments, and all our efforts to teach, preach and catechise, are shaped and nourished by some theology or other. When that theology is all about sin and redemption, then our relationship with God will be deeply affected by how awful we are for somehow being part of the original sin that forced God to become one of us. And, because of that, for causing the crucifixion of Jesus. Our catechesis, our liturgy, our teaching and preaching, our hymns and our public prayers, will then be bound to carry this heavy shadow – the shadow of fear, unworthiness, guilt. Many would hold that such is the way it still is.

When, however, the theology that inspires us is coloured and textured by a love-story of God's utter delight in creating us, in becoming one of us, and in finding divine happiness by living intimately with us now, our prayers, celebrations, evangelising and homilies will carry an entirely different energy and intimacy. Unlike the dualistic, divisive impact that doctrines about how bad and unworthy we are have on our mostly-unsure and wavering hearts, the reassurance that we are already shining with the presence of a God who is utterly at home in us and with us, is positively transforming for human beings.

This doctrinal stance springs from what is called a theology of nature and grace. Full of intense compassion, God wished to create out of pure love, and then, in time, to become that creation. That becoming happened in Jesus Christ. In him it was revealed that God's heart beats in all our hearts, that all our bodies are temples of the Holy Spirit, and that every creature is a divine work of art. Revelation (and evangelisation) is about the unbelievable possibilities of humanity, graced at its centre from the very beginning. It is about God's desire to be known and loved in the humanity of Jesus Christ. It is about God's delight in being visible and tangible in human form.

Gone, then, forever, we hope, will be the dualistic and misleading view that would separate creation from grace, the natural from the divine, perceiving our time on earth as a painful preparation for, and costly return to, a lost paradise. This kind of teaching, which still abounds - a teaching with which many of us are only too familiar - is a travesty of the story of God and Jesus. It has been referred to in this very journal as a type of 'spiritual abuse'. And so it is. It has caused irreparable damage to sensitive souls. And there are so many who would still defend it as traditional orthodoxy.

It is so important here to clarify the unambiguous reality of original sin in each one of us personally, and in humanity as a whole. To be deeply flawed and attracted towards sin is part of the definition of being human. And that is why we sorely need saving from self-destruction. We do terrible things to each other as individuals and as nations. Our theology is a theology of redemption. We must make no mistake about that. What is important to remember, however, is that there is more to the story than a divine rescue-operation. The original revelation is of a God who was moved to create out of intense love, to become a part of that creation, to die out of love for us, and to remain with us forever in our deepest hearts. A theology of sin and redemption needs the wider horison of a theology nature and grace to reveal its true context and meaning.

In the beautiful theology of creation and incarnation, of nature and grace, the fleshing of God has revealed, once and for all, what it means to be truly human. We achieve our true humanity, not by running away from the world and its joys and pleasures, or by turning our backs on it in fear or doubt. Christ does not reveal what it is to be divine but what it is to be human. It is often said that we are not human beings trying to become spiritual. We are spiritual beings trying to become truly human. That our often-faint God-likeness might become purified, intensified and completed in us, is the purpose of creation and incarnation.

This completion, this transformation is not something added on from the outside, so to speak, to our 'mere' human nature – a kind of divine layer on top of our ordinary humanity. It is rather the revelation of the intrinsic meaning of our very lives. The graced unfolding of our lives is God's dream within us becoming true. The Second Vatican Council was so clear about all of this. Through God's desire to become human, the incarnation revealed the meaning of the humanity of all of us. And that is that we are all sacraments of God's love. *The Church in the Modern World* reminds us that because Jesus 'worked with human hands, thought with a human mind, acted by human choice, and loved with a human heart' we are all ordained to share in that same grounded priestliness (para 22).

There is a lift and lightness about a theology of nature and grace. It discerns the free movement of the Holy Spirit wherever people are committed to genuine human values and humanitarian pursuits. It identifies the longing for God in all human longing. It sees God's spirit ranging across the whole spectrum of creation, of history and of individual experiences in ways far beyond the constricted and limited places, people and things to which many of our text-book theologies, catechisms and homiletic suggestions would restrict it. It takes its shape and texture from the passion of Jesus for making possible for everybody, the actual here-and-now experience of the abundant life. And whatever we may mean by evangelisation, the moment it loses that life-giving empowerment as its main thrust, then it has lost everything.

In a recent homily, moral theologian and parish priest Fr Kevin Kelly said, 'Evangelisation is really about something very simple, wonderful and exciting. It is about being truly human, each in our own unique way, and thus translating and interpreting God's love story in the language of our modern age – and so helping people read that same story in the wonder of their own being and even in the ambiguity of their lives.'

## TWO APPROACHES TO EVANGELISATION

Such an earthy, healthy theology is the reason why there should be something instantly recognisable as good news whenever we are engaged in evangelising, catechising or spiritually forming those we serve - as there was in the life and relationships of Jesus. The whole point of his coming was to bring an abundance to people's lives by his very presence - a presence that captured hearts and minds and bodies in a way that arguments and progressive stages of knowledge, as the early Jesuits realised, never could.

Jesus did not measure his friendship, or the deepening trust of his disciples, or the emotional bonds within his followers, in steps and compartmentalised progressions. Living relationships are not like that. They do not subject themselves to analysis as worked-out plans and theories do. People were simply drawn to his company, attracted by his humanity. Their hearts expanded in his presence; the best in them was touched. You could say that they felt so good about themselves just by being around him, by being loved by him. When that central excitement is withdrawn, denied or lost from the very centre of the process of evangelisation, or catechesis, or preaching, then, whatever else we may think we are doing, we are not presenting the human Christ as he was, we are not telling the whole truth about the Christian story.

Evangelisation is not primarily about mental assents to sets of beliefs, or about telling people things that are completely new and essentially different, adding to their knowledge, coming to them from the outside, so to speak. It is more about convincing them of something they already suspect, of assuring them that the faint dream they carry is, in fact, true, and that the intuitions of their heart about the mystery of their being, are confirmed and guaranteed by Jesus Christ. It is true to say that people's own hearts recognise, and delight in, and are transformed by, the authentic validity of such evangelisation.

There is no denying the reality of this kind of life-transforming good news. Only those who are deeply moved themselves by it can ever be true teachers and facilitators of the 'two-edged sword' that reaches to our inmost places. Christian leaders today repeatedly call for more fire and vision in those who are privileged to be part of the various pastoral ministries in the Churches. A whole-hearted commitment to evangelisation would suggest some of the following aims as central summaries of that passionate work of pastoral faith-education;

- Jesus is revealed as the language, the body-language, the human body of God. When God enters our space and time, our loving Creator emerges in the person and personality of Jesus. It follows that all human beings, then, without exception, are God's language too. And it is God's delight to be dwelling within us. A huge dimension of evangelisation, then, is to keep telling this astonishing story in the music, dance and poetry of a living sharing, in the revealing to people the truth about their own divine identity, in telling them who they really are.

- How to convince people that they are unconditionally loved by a God who is so delighted to be intimately one with us? It takes a huge paradigm shift in our innermost spirit to transcend the negativity and dualism of so much of our inherited understanding of the Church's laws and teachings. Many of us need a deep conversion before we can reach into, and experience, the freedom of the daughters and sons of God. The fragility and tenderness of God's desire for our total trust and surrender have been lost in translation and interpretation. Evangelisation is about singing faithfully and accurately the saving song of Jesus.

- Evangelisation reaches in to the dark places and demonic powers within us, and within our society and world, so that we can name and dismantle those spirits, finding a new courage, a new heart, to continue on, no matter what. Jesus saved people's lives by filling them with redemptive hope. The first concern of Jesus was to set people free from their despair and their fears, to bring the light of joy into their daily lives, to enable them to live a more abundant life in the here and now. Persistent images from the past of a hard God still make it so difficult for us to trust ourselves to the personal, human, constant and unconditional divine love revealed in Jesus.

- Central to any context for such a liberating, comforting and life-giving understanding of the Christian revelation is the humanity of Jesus. Any true evangelisation can ever only draw its wisdom, its justification and its never-ending inspiration and nourishment from that first principle of Incarnation – the humanity of God as personified in Jesus. This is the humanity through which we are saved; the humanity that attracted people to follow Jesus, forming his first community of faith; the humanity that people fell in love with, and their lives were changed forever. It was an 'ordinary' humanity in which he suffered much, lived life to the hilt, lost his good name, felt abandoned by his father, confronted and redeemed his darkness. This was the kind of needy and authentic humanity chosen by God as the designated moment and context for the fullest revelation of the nature of divine being.

- Christian evangelisation amazes us by insisting that this revelation is still taking place in every single one of us, day in, day out. The work of evangelisation is to provide us with the sacramental vision to believe this, to find God's signature in every event of our lives, God's footprints in every situation and experience that comes our way, God's presence in all our comings and goings. There is no exception to the truth of this revelation about the immanent holiness of God's intimate energy. Perhaps nowhere more than in the heartfelt dynamic of married life, where the human spirit stretches itself, in its trusting and letting go, to the limits of its potential, is this expression of incarnate love more clearly sacramentalised. We discover, to our astonishment, that every ordinary human home is the unexpected place where God dwells, whether this be recognised or not. Even where there is suspicion and deceit, married life must remain an epiphany of mystery; a participation in God's own challenging essence. Anytime we say 'I'm trying to forgive you' or 'I still believe in you' to each other, that is also the ever-present expression of God's incarnate covenant within us, constantly healing and completing all that is imperfect.

## TWO LITURGIES

The liturgical celebration of the astonishing vision revealed in the Incarnation is a central dimension of Christianity. Without it we forget to recognise the presence of God in the midst of life. It is for a good reason that we are encouraged to avail ourselves of sacramental participation as often as we can. The pervasive presence of original sin keeps blinding us to the good news of the precious potential of our humanity and of our world.

However, the whole meaning, context, structure and self-understanding of liturgical celebration will be radically coloured by our theology of salvation. A sin/redemption-based theology will tend to focus on the quality and good order of the celebration itself, emphasising its intrinsic holiness, its distinctiveness and independence from created things; a nature/grace understanding will emphasise the truly sacramental nature of the celebration, pointing away from itself towards the already-holy humanity which it prays to purify and celebrate. Can both emphases be held together?

I find it helpful to refer to two liturgies - the liturgy of the world and the liturgy of the Church; the sacrament of the universe and the sacrament of the Mass; the table of our lives and the table of the bread and wine. We need to celebrate the one as we celebrate the other. If we are not in a holy communion with the God of Life in the routine lives we live, we will hardly experience a great intimacy at the Holy Communion of Mass. The theologian Karl Rahner reminds us that the Christian 'receives under holy signs the true Body of the Lord, knowing this to be worthless, were he not to communicate with that Body of God which is the world itself and its fate; he partakes of the one Body so as to remain in communion with that other body which is the reality of his life.'[2]

The first aim in an authentic liturgical catechesis is, as we have been emphasising, to present the sacraments as of a piece with our lives in our world; to see them in the context of a world already permeated with God's presence, encompassed by divine love. In the very person of Christ himself, this intimate unity has taken place. The human is now the address of the divine, the raw material of our redemption. 'Salvation' wrote Tertullian, 'hinges on the flesh.' The art is to enable this revelation to be known, gladly accepted, and celebrated; to enable people to accept and to become 'who they already are'.

To the analytical mind sacramental grace is a complicated phenomenon which needs many terms and treatises; to the more 'feeling' mind it is a simple, rich and enriching experience bringing the kind of knowing that surpasses all knowledge. To the calculating mind the notion of the sacramental imagination is too undefined and risky, too vague to measure, too unreachable to possess; to the contemplative mind it is the beckoning horizon of love and meaning that transforms the soul and enlightens the wavering heart. There is a functional paradigm of rubrical uniformity; and there is a liberating paradigm of life-giving worship. Many contemporary liturgists believe that our sacramental celebrations could do with the services of our best theatre-directors, and our teaching and preaching with the best of our poets, playwrights and actors!

Vatican II's *The Church in the Modern World* makes it clear that in the past we over-emphasized the notion of two distinct worlds – one profane, the other sacred. Gregory Baum, a *peritus* at the Council, explains; 'The radical distinction between sacred and profane, between nature and grace has been overcome in the person of Christ. In Christ it is revealed that the locus of the divine is the human. In him it made manifest that God speaks in and through the words and gestures of people. Christian liturgy, therefore, can no longer consist in sacred rites by which people are severed from the ordinary circumstance of their lives. The liturgy, rather, is the celebration of the deepest dimension of human life, which is God's self-communication to all humanity. Liturgy unites people more closely to their daily lives. Worship remembers and celebrates the marvellous things God works in the lives of human beings, purifies and intensifies these gifts, makes everyone more sensitive to the Word and Spirit present in their daily lives.'[3]

It is vital for pastoral ministers, if their educational work is to bear lasting and transforming fruit, and if they believe that grace reveals the true essence of nature, to be true to this insight in the way they catechise and explain the connection between liturgy and life. If the presence of the Creator is not sensed in the ordinary events of each day, then the odds are that God will not be sensed in sacramental celebration either. If we find no hint of divine immanence in the emotions and experiences of our lives, then, it is highly unlikely that we will touch the closeness of God at the liturgical assembly.

When the liturgy is celebrated with this understanding in mind, heart and body, a new horizon is opened up. The celebrant and pastoral liturgical team will be deeply familiar with the significant moments in the life of the parish and its parishioners. Then all kinds of things - the beauty, goodness, tragedy of our lives, - can be a compelling opportunity for the disclosure of the presence of God to be recognised and high-lighted, where appropriate, in the liturgies.

The profound relevance of redemptive grace to each person's condition will inspire hearts with a new urgency for a deeper kind of loving and living. This heightened awareness is a huge step in claiming and living the promised, abundant life. That is why liturgy has such a potential for transformation. Shortly after his inauguration, Pope Benedict called for a greater sense of beauty in achieving this promise. 'If the Church is to continue to transform and to humanise the world, how can she dispense with beauty in her liturgies, that beauty which is so closely linked with love, and with the radiance of the Resurrection'.[4]

## TWO LANGUAGES

The sensitive care in the preparation and celebration of the liturgy that Pope Benedict desires, applies too, to the language we use in presenting the good news. Too often we settle for mediocre ritual and obsolete phrases to convey a glimpse of the unutterable beauty of Christian revelation, of the astonishing fact that God loves us so dearly. Only the best language is good enough to reflect God's compassionate heart. No effort is spared in crafting a love-letter. Spiritual writers and speakers have taken endless pains to get the weight and texture, the shape, sound and rhythm of their words as perfect as can be. They believe that since God, and the things of God, are at the heart of our lives, then we should create the most beautiful way of speaking and writing about the Gracious Mystery.

It is such an exquisitely delightful thing to be doing, to be waking up the hearts of young and old to the reality of how beautiful they are, and how extravagantly desired they are by a Tremendous Lover. At a recent conference at Ushaw College, Durham, a number of international theologians spoke of the need for a poetic, lyrical and attractive language and imagery for spreading the amazing revelation – that there's no part of our lives or world that isn't already everlastingly graced and blessed by God's beauty. What is needed, they agreed, was a language that touched the heart. It is called the language of love.

This applies especially to the ministry of evangelisation. This work is profoundly sacred. You don't, for instance, let just any old interior decorator loose on the Sistine chapel to restore and reveal the exquisite details of its breath-taking beauty. Only the best in the world will do for such ultra-special work. We, too, need to test and filter every expression we use to make sure that the language is fresh, relevant and true to the original revelation of God in Jesus. We need to look at the ideas and insights of our best theologians, educationalists, poets and playwrights, past and present, to make sure we are not short-selling that captivating story that God wants every human heart to hear.

It was probably never more difficult to communicate meaningfully than it is today. Here again in our calling to evangelise, we need to replace an outdated language with a more appropriate one. How do we ensure that the 'sacramental vision' of a reclaimed 'Catholic humanism' will engage with the crisis of communication – of translation, transmission and relevance – probably the greatest current challenge for a multi-cultural, post-modern Catholic inner-city parish or school today? Writing about 'sacramental abundance', theologian Fr. David Power asks, 'How can we, in a time of computerisation and remote control, get beyond the stranglehold that technique and concept have on language, so that it may speak "in, with, and under" bread, wine, oil and water, through a poetics that allows the things themselves to come to speech, and through them, the gift of divine love and divine life that Jesus and the Spirit have poured into them?'[5]

In general terms, then, what would a concept of spirituality, or of evangelising look like in a highly technological, multi-religious, deeply pluralistic age? This is a huge concern and challenge. Our best prophets struggle with the way forward. John O'Donoghue believes that much of the language of religion is caught in a time-warp. It attempts to speak with the voice of a vanished age to a fragmented culture that has outgrown it. Far from being an imposition of the gospel on people, evangelisation will aim at touching the deepest origin, memory, identity and destiny of the human individual and of communities. It is good news. 'This news comes from the very well of life itself. It encourages life to celebrate and honour all its possibilities and risks. This is the news that life itself is the primal sacrament; that life is the home of the eternal, albeit in veiled form; that the life of each person is a sacrament, wherein the eternal seeks to become visible and active; that each individual is chosen for a creative destiny in this world; that each one incarnates a different dimension of God; that at death, life is not ended, but elevated and transfigured into another form; that we are not outside, but within, God.'[6]

It is this kind of sacramental vision into the love and meaning already at the 'well of life itself' that will bring a new insight and courage to the work of evangelisation. Vincent Donovan reminded us many years ago that we do not bring God to people. 'We awaken the presence of God in them. This is the heart of the spiritual journey, to bring that presence to awareness. This is a delicate and sensitive work. Awareness cannot be forced; it can only be awakened.'[7] A tentative definition of evangelising might see it as bringing to consciousness in people a sense of God's presence within them; an awakening of people's slow awareness of who they really are. It is this awareness then that motivates a passion within us to relieve the poverty and pain of a world for which we are all, by virtue of our birth and baptism, forever responsible.

## NOTES

1   Holman, Michael, "St Francis Xavier and Today's Mission in Europe," *The Tablet,* December, p.6 (2006).

2   Rahner, Karl, "Secular Life and the Sacraments," *The Tablet*, vol. 225, p.267.

3   Gregory Baum, *Man Becoming* (New York: Herder & Herder, 1973), p.75.

4   Pope Benedict XVI. From a talk after his Papal Inauguration, 2005.

5   Power, David, "Sacramental Abundance: An Economy of Gift," *The Way Supplement*, 1994, Spring, p.90.

6   O'Donoghue, John, "To Awaken the Divinity Within," *The Way*, 34, no. 4 (1994), p.267.

7   Vincent O'Donovan, *Christianity Rediscovered* (New York: Orbis, 1978), p.99.

# Part Two:
# Home and Parish

# Chapter 4

## FAITH IN THE FAMILY

### JOHN SULLIVAN

In this chapter I reflect autobiographically on how, as a child and young person, I learned the language of faith, starting from home, taken into the church, and show how these fed into each other, mutually reinforcing the way I found myself surrounded by a world where faith was at work. Then, with the perspective of a parent seeking to bring up his children in an atmosphere conducive to faith, I focus on the practice of prayer in the home, in particular on how the different kinds of talking that form family life provide an appropriate soil in which prayer can flourish. Finally I consider some of the features of faith in the family setting. Implicit in all these is the belief that the holy and ordinary are inseparable.

### 1. FOUNDATIONS OF FAITH

When I think of how I learned the language of faith, it is clear that the order in which this developed began with doing, engaging in a set of practices, leading to belonging, gradually prompting believing. It is just as clear that any attempt to separate out the religious from the rest of life is artificial. The life of faith is not a marked-off one, with a large, ordinary, shared-with-everyone aspect, to which is added a special, extra aspect, one limited to a close circle of fellow-believers. The life of faith is simply life, ordinary life, experienced in the light of faith. Thus eating and drinking, seasons and celebration, temptation and forgiveness, stories and meaning, sickness, death and new life, all intermingle in an undifferentiated whole. The life of faith grows, as does all life, in the midst of the tangible and the sensuous, with sounds, sights and smells (and all the feelings aroused by these) preceding, but later meshed into, emergent beliefs and embryonic concepts.

Many things played a part for me: the bells that called us to church or that alerted us to a special moment in the liturgy, the smell (and sight) of incense that rose up in the air as a sign of prayer reaching out to God, the candles that flickered, attracting attention both to the way they sway back and forth with the breeze and also to the mixture of illumination and shadows they cast around them, and, not least interesting to a child, the dripping of wax with its briefly wet and hot but quickly becoming cool and soft and malleable texture. Then there were the brown wooden benches on which we sat while in church, at the end of which rested the pile of maroon hymn books, from which, when they were picked up and used in response to the organ, emerged a faltering yet hypnotic sound that, despite the strange words, still managed to convey sentiments of praise, gratitude, sorrow, pleading, surrender and trust. The grey holy water stoop as we entered the church, the layout of the building, the way the light was filtered through its stained glass windows, the columns that reached up to a high ceiling, the pulpit, altar, organ, holy images, sacred icons, carving and pictures – all these registered both separately but more importantly as a cumulative whole to create an atmosphere of being in a special place, where God was invoked and his presence was evidently felt by others around one. Indeed, their bowed heads, their fumbling with rosary beads, their muttering of prayer, their closed eyes, their concentration on the sacred actions of the priest, their close following of a missal and their hushing of the words and muffling of the movements of small children all conveyed the need for quiet and reverence: here we were at the gateway of God. Then there was the texture and colour of the priest's vestments, matching the seasons of the liturgical year, plus, when I was young, the cadences of a Latin language and the ritual gestures that aroused a sense of precious awe and reinforced the particular message being mediated at that point: humility, adoration, blessing, thanksgiving.

At home I first encountered the sign of the cross, where the explanation mattered less than getting the action right, together with the regular practice of prayer, especially by the bed at night. Here I learned how to link all the people I knew, and life's ups and downs, with God's mysterious presence, power and purpose. At Christmas the setting out of the crib in the front room – and the visiting of cribs in churches – played as central a part in the season of celebration as making decorations and designing cards. The telling and re-telling of the Christmas story, with what soon became its prescribed vocal intonation, its pauses and the associated sparkling eyes and linked body-language, supported on occasion by singing of a carol, provided an ambiance for the ritual of giving and receiving of presents, a context which qualified and partly limited the importance of such gifts, even though often these seemed the driver of excitement. I was taken regularly to Mass and Benediction, the latter offering a possibly richer source of sensuous images and symbolic gestures than the more word-dependent Mass at the time. I was conscious of the rhythm of fasting and celebration, so that breakfasts were delayed until after Sunday Mass but were then bigger and I was well aware that crisps and lemonade outside a pub often followed attendance at May processions and summer feast day Masses. The Rosary punctuated our evenings and provided a prologue to longer car journeys. Priests frequently visited our home and were familiar with family events and issues, indeed, seemed to be honorary members of everyone's family. I enjoyed looking at illustrated books telling the lives of the saints, often reading these to the brother with whom I shared a bed before we went to sleep, sometimes with a torch, because it was officially well after lights off time. The pictures in these and those on holy cards and little statues, all left a real impression; they went beyond mere decoration.

For ten years, from the age of eight, I served on the altar, bringing me especially close to the 'holy action'. I was inducted into the ritual, saw at close hand the melding of the normative and the idiosyncratic in how it was conducted – in other words, I could see the hold of the rules over the clergy yet the space this left them to put themselves into the action in a personal way. Through their occasional grumpiness and ill-humour, I experienced at first hand and felt intuitively the teaching about *ex opere operato*: perfection was not required to participate in the sacred rites; it was the doing that counted; sometimes we seem to go through the motions, but they are worth going through; sometimes we are carried by habit, rather than by emotion or decision – and often this is enough. God knew we could do better; we knew we could do better; but God accepted what we had to offer for now; we resolved to do better another time. The experience of altar serving also provided an opportunity to learn different roles, to become accustomed to special clothing without being unduly self-conscious, to participate in teams, to share banter in the sacristy, easily mingling the holy with all the ordinary concerns and interests of a boy and adolescent. Through the rotas allocating duties across each month and through the increasing leadership role I was asked to play in co-ordinating the work of several other servers and in ensuring the smooth running of the liturgy by arranging everything in its proper place and making sure that actions were carried out at the proper time, I learned habits and attitudes that served me well in other walks of life at a later stage.

Because I attended a non-denominational, state grammar school, my religious education throughout my secondary school years took the form of Friday night instruction in a room in either the presbytery or church hall. My memories of this are blurred. Although some priests clearly followed some kind of syllabus, with others it was hard to tell what was going to happen or the rationale – although this did not seem to matter. We learned prayers, we saw slide shows of the lives of the saints, we discussed all kinds of issues and we were introduced to various elements of doctrine. Above all, we grew together, gradually maturing in life as in faith, keeping the conversation going, maintaining familiarity with the language and life of faith without this being too separated from everything else that was going on in life. Mass and sacramental practice accompanied this weekly instruction and visits to the home by clergy also continued. I remember being challenged by other pupils in school about the peculiarity of my faith and learning to develop rough and ready forms of apologetics in response, arguments partly drawing upon what I learned in Friday night instruction, but also partly experimental and personal – and probably erratic and unorthodox in parts.

My final memory of learning the language of faith before going to university was a diocesan pilgrimage to Lourdes, without my parents. The giddy experience combined a sense of independence, uncertainty about French food, the powerful and lingering effects of a litre of lager, the lulling effect of constant praying, either of the rosary or in silent meditation, the dizziness following staying up all night at the grotto, the fits of giggling in a darkened church prompted by Dave, a fellow-student's comments as we sought to out-do each other in witty comments on what was going on, even as at the same time we were not really mocking it at all. There were also the tears brought on by witnessing the deep faith of the sick and that of other pilgrims, the shivers induced by being fully immersed under the waters in the baths, briefly naked, on a very cold March day, the moving caravan of candle lights in the evening, processing around the roads like an enormous animal, made up of (it seemed) thousands of people, all united in song and prayer. The shops were filled with holy pictures and cards, of rosaries and holy medals, of paraphernalia that I recognised as simultaneously trashy and tacky yet faith-reinforcing for many. I think I slept most of the flight home, thoroughly exhausted. How much of that experience was 'secular' and could be had from any young person's first nights away from home and how much was 'religious' is hard to distinguish. The class-mate I shared the pilgrimage with, Dave, was the drummer in the rock-band for which I played rhythm guitar at dances on Saturday nights. For each of us, I think it is fair to claim, faith and fun, intellectual questioning and simple devotion, the foreign and the familiar, emotion and prayer, the physical and the spiritual, the sense of belonging to something much bigger than us and yet the deep sense of personal engagement, were all at play and intermingling.[1]

## 2. TALKING AND PRAYER IN THE HOME

In most families there is a rhythm of routine and spontaneity. Much of what we do each week and, indeed, every day, is fixed, regular, easily recognised and to be expected. Washing, dressing, shopping, going to work, meals, visiting Grandma, watching the news, times for getting up and going to bed, all these become familiar foundations for a family's stability. Their very familiarity means that they can be both anticipated and remembered from a very young age. Yet into these patterns of daily life come moments which interrupt, causing us excitement, fear and wonder. For a child who falls over and hurts herself, or who goes to a strange place, hears a fresh sound, comes across an unfamiliar object, then the routine responses do not suffice. Crying aloud for reassurance, attending to our surroundings with awed concentration, tentatively experimenting – all these are moments for spontaneous, that is, unplanned behaviour, and moving beyond the boundaries within which we had been safe and restricted.

The life of prayer should surely embrace both of these essential elements in our lives, the routine and the spontaneous. We should never despise the role of habit. Regular responses to many areas or options prevent us from having to go through agonies of choice about every decision. They relegate to the edges of our minds the less important aspects of life which can validly be carried out without much thought, since they have become part of the way we act and the kind of persons we are. This frees us to give more attention to a smaller number of matters which require careful reflection. People without regular habits and patters of behaviour face an endlessly nerve-wracking and stressful existence. They are taut, unresting, overstretched and so their appreciation and enjoyment of life is seriously impaired. If we are supported by routines and habits we are less at the mercy of moods. It is easier for us to carry out certain actions, even if at the time they are unpalatable, awkward or embarrassing, if we are 'programmed' as it were, to do them. This can be true when we have to go somewhere that feels unattractive to us today, for example, to school or to work, or when we have to say something that does not match the way we feel, for example saying thank you or sorry. It is also true in our coming to prayer. Habit is the motor which keeps us on the road, allows us to operate on 'automatic pilot', to be in a situation without our whole self being engaged. To be minimally present in this way is not the height of manners, nor is it the best way to pray: but to be present at all is a beginning, and an essential foundation without which further progress is impossible.

Talking within the family also rests upon conventions – relating to time, occasions, topic, frequency, length and degree of depth and openness. This is easily seen when we visit other families who do things – and say things – differently. What is taken as aggressive or hostile language in one is taken as a natural and non serious exchange in another. What is considered normal politeness here is considered 'posh' elsewhere. What is taboo in one home is frankly talked about in another. It is interesting, too, to note who starts, who controls and who stops conversation in families. Without such (probably unspoken) conventions or 'rules', family life would become a battleground, erratic and uncertain. These common assumptions and familiar expectations are the building blocks for domestic life.

But, as is well known, a house is not necessarily a home. We might know where we stand, we might be aware of what we must do, we might feel clear about the limits allowed for comment and behaviour, without feeling 'at home' in this situation. If family life is to nurture all its members, to encourage growth and development, to foster creativity, to cherish questions, to promote exploration, openness and wholeness, then routines must leave space for spontaneity. Otherwise a home becomes a prison – emotionally, socially and indeed spiritually confining us. Conversation within the family is given structure and a framework by conventions. Our conversation in prayer with God is likewise given structure and framework by our religious 'routines'. We cannot, however, guarantee life, quality or growth by relying on such habits, even though they are necessary. For without a nourishing of the inner life our conversation is in danger of remaining stilted, shallow, repetitive and empty. Paying attention to the quality of our talking at home is one of the ways we can release the potential for growth in us all and increase our receptivity to each other and to God's individual word for all of us. It will also enhance our ability to respond more maturely to God's call with *all* the dimensions of our nature gradually becoming integrated and brought into conscious relationship with God: our bodies, our feelings, our hopes and fears, our questions and concerns; our choices and priorities at home, at work, at leisure, in politics and society, and, most importantly, our relationships.

How can we play our part as parents in this process? Mostly we do it without thinking, certainly without reference to the notion that fostering 'good' conversation is a necessary prerequisite for true prayer. It is right that this is so. It is not because talking things over in the family helps us to pray, nor because such talking provides a suitable soil in the depths of our lives, one that is sufficiently fertile and nourishing for the seed of prayer to flourish, that we should attend carefully to cherishing conversation. It is because it is good for *us*, rather than because it pleases God, that it matters. We are God's children. God wants our flourishing, just as we desire the flourishing of our children for their sake, not just wishing their progress and 'success' to please us. The promoting of talk of all kinds is beneficial whether or not it leads to explicit prayer. In a sense our task is to prepare the soil, irrigate it with love and try to prevent weeds from taking root or from choking or strangling tentative growth. God provides the seed and in plenty. Forced, artificial preparation does not support a resilient and natural development. God is not in a hurry to 'catch' souls. We must not rush to 'achieve results' in this aspect of our lives. There is not a time when everything has to be known, when our vocabulary, or that of our children, has to be complete. Nor is any apparent set-back the last opportunity. Defeats are part of a life-long campaign of retreat and advance, of growth, self-reliance and interdependence.

Not only is it important to stress that we should not be burdened by looking upon the promotion of talking as a duty rather than as a process which is essentially beneficial and natural, one that has no time limits or deadlines; we should recognise from the very birth of our children that they are not puppets to be manipulated - even for their own good. They are human beings, soon to be independent centres of initiative, original in their own way and answerable for themselves, with a separate existence, however close to us they remain. Space for this movement is essential. As parents we cannot guarantee anything about our children's future. They are, as we are, vulnerable. Our responsibility for them is real; but it is also limited. Their willingness to return what we offer, to grow into reciprocal and mutual relations with us, must come from within, rather than be imposed, and it relies on an ever-advancing degree of freedom .We must love and let go.

Normally, talking is a by-product of joint activity. It starts in a family long before a child can reply; in fact we constantly talk *to* children, not just about them, at least from birth, if not before. At first the child is a passive partner carried along rather than a real participant. But ever so slowly and gradually that chatter about what 'we' are doing when we get in the high chair or on a bus, sit on a trolley at a supermarket, use a potty, wash our hands and, eventually, dress ourselves, does become a purpose and a practice that I can share in, one that I can describe and comment on as part of my passage to a larger world rather than being something nameless that is done to me.

Over the years we have found that playing games has brought us together in a setting that has both boundaries and room for self-expression. The talking and arguing, the cooperation and competition, have allowed us to try each other out. An important part of this process is the practice of learning to compromise, of choosing a variety of games which allow for different members of the family to have opportunities to excel or have favourites. Arguments about what is cheating, what is fair, about winning and losing, loom large. An important stage is reached when children can play without help, when they are, in the game, real opponents, and especially when they can win without a benign bending of the rules. The games are a platform for mutual exchange, intense involvement, for joint fun as well as for the exercise of patience. This applies to board games, card games and a variety of sports and outdoor activities. It is not just our bodies which benefit from family football, cricket, swimming or hide-and-seek. It is vital that our foibles, follies and failures in these can be joked about and referred to, without offence. Moments of silliness and 'letting go' are as important as sharing enthusiasms and expressing passions.

With such a background of regular family routines and of fun and games the opportunity for talking things over (and the coming to terms with experience that this allows) arises more naturally than in an environment which is insecure, unpredictable, inhospitable and over-stern. It is so easy to stifle inquisitiveness on the part of children, to create a climate where questioning is repressed. Asking what and why is an endless process; it requires continuity. If you cannot ask the little and apparently trivial questions, you cannot feel free to broach the more difficult, threatening or embarrassing ones. Keeping the conversation going - in the sense of not closing down any particular topics, and not crushing someone apparently in the wrong - I consider one of the most important parts of a parent (and of a teacher). An atmosphere of approval and affirmation is essential, for confidence and honesty to survive.

Talking things over helps us, at any age, to achieve some purchase on our world. Learning to articulate our questions and to express our feelings opens up communication. If we cannot do this with each other at home, when we are not thrown together because of our status, our job, or our achievements, but simply because we belong together and we are dear to each other, then we will not do it in our individual conversations with God. Telling off, upsets and arguments are one facet of this talking things over; they are an integral part of family life. Rather than feel guilty about such features we should as parents perhaps try to see them as growing points; even in anger we can be expressing love and concern. And so can our children.

"Do you remember when?" The sharing and repetition of the past within the family, some part of its tradition, can be a healthy opportunity to explore continuity-despite-fallibility, the sense of belonging, of inheritance and of progress. The idiosyncrasies of some relatives, key incidents, funny mistakes or misunderstandings - all can be shared as part of a bonding process.

"What did you do today?" We can encourage a degree of reflection and can assist children in finding some significance in the daily events of their lives - so long as we are open to the same questions. Sometimes a sharing of one's past experience can be painful; this does not have to be disguised. Having the 'right words' and the ability to talk smoothly about something painful is not important; being willing to be vulnerable and to share is a priceless gift we can all offer to our families. One critical example of this for me was when I touched a raw nerve within by sharing with two of my children (on separate occasions, in a one-to-one situation) how I had, as a child, sold a special and (to me) precious collection of coins in order to buy a pencil case needed for school. The hesitant description and evident grief of this provided a potent encounter with disappointment which was the issue of that moment. I felt exposed, revealed, hurt and yet helpful in this 'flashback' conversation. It certainly did not reduce in importance the current cause of concern felt by my sons, nor did it make it go away; but perhaps it assisted them in naming their own wounds and coming to terms with them.

Since I am not very practical with my hands and fairly hopeless at mending things, I have had to concentrate on other ways of encouraging conversation as a by-product of some joint activity. We certainly talk, as we eat, about items that are mentioned in the news and sometimes far-ranging and quite deep exchanges are enjoyed before or during the washing up. Reading stories, such as E.B. White's *Charlotte's Web*, or Michelle Magorian's *Goodnight Mr Tom*, or her later book, *Back Home*, establishes a context and provides a shared experience for sensitive joint exploration of many important questions. With so many other attractions now, this is harder for many families than it was two or three generations ago, but I firmly believe that the benefits of this activity are so great that we should put in every effort to make it possible within family life for as long as it is acceptable. Being wanted, facing disappointment, overcoming fear, exploring the unknown, combating temptation, breaking down barriers - all these can be sensitively and safely entered into at second hand through much easily available and appropriate literature.

Then there is the family 'consultation' about possible courses of action which will affect other members of the family. This could focus on a clash of preferences for television, or on moving house, or where to go on holiday, or whether to buy an expensive item, which exam subjects are to be taken at school and so on. Discussing the points for and against various possible courses of action helps children see situations in a broader way, exposes values implicit in choices and affirms priorities worth serious effort. The quality of regular discussion between husband and wife - by which I mean, for example, the depth of exchange, the mutual respect and the genuine openness that is evident - will be overheard and, at least to a limited extent, be internalised as a model by children both old and young.

Talking things over is not, of course, prayer. It does not always solve problems. Sometimes it is too hard to say or to hear the word 'sorry'. Sometimes we do not want to be sociable or reasonable. We want, as adults or as children, our 'rights'. Or we want to be left alone, perhaps to sulk. We need a space and a release from talking or explanations. So long as silence is part of a wider rhythm of involvement and detachment within a family, it is healthy and indeed a necessary ingredient in the developing depth of conversation that is possible. If it is part of finding out who we are, what we really want and what is of central importance for us, then it is part of an internal dialogue - and God is closer to us than our innermost selves, and he is to be found speaking from our innermost depths. To recognise his voice, however, we usually need to have the model and practice of a more external dialogue; certainly the potential of family conversation for assisting us in an ever-developing conversation towards God is limitless.

## 3. FAITH IN THE FAMILY

For most human beings on the planet, the most important thing they do in life is to bring up children. The importance of the job of a mother and father cannot be overestimated. Throughout its history, the Catholic Church has regarded the family as the most influential factor in shaping and nurturing the faith of each generation. The official documents of the church all confirm that parents are the first and primary educators of the faith for their children. Both Catholic and Protestant theologians have emphasised the central role of parents in bringing up children in faith. Much of my thinking about this comes, apart from my own experience as a father of four children (now aged 37, 35, 34 and 22) and grandfather of three more (aged between thirteen and two years old), from my life and work and reading in the Catholic tradition. But let me mention three Protestant thinkers. Martin Luther in the sixteenth century referred to mothers and fathers as apostles, bishops and priests to their children. Karl Barth in the twentieth century outlined the duties of parents as teaching their children how to pray, to observe the Sabbath, to become biblically literate, and to struggle for justice. In the nineteenth century Schleiermacher suggested that children keep adults fresh and cheerful and thus assist them in advancing along the path of sanctification.[2]

Family life is a privileged place for encountering God in everyday circumstances. Faith nurturing opportunities can arise spontaneously within the daily events of family life. The *General Directory for Catechesis* says that catechesis within the home is more witness than teaching, more occasional than systematic, more daily than into structured periods.[3] Thus, it is not like school (or university).

Let me mention four features of a family. First a family is a mixed age or intergenerational place (like a parish). Second, it is an enduring, long-term community, open 24/7/365. Third, it is an informal and intimate community. Close proximity, regular touch, constant and unscheduled verbal exchange, mutual accommodation, frequent sharing, rhythms of argument and reconciliation, times of undisguised vulnerability and disappointment punctuated by occasions of elation and celebration – these are all part of the pattern of family life. Fourth, it is a place where one feels at home, where one experiences acceptance, where one belongs, where one can be relaxed and natural. Here you can express your feelings, expose your fears and explore your dreams. Here one is loved without condition, regardless of achievement. Each member of the family is recognised for his or her idiosyncrasies, specialness and uniqueness, with a mixture, probably, of appreciation and respect, irritation and tolerance, amusement and wonder.

At different times children have been seen as commodities, consumers and burdens, as bedevilled by original sin, as well as made in the image of God, and offering adults a true pattern of Christian existence. Children are not only to be formed; they are also to be imitated, according to St John Chrysostom.[4] The spiritual benefits of family life flow back and forth between parents and children, not in one direction only. Children can be models of faith, from whom we should learn; they are not just 'targets' for faith, to be taught.[5]

There is likely to be a strong link between the understanding of faith held by the parents and the way faith is nurtured within the context of their homes. I do not just mean *what* parents believe but also *how* they believe; there are different ways of holding or living in a faith. Some people sit more lightly to their faith. Some sit more rigidly. Some continue to grow in maturity with regard to faith. Some get stuck with the faith from their past but this does not match how they have matured in other ways. Some are more questioning about their faith. Others are not willing to pose questions or to face other people's questions; they find questioning unsettling and painful. The kind of faith I have will influence how I seek to convey faith at home.

There is an intimate connection between the child we are at the early stages of life and the child we carry around within us thereafter and into all stages of later life. Perhaps we should appreciate this more when we are perplexed by someone's behaviour and attitudes. Sometimes it takes the insights of other people to help us recognise how wounds from our past can weaken our vision, inhibit our capacity to be open to others and undermine our willingness to be generous today.

Would it be fair to suggest that some (perhaps many) parents are not confident that they know enough to pass on a faith properly? They might not be familiar, for example, with the Bible and therefore feel that they are not equipped to instruct their children in its stories and teaching. A lack of confidence because of perceived inadequacies or because of their own perceived lack of religious knowledge, affects some (perhaps many) parents as they face the task of nurturing the faith of their children within the home. One of the reasons for this is that they associate successful faith development with religious knowledge. I want to suggest a different emphasis on what is entailed by communicating faith in the family.

Before I do that, let me comment on teaching about children in Scripture. In the Gospels, adults are told that they should become like little children, that children have a privileged place in God's Kingdom, that children should be seen as models for disciples, models who have much to teach their would-be teachers. It was unheard of and unparalleled in classical thought for a sentiment such as 'unless you change and become like children, you will never enter the kingdom of heaven' (Matthew 18:3) to be uttered. What is it about children that Jesus is alerting his followers to? Children are unselfconscious, receptive, trusting, dependent, flexible, open to learning new ideas, responsive. They know that they have not deserved the gifts offered to them, but nevertheless they are willing to receive these gifts gladly. Children display the capacity for spontaneity, playfulness, wonder, delight, marvel, amazement and joy. Such capacity can sadly become atrophied as we get older and we would do well to tend to its wellsprings within us if we are to remain capable of welcoming the gifts of creation and grace. Our self pre-occupation can also make us blind to the needs of others. Receiving the child is a radical version of what it is in the Gospels to receive any outsider, anyone weak, unclean, at the margins, or under the domain of others. We might link our ability to respond sensitively to children to our readiness to respond adequately to anyone in need, regardless of their status.[6]

The interaction between the grace of God and the mystery of each child is mediated by biology, family upbringing, culture, education, peer groups, choice and accident, as well as by religious faith, practices and institutions. In the provision of care, we adults should be vigilant about our interventions, in case we try to become controlling and fail to appreciate the inherent mystery residing in each child (and person).

I believe very firmly that the handing on of holy things is inextricably linked to the handling of ordinary things. We sometimes separate what we think is holy or sacred from what is ordinary, as if God was reserved for holy places, holy times, holy people, holy activities. But if God is God then all places belong to God, all time belongs to God, all people are called to be holy, all actions are open to the grace of God. We do not get to God in by-passing the ordinary but in how we treat it. Here my focus is on the family as the domestic church. The domestic church is where biology opens up into biography and then into sharing God's life. We start with what earth has given; then with what human hands have made; then we open ourselves to God's transforming love. The family is where community (not on the basis of self-selection – you do not choose the family you were born into) can open up into church. In the domestic church the 'liturgy of life' includes bodily functions (their development and decline), eating and drinking, sexuality, sharing things, play and experiment, reconciliation, disciplining of our affections (learning to love things in the right way), story and celebration. We might say that the curriculum or the syllabus of communicating faith in the home includes: body and touch; food and meals; routine and habit; play and exploration; children and the elderly; celebration and our use of time; conversation and stories.[7]

We can speak of child-rearing as a spiritual practice. This shows itself in the kinds and qualities of receiving and self-giving, of waiting and patience, of forgiveness and forbearance. It is revealed in the act of sticking up for what is right even if this is unpopular or costly. Child-rearing and family life provides a context for gratitude and wonder, for trusting and letting go, for the display of both accepting and transforming love. These are all integral elements in learning the language of faith.[8]

## NOTES

1   For valuable insights in theology from a child's perspective, see *Through the Eyes of a Child*, edited by Anne Richards & Peter Privett (London: Church House Publishing, 2009).

2   See chapters on Luther, Schleiermacher and Barth respectively by Jane Strohl, Dawn DeVries and William Werpehowski in *The Child in Christian Thought*, edited by Marcia Bunge (Grand Rapids, MI: Eerdmans, 2001).

3   Congregation for the Clergy, *The General Directory for Catechesis,* (London: Catholic Truth Society, 1997).

4   See chapter on Chrysostom, parenthood and children by Vigen Guroian in Bunge, 2001.

5   See *The Vocation of the Child*, edited by Patrick McKinley Brennan (Grand Rapids, MI: Eerdmans, 2008).

6   See chapter on children in the New Testament by Judith M. Gundry-Volf in *The Child in Christian Thought*. Also *The Child in the Bible*, edited by Marcia Bunge, Terence E. Fretheim and Beverley Roberts Gaventa (Grand Rapids, MI: Eerdmans, 2008).

7   For a more developed approach to Christian parenting than my brief sketch here, see Michael W. Austin, *Wise Stewards* (Grand Rapids, MI: Kregel Publishing, 2009).

8   See Bonnie J. Miller-McLemore, *In the Midst of Chaos,* (San Francisco: John Wiley & Sons, 2007. This book is sub-titled 'Caring for Children as Spiritual Practice' and complements her earlier work, *Let the Children Come* ( San Francisco: Jossey-Bass, 2003).

# Chapter 5

## COMMUNICATING FAITH ECUMENICALLY

*KEVIN T KELLY*

### 1. COMMUNICATING FAITH ECUMENICALLY
### – IN A SHARED CHURCH

The shared church I am describing consists of a particular group of Anglicans and Roman Catholics living in an area called Hough Green in the town of Widnes in the north of England. In that sense it is unique through its local situation. It is also fairly unique in the way they share so much of their lives ecumenically. But it should not be unique in terms of its ecumenical commitment. For Cardinal Walter Kasper, (in his address to the 3rd European Ecumenical Assembly, Sibiu, Romania, 5th September 2007) ecumenical commitment must be the hall-mark of every parish: "There is no responsible alternative to ecumenism. Anything else would contradict our responsibility to God and the world."[1]

'Communicating Faith ecumenically' would be a fairly accurate description of the parish which is the subject of this chapter. St Basil and All Saints church was built as a shared church over 25 years ago. It stands on what was originally a green-field site and which in the early eighties was beginning to be developed to house people who were being moved out from the Dingle in Liverpool and from parts of Widnes devastated by the chemical industry. Although the development plans included sites for two separate churches on opposite sides of the road, the two local clergy at the time believed that such a project would hardly be in keeping with the Gospel message of unity, especially as understood by Christian churches today. The people moving into the area were consulted. By far the overwhelming majority were in favour of a shared church. The church was formally opened in 1983 by Derek Worlock and David Sheppard, the two Liverpool bishops who were internationally renowned for their deep commitment to 'communicating the faith ecumenically'. They put their commitment into practice as bishops in the way they shared a unique leadership role in the city of Liverpool in conjunction with Methodist and Free Church leaders. Nevertheless, although St Basil and All Saints had the full and enthusiastic support of the two bishops, the initiative itself was due to the way the two local clergy, Pat Conefrey and Bill Broad, and both congregations were determined that the right way forward lay in the direction of communicating their faith ecumenically.

The people of St Basil and All Saints see their shared church as a symbol of their desire and commitment to live and share their faith as closely as possible while respecting the disciplines of their two Churches. As well as developing deep friendships with each other, they accept joint responsibility for the upkeep of the building and for the overall life and mission of the parish through the Joint Church Council. Adult Christian education is a shared undertaking, whether through ecumenical Lenten house groups, Advent reflective prayer evenings and helping people find comfort, support and inner healing through annual shared services of healing and remembering our dead. At key times in the Christian liturgical cycle when both communities needed the church at the same time, 'simultaneous Eucharists' were celebrated. This practice ceased in September 2008 on the insistence of the Roman Catholic Archbishop of Liverpool. These 'simultaneous Eucharists' had enabled the parish to celebrate such feasts as Holy Week and Easter together without contravening regulations forbidding concelebration or intercommunion. Such limitations were obviously occasions for shared pain but such pain can be healthy and even healing when experienced together at the same time and in the same place. Sadly the separate schools were built prior to the shared church but every effort is being made to draw them closer together.

The phrase, 'communicating faith ecumenically' is ambiguous. It could be understood in the sense of one church sharing with its ecumenical partners the 'one true faith' which they believe their partners do not have. That would be a totally unacceptable meaning and is a million miles from the experience at St Basil and All Saints. The two congregations would understand the phrase much more along the lines of 'being in communion (communicating) through faith'. This being in communion is nourishing because it involves mutual enrichment as parishioners of both communities help each other to appreciate (and live) their faith more fully by seeing it through other eyes and through sharing different forms of liturgy, prayer, church life and social involvement.

Until I retired at the end of June 2008 I had been parish priest for ten years and a few years previously Revd Peter Dawkin had joined me as vicar, replacing Revd Guy Elsmore who had come to the parish at the same time as myself. Peter has continued the practice originally established by Guy and myself of exchanging pulpits four or five times a year, a very personal way of 'communicating faith ecumenically'. It has given each of us the opportunity to experience and learn from the faith of each other's congregation as it expresses itself in the liturgy. It has also given us the privilege of listening to how our faith is nourished by the Sunday readings from the Word of God and how we communicate that to the assembled congregation – and the response that communication of faith seems to evoke from them. On the occasion of Archbishop Kelly's parish visitation in January 2007, it was my turn to preach at the Anglican Eucharist. The Archbishop very kindly volunteered to preach in my place and Peter's congregation were delighted to have this additional experience of 'communicating faith ecumenically'. The fact that Guy Elsmore and I arrived at the parish at the same time offered a further occasion of 'communicating faith ecumenically' since we were able to plan together and share a joint induction by both area bishops.

## 2. COMMUNICATING FAITH ECUMENICALLY
### – THROUGH 'RECEPTIVE LEARNING'

In January 2006 I had the great privilege of participating in an international Ecumenical Colloquium held at Ushaw College, Durham. (Revised versions of the papers are published in Murray, 2008). The Colloquium was on the theme of 'Receptive Learning' and coincided with Durham University's conferring an Honorary Doctorate on Cardinal Walter Kasper, President of the Pontifical Council for Promoting Christian Unity.[2] The Cardinal played a very active part in the Colloquium which comprised 140 participants, young and old, from 10 different countries and representing a variety of churches. Not by accident it was held in the middle of the Week of Prayer for Christian Unity.

I found the insights shared on 'receptive learning' immensely enriching at a personal level. However, they also helped me to appreciate the very privileged context of our shared church in which I was being asked to live out my faith and ministry.

Receptive learning was understood to mean churches being open to learn from each other precisely as churches. While the make-up of the group was ecumenical, the actual focus was principally on the Roman Catholic Church. In other words, it was seen as an occasion for the Roman Catholic Church to commit itself to the process of receptive learning and ask its ecumenical visitors to help it be open to learn from them. To opt into this process the Roman Catholic representatives really had to accept that they had much to learn from other churches about their own church's Christian faith, life and mission as a church. That implied also accepting, to quote *Ut Unum Sint*, that some of these other churches may have 'more effectively emphasised' certain features of the Christian mystery[3] or may have 'come nearer ... to an apt appreciation of certain aspects of the revealed mystery or expressed them in a clearer manner.'[4] In other words, it meant accepting that the Roman Catholic Church, while not lacking essential truths, can still grow in its understanding of the Christian mystery. Moreover, insofar as it can fall short in its living out of aspects of the Christian life, the Roman Catholic Church can benefit from learning good practice from other churches. It also involved the representatives of other churches being prepared to be sufficiently open and honest to share aspects of the faith which they felt they had and which Roman Catholics failed to appreciate or to which they had not given enough emphasis.

Nevertheless, it was no accident that the meeting was called a colloquium (conversation). Any genuine 'conversation' involves mutual listening and sharing. Hence, although the principal focus was on the Roman Catholic Church, there was no way it could develop as a genuine conversation if it was totally one-sided. One of the contributors, Margaret O'Gara, shared with us the beautiful and very helpful phrase, "an exchange of gifts",[5] explained so movingly by John Paul II in terms of mutual self-giving in his 1995 Encyclical on Ecumenism, *Ut Unum Sint*.[6] Our colloquium would hardly have been the positive and rich occasion it proved to be if it were only the Roman Catholics went home with their hands full of gifts. The other ecumenical representatives were equally keen to receive gifts. Receptive learning is a mutual process. And that was precisely how the colloquium developed.

Prayer and liturgy were at the heart of the whole process. This brought home to us our shared belief that the real gift-giver is the Holy Spirit. That is why there was no need for any of us to be afraid to acknowledge that we are in need and lack gifts that others have. To be open to this process of gift-giving/gift sharing is to be open to the Holy Spirit. I found this a much more creative way to understand ecumenism. Ecumenism is not a kind of melting pot, boiling away all differences and distinctions and producing a bland common denominator. It is much like a mosaic. Each little part, however tiny, is needed for the beauty of the full picture. Paradoxically, the Roman Catholics among us quickly realised that we need gifts from other churches to make us more truly 'Catholic'.

The word 'catholic' was used a lot in the colloquium. This was not in any excluding sense - Catholic as against non-Catholic. Rather it was used in its more basic and original meaning of 'universal' (Greek: 'kata holos' – according to the whole). In other words, it meant embracing others, all-inclusive. Philip Sheldrake shared a fascinating paper on this theme entitled 'Becoming Catholic Persons.'[7] He suggested that God is the key to our understanding of what it means to be 'Catholic'. Unity in communion lies at the very heart of God. God is one in diversity. As unique images of God we are individuals, but not in any isolationist sense. In no way are we called to be closed in on ourselves. Communion with others is part of our identity as persons. We cannot exist without others, just as others cannot exist without us. At the very heart of our being made in the image of God lies our being 'one in communion'. A 'catholic' person means someone sharing God's catholicity in and through Christ. Paul expresses this very powerfully, "In Christ, the whole fullness of the Godhead dwells bodily, and you have come to fullness in him" (Col 2, 9-10). John uses different words for the same truth, "From his fullness we have all received – grace upon grace" (Jn 1,16).

In one of a number of prophetic interventions the Hungarian Jesuit, Ladislas Örsy, made from the floor, he insisted that we do not belong to a divided church.[8] In other words, we are not each members of a different part of the church, separated from the other parts. Rather, we all belong to one wounded body of Christ. As such, we all need healing – and that healing has to be shared with each other.

This made me face up to a question which I experienced as a very special gift of this experience of 'communicating faith ecumenically'. It was the question: 'Am I really Catholic?' Another speaker put it slightly differently but no less forcefully, 'To be more truly Catholic, we need to be open to learn from other churches'. This is another way of saying that we are incomplete. We have to be open to growth and change. We have to be prepared to let go and venture into the unknown. This is especially true in terms of embracing the stranger, including those whose life-style might disturb us. Being truly catholic can be very uncomfortable. Sheldrake ended his paper with the disturbing challenge: "The catholicity of God revealed in Jesus embraced precisely what those who saw themselves as spiritually pure preferred to exclude and reject."

This led me to reconsider what I mean when I describe myself as a 'catholic priest'. I suspect that, unconsciously, I probably mean – I am a priest of the Catholic Church, rather than of the Anglican, or Orthodox or Methodist church. Perhaps that is a very unchristian use of the phrase, 'Catholic priest'. I am beginning to think I should mean something much broader and more open and all-embracing than that!

Mary Tanner, an Anglican woman who has been a leading light in the ecumenical movement over many years, gave a brief overview of all the dialogues and agreed statements between the various churches.[9] Despite the progress made at the 'head' level of mutual understanding, she stressed that receptive leaning needs to go beyond the 'head' and embrace 'real-life experience' at grass-roots level. She mentioned IARCCUM, the International Anglican/Roman Catholic Commission for Unity and Mission, set up in 2001 to promote this. She instanced such phrases from its documentation as "a new state of committed relationship", "openness to one another", "get to know one another/open to learn from each other" and "share in mission together".

In 2007 IARCCUM issued an 'agreed statement entitled, 'Growing Together in Unity and Mission: Building on 40 years of Anglican-Roman Catholic Dialogue'. It is described by its authors as "a call for action" (p.4). A few sentences later they go so far as to speak of "intensified action". It can truly be described as an exercise in 'communicating the Faith ecumenically' since the first and major part of the statement consists in a very beautiful and helpful overview of the various agreed statement or ARCIC I & II and is headed, 'The faith we hold in common'. Its second part opens with the words: "Genuine faith is more than assent: it is expressed in action". It then proceeds to challenge both churches to very practical action under four main headings: (1) Visible expressions of our shared faith; (2) Joint study of our faith; (3) Cop-operation in ministry; (4) Shared witness in the world.

While Mary Tanner was speaking, I could not help thinking that this kind of grass-roots ecumenism is precisely what had been going on in St Basil and All Saints for nearly 24 years! This made me much more conscious of the immense privilege I have been given of serving as a priest in this very gifted community. When I returned to the parish after the Colloquium I could not resist challenging our shared community with the following words:

> Do we really appreciate how gifted we are? Do we cherish this gift – every single one of us here in our community? Or do some of us just put up with it and even hope that it might go away and we can get back to being like an ordinary 'Roman Catholic' or 'Anglican' parish!!! We hold this precious gift on trust. We have a shared responsibility for it. We cannot feel complacent about it or hide it away like buried treasure. Our prime responsibility is to let it live and grow in us. It is not for nothing that God's Spirit, the driving force of Christian unity, the giver of all gifts and the life-principle of the church, is often portrayed as a strong wind or burning fire. Jesus did not promise an easy life to those to whom he gave the gift of his Spirit.

At present in Liverpool Archdiocese we are going through a process called 'Leaving Safe Harbours'. It is about putting ourselves on a stronger footing to be a truly missionary church to the modern-day world. Some of the process involves rethinking the way individual parishes relate to each other within the one deanery (henceforth to be called 'pastoral areas'). It is highly likely that some neighbouring parishes will be sharing their resources – and their priest – and may even be merging into one new community. The shared church of St Basil and All Saints does not fit easily into such a process. The way forward is not clear. One temptation would be to abandon our almost unique experience of 'communicating the Faith ecumenically'. To me that would be a sin against the Spirit. It would be rejecting the special gift we have been given, a gift to be treasured and shared, not to be buried in the ground as though dead and lifeless. Another temptation would be to ring-fence what is going on in our shared church, as though it was a museum piece or an oddity which has no relevance for the wider church.

If the shared church experience is truly a Spirit-filled one of 'communicating the Faith ecumenically', perhaps 'receptive learning' might give some kind of clue to where God, the giver of all gifts, might be calling St Basil and All Saints. They are certainly living in a rapidly changing world and the Christian church is within that world, not outside it. Just as the church in general has to be receptive to change, so too should be the shared church. Yet the learning dimension is also crucial. Perhaps the presence of St Basil and All Saints in the Widnes Pastoral Area (former Deanery) and in the Archdiocese is a kind of 'learning experience'. As a shared church St Basil and All Saints parishioners need to learn from the changed situation they are living in; and the Pastoral Area and Archdiocese need to learn from the gift of shared experience. If they can be receptive to each other and truly open to learning, together they will be in a better place to accept the mutual gifts they have to share.

Since the above two paragraphs were written, it has been decided that St Basil and All Saints should be served by a team ministry of three priests, all comparatively young, whose ministry also covers four other parishes in the town. Despite a number of obvious difficulties involved in this solution, it has the great advantage of drawing our ecumenical experience into the main stream of Roman Catholic life and ministry in Widnes.

Despite that, there remains one major weakness in the whole process. 'Leaving Safe Harbours' is an exclusively Roman Catholic process within the Liverpool Archdiocese. This seems alien to the basic theme of this chapter, 'communicating the faith ecumenically'. Perhaps part of the learning experience provided by St Basil and All Saints is to alert our two dioceses – and the wider church – to the fact that renewal processes like 'Leaving Safe Harbours' face a very special danger. If they are initiated and implemented in isolation without join consultation and planning between the churches, they run the great risk of being contrary to the basic principles of ecumenism and so against the flow of the movement of the Spirit. It is not impossible that this might be the very special 'learning experience' the Holy Spirit is offering our two churches (and beyond) though the irritant-gift of St Basil and All Saints.

While there are serious challenges still to be faced in relationships between churches, for example, in relation to intercommunion, marriage between spouses from different churches and differing interpretations and emphases on ethical issues, it remains the case that the kind of sharing of parish life described in this chapter is not only possible but also live-giving and mutually enriching. Such examples should encourage Christians from different churches to invest more of their energies in mutually receptive learning (communicating faith *ad intra*) as an integral feature of their discipleship and as an essential foundation for more effective communication of faith to outsiders (*ad extra*).

In his paper to the Durham Colloquium, Cardinal Kasper insisted that the unity we are striving for is not a return to how things were in the past. Rather it is moving to a new reconciled form of unity in the future.[10] That does not mean being a 'new church'; but it does mean being a more developed and more enriched church, insofar as we have mutually shared each other's gifts. According to the Cardinal, this is the "one, holy, Catholic church" we profess in the Creed – which is saying that we believe in the future. Kasper ended with the words: "When, how and where that occurs we can confidently leave to Another. I am convinced that He will bring to fruition that which He has initiated."

## 3. CONCLUSION

On the base of the shared baptismal font in St Basil and All Saints are inscribed the words of the well-known text from Ephesians 4.5: "One Lord, One Faith, One Baptism". This is surely saying that 'communicating Faith ecumenically' is not a pastime for a few ecumenical enthusiasts. It is about an urge, a 'fire in the belly', implanted by the Spirit deep in the heart of every Christian. It is an essential dimension of our very being.

Cardinal Kasper made this point very forcefully in his address to the opening session of the 3rd European Ecumenical Assembly (5 September 2007) held in Sibiu, Romania:

> For us, ecumenism is a task given us by Jesus Christ, who prayed 'that all might be one'. It is set in motion by the Holy Spirit and answers a need of our time. We have stretched out our hands to each other and do not want to let them go again.
>
> We ought not to take the divisions between us as something normal, get

used to them or gloss over them. They go against the will of Jesus and as such are an expression of sin.

There is no responsible alternative to ecumenism. Anything else would contradict our responsibility to God and the world. The question of unity ought to disturb us; it needs to burn within us. [11]

## NOTES

1   From a private translation of Kasper's address, courtesy of Fr Peter Fleetwood, who helped organise the Cibiu meeting.

2   Revised versions of the papers of that colloquium were subsequently published in Paul Murray (ed), *Receptive Ecumenism and the Call to Catholic Learning* (Oxford: Oxford University Press, 2008). This chapter draws upon memories of the papers as given on the occasion, not the subsequently published versions in Murray.

3   Pope John Paul II, *Ut Unum Sint* (London; Catholic Truth Society, 1995), # 14.

4   Ibid, # 57.

5   See Margaret O'Gara, "Receiving Gifts in Ecumenical Dialogue," in Murray, op.cit., pp.26 – 38.

6   Pope John Paul II, op.cit., # 28; 57.

7   Philip Sheldrake, "Becoming Catholic Persons and Learning to Be a Catholic People," in Murray, pp.52 – 62.

8   Ladislas Örsy, "Authentic *Learning* and *Receiving* – a Search for Criteria," in Murray, pp.39 – 51.

9   Mary Tanner, "From Vatican II to Mississauga – Lessons in Receptive Ecumenical Learning from the Anglican-Roman Catholic Bilateral Dialogue Process," in Murray, pp.258 – 270.

10  Walter Kasper, "'Credo Unam Sanctam Ecclesiam' – The Relationship Between the Catholic and Protestant Principles in Fundamental Ecclesiology," in Murray, pp.78 – 88.

11  See note 1.

# Chapter 6

# LAY MINISTRY

*PAT LYNCH*

"For where your treasure is, there will your heart be also." (Luke 12:34)

Faith is that which gives meaning and value to our lives. It is having a "treasure" which enables us to get out of bed in the morning or to keep going when the going is difficult. Fowler defines this 'treasure' as a centre or centres of value and power which give our lives meaning and unity and make them worth living and to which we give our loyalty and commitment[1]. These centres are many and varied and everyone has a range of them. When they arise from self they focus on such things as money, fame or power. More nobly they can focus on churches, ideological movements or political parties which call for sacrifice and a high degree of commitment but these are still finite centres and do not have ultimate value. At best they supply us with finite goods and tribal gods. To commit only to such centres risks idolatry.

When the focus is on the transcendent, which Fowler categorises as loyalty to "the principle of being and to the source and centre of all value and power"[2], it is focused on an infinite centre with ultimate value. Such a centre does not arise from the personal or the group ego and, by it, all our other centres are relativised and ordered. Fowler names this type of faith pattern as radical monotheistic. In the past, such a centre was understood, in our culture, to be the one God, the transcendent creator, and sustainer. Many today would argue that they do not believe in God and have no vision of ultimate meaning. Even so, they do find the energy to get out of bed in the morning and some demonstrate a remarkable ability to live through times of great trial and difficulty, which shows that they do have faith as defined above. As Fowler argues, the opposite of faith is not doubt but nihilism, "the inability to imagine any transcendent environment and despair about the possibility of even negative meaning".[3]

Faith is not synonymous with religion but it is reciprocal. Wilfred Cantwell Smith defines religion as 'cumulative traditions', that is, the various expressions of the faith of people in the past.[4] These may or may not speak to us today and certainly they have to be interpreted for this time and place, but, if they are living traditions, they are capable of awakening faith in contemporary people and nurturing it. For Fowler, faith is deeper and more personal than religion, but both share certain qualities. They are both universal, integral to being human; they are relational and both need community; they are dynamic, linked to stages in personal development and experience and they either grow or wither. Studying faith in various cultures and religions shows that similar patterns exist. The desire to look for and find meaning is a human phenomenon. Radical monotheistic faith, as Fowler points out, calls people to identify with a universal community and "in a sense, depicts our universal coming faith"[5]. This bodes well for living in the global community of the future.

As social beings we live in relationship with others, so too, our faith is relational. We are born into families where we have our first experience of the world and gain our first impressions of whether it is trustworthy and dependable or arbitrary. Initially we absorb uncritically the myths, the values, the ideals of our families. It is as we grow and come into contact with different myths and values that our original concepts are modified or changed. The mutuality of faith and religion means that our religion, also, is inherited, initially, from our family and develops and changes under the influence of our experience and development as persons. It is in the context of religion that I, as a lay ecclesial minister in the Roman Catholic Church, am involved in communicating Christian faith.

The ultimate environment that the Christian faith envisages is symbolised by the concept of the Kingdom of God. This symbol speaks of an ultimate environment which is inclusive, at hand but to be realised fully only eschatalogically, liberating the oppressed, promoting justice and peace and uniting all in love. To love God and neighbour today is the means whereby the eschaton is made present and meaning is given to our present lives. As religious practitioners we take the inherited traditions of our forebears, themselves interpretations, and re-interpret them into meaningful understanding for us today. Some expressions of traditions have lost their meaning and require radical translation. An example would be the traditional devotion to the Sacred Heart, which symbolised the belief in the sacrificial love of Jesus in an image of Jesus displaying externally his bleeding heart. This was an image which spoke powerfully to our nineteenth century forebears. Our belief in Jesus' unconditional love is unchanged but, in twenty-first century England, it needs a different expression.

Although this reflection on sharing faith through the role of lay ministry is in the context of the Church in England and Wales, the mission of all the local churches and parishes throughout the world is the same, namely to witness to, serve and realise the Kingdom of God. The difference lies only in the inculturation necessary to make it relevant in the particular locale in which it is carried out.

A task that all the baptised are called to engage in stems from our share of the prophetic office of Christ. As prophets we are called to present an alternative vision to that presented by the dominant culture, using our prophetic imagination as Walter Brueggeman calls it.[6] The alternative vision critiques the prevailing system with the intent to dismantle it in order to allow a new reality to emerge. The Second Vatican Council did this by looking at the then church structures and remembering the Church's origins. The reminder that baptismal vocation calls all the people of God to build up the Church, to be holy and to be there for the whole world has changed, in varying degrees, the culture of the Church. The subsequent proliferation of the involvement of the laity in worship, in catechetics and in working for justice and peace is proof.

To bring about change it is necessary to have power, which is a concept greatly misunderstood in the institutional church. The power we have comes, we believe, from the Holy Spirit, it is God's power, not our own and is mediated through the community. Historically, for many centuries, it was understood to be conferred solely on the ordained. But, Jesus, reportedly, while on earth, shared his power to teach and to heal with the apostles (Luke 9:1-2) and the seventy disciples (Luke 10: 1-20) and sent them out to use the power so conferred. The account of events at Pentecost demonstrates the power of the Spirit to transform ordinary, frightened men, fishermen and ex-tax collectors into confident and successful preachers. The selfsame power is given to every one in baptism. If we are aware of our power, coming from God, and the way power functions in our organisation, we can learn to use it wisely and consciously.

Roy Oswald[7] has identified four power bases from which people can exercise power in an organisation. The first is structural power, which is not very great for lay minister in the Church of today. The ordained inherit a historical legitimacy which enables them to take up a leadership role in the parish community. The lay leader, authorised by the Bishop, has a degree of legitimacy and may be endorsed by the community but only after a period of giving generous and effective service. This Oswald names as reputational power. It is what Evelyn Whitehead refers to as "a seasoned authority developed on the job".[8]

Oswald's third power base is communicational power. As lay ministers working with groups within the parish community and with other groups in the local community and beyond we form communication networks and opportunities to communicate our faith by deed and word. It was St. Francis who exhorted his followers to preach constantly and to use words if necessary. These groups provide us with coalitions which not only give us a communication platform but also a coalitional power which is Oswald's fourth base. Working in groups not only produces more effective action, but it also provides mutual support and encouragement. Reflecting on and evaluating initiatives in a group helps with ongoing discernment and with refining and developing modes of working effectively.

As human beings it is impossible not to communicate. One's presence or absence, the words one uses, the tone adopted, one's actions and the manner of acting all convey messages which are interpreted by those around us. In this way we cannot fail to communicate our faith to a greater or lesser degree to those we live and work with, a communication which they interpret. Even if we actively concealed our religious beliefs, the way we treat one another would indicate our understanding of who we are in relation to each other and to the rest of creation, unless, as consummate actors, we set out to live a role alien to ourselves.

The power of communication by authentic lived example can be very great indeed. A drop-in location for the hungry and homeless centred on a parish in the middle of Manchester employed volunteers of different faiths and none. One volunteer, a professed atheist, was so impressed by the way that the Christian volunteers treated the clients that he converted to Christianity. He was convinced by the way that every client, no matter how demanding or difficult, was treated with respect, politeness and concern.

We communicate our faith in two directions, firstly within the parish community and secondly, together with the whole parish community, outwards to those who do not belong to it. The second should flow naturally from the first as a consequence of the injunction to love our neighbour as ourselves.

As people of Christian faith we are called into community. We are born into families as social beings and through our religious faith are called into community with other believers to live out faith together. Together we are on a faith journey and together we communicate our faith, to each other and also to those not of our faith, but with whom we live. The faith community we are called into we name church. It is in the parish that most people experience church and it is as being part of a parish community that most people understand themselves as belonging to a church. It is attendance at the weekly parish gathering which brings us to the notice of our immediate neighbours.

The Second Vatican Council in its *Dogmatic Constitution on the Church* reminded the laity that, through baptism they belong to the People of God and share in the priestly, prophetic and kingly office of Christ. Furthermore, the laity are called to use their talents for the building up of the Church, the Body of Christ,[9] in collaboration with Bishops, priests and deacons and to participate in the mission of being "church for the world". This call to active participation in the church produced a radical step change in their role as it had been practiced for the four hundred years preceding the Council, a role which required lay people to be active in an apostolate in the world but passively receptive inside the institutional church.

Today, in the parish, lay people are active in various roles that formerly were filled by the ordained. Lay ministers take communion to the sick, they work as catechists helping people wishing to come into the church, or wishing to receive other sacraments. They participate actively in the liturgy as welcomers, as readers, leading children's liturgy, presenting the gifts, as eucharistic ministers as well as filling the more traditional roles of collector, cleaners, altar servers, flower arrangers, members of choirs and musicians. This is a consequence of the teaching of the Council that, the laity through baptism are responsible, working in collaboration with the ordained, to build up the Church.[10] That the parish should be an open, welcoming, inclusive, community, acting justly, supporting one another but also reaching out into the local and wider community to help those suffering oppression, is not optional, because the parish needs to be a model, as far as possible, of the kingdom of God, our ultimate end.

Where we are now, it is possible to name three factors which hinder faith communication within the parish and three factors which promote it. The former are the communication systems within the church, the power of the parish priest, and the history of lay-ordained relations. Three factors which encourage active lay participation in the parish and the kind of faith that communicates are the shortage of priests, universal education and present day culture.

Communication in the church has been, for a very long, from the top down. Without an effective channel for disseminating the teaching of the Council coherently throughout the church it has reached the laity patchily. To put this teaching into practice at a local level, parishioners needed extended instruction from their ministers who, in turn, needed time and the means to understand the changes so that they could pass on such understanding. Twenty years after the Council it was possible for a sixty-year old priest to say, regretfully, "This is not the Church I joined". In the parish that he led, the changes in the liturgy had been implemented, because directives to do so had been communicated. The how and the why of working with the laity, collaboratively, however, had not, because either there had been insufficient opportunity for formation or there had been resistance to receiving the formation and implementing it. Consequently, the considerable talents and the willingness of the parishioners to be involved were not being used. Without the leadership of the ordained leader the ability of the lay to initiate changes at that time was limited and still is.

The degree of parish activity and lay involvement in a particular community still depends on the parish priest. In fact, nearly forty years after the Council, it is possible for a newly appointed parish priest to come into a parish and close down existing structures and remove all those involved in different ministries, even those preparing for the permanent diaconate. Not only are there no sanctions available to the lay other than their withdrawal from the community, the residual deference to the priest, left over from previous generations, prevents lay people from making legitimate protest at the situation as they probably would in similar circumstances outside the church.

In addition to the consequences of the historical passivity of the laity as noted above, the institutional Church of the past wanted the lay to remain at a faith stage which Fowler names as synthetic-conventional faith, suitable for adolescence. In this stage there is no critical reflection or inquiry and the authority for belief comes from the institution. The believer is expected to take ownership of the teachings and standards handed down by the magisterium. Faith is dynamic and develops as we develop as persons. A growth in personal development leading to a corresponding movement in one's faith stance could leave an individual feeling uncomfortable within the institution.

Changes in the liturgy and in parish life after the Council, despite falling short of what seemed initially possible, nevertheless have led to more and more lay involvement liturgically, catechetically and in administration in the parish. The shortage of active priests has encouraged and augmented this. Any parish which wants to function as an active worshipping community in our present context has to draw on the time and talents of all the members or fail to actively live out its calling. Experiencing active participation in community life makes individuals unwilling to accept anything less. This counters the historical passivity of the laity, which can still linger, and encourages members to shoulder responsibility for the situation and act against moves to return to an earlier outmoded way of being community.

With present day universal education lay people have been taught to question and think for themselves. The prevalence of such means of communication as television and the internet, together with the multicultural and multifaith society in which we live broadens one's world view. The post modern culture with its suspicion of meta-narrative leads to the valuing of other narratives. It leads to an openness to other possibilities, other ways of being and doing. This means that the Christian story cannot be universally accepted as the only story, as was true in the Middle Ages. On the plus side, this is countered by the fact that the Christian narrative has its place alongside other narratives and is on offer to provide an answer to a search for meaning.

The concept of lifelong learning is current in our present society which has led to the provision of courses in a wide variety of subjects for people of all ages. This also obtains in the Roman Catholic Church. Today there are many opportunities to deepen our knowledge of what we believe and to reflect on our understanding of our faith. Not everyone can take up the offer but those who do deepen their understanding of their faith and this has an influence on their communities. Their changing attitudes affect the general mind set of the whole. This makes it easier to articulate an adult faith and share our experience of discipleship with others in and out of the church. It helps the living out of our faith - our discipleship - to be meaningful for today's culture.

It is no longer possible for every parish to have a resident priest. This leaves two options: either amalgamating parishes with the closure of one or allowing both communities to continue to function as worshipping communities. The latter choice leaves both communities with only partial support from an ordained minister, usually a reduced number of services and a potential deficit in leadership. One option is employing lay people to co-ordinate the individual community under the leadership of an ordained priest or priests who are not resident. In this situation parishioners need to take responsibility for their community or fail to be the communities they wish to be.

The lay ecclesial minister, whose purpose is to be the co-ordinating figure in the parish community so that the community fulfils its mission, has a vocation which is more than a baptismal vocation. It is a call to lay leadership in the parish, with the understanding that leadership is service as modelled and taught by Jesus. According to Matthew's Gospel, Jesus taught that "anyone who wants to be great among you must be your servant, anyone who wants to be first among you must be your slave" (Matt. 20:25-28). Other root metaphors for leadership offered by Jesus are shepherding and stewardship. Shepherding as a metaphor needs treating with caution in the present day. It carries overtones of the faithful - the flock- obediently following the leader - the shepherd. However, the style of shepherding presented is that of one who not only looks after the flock but has a particular care for the one who strays, and is prepared to lay down their life in doing so, as Jesus did. Stewardship requires one, not only to act as servant, but also to make responsible decisions when the master is away, calling for a seasoned reliability and inner authority developed on the job.[11]

The faith life and practice of a community is all important, because it communicates, in the most powerful way, to each other and to those who are not members. Lay ministers can serve as models in two ways. They can model an adult style of Christian faith, which enables those, who still feel required to remain stuck at an early stage of faith, that growth is good and allowed. Secondly they can also be role models for lay participation in the community. It becomes normal to see lay people taking responsibility for and being active in roles previously performed only by the ordained. Part of the power of the modelling comes from the fact that the lay minister is 'one of us', a lay person and not one of the ordained, a priest or deacon, often regarded as a man set apart.

Everyone is born into a family in a particular time and place. Baptism initiates a person into the People of God, the Church, into a particular portion of it, the local parish community. Through inherent talents and abilities, in the circumstances of one's life, all the baptised are called to live out God's eternal plan for them. This involves a lifelong journey in faith, a journey which calls for action using these talents. This vocation is in the world and for the world and requires action and involvement in those areas which promote the common good locally, nationally and internationally. Without community the task would be overwhelming and the individual would feel powerless. Most parishioners are too over stretched with work and care of families, including care of ageing relatives, to have the time and energy to devote to the task. Together it is possible to take effective action and achieve results using coalitional power. It is often lay ministers who enthuse, co-ordinate and lead these groups. This action communicates to the world, near and far, the importance of freedom, dignity and justice for all people. It also can lead to an accusation of meddling in politics.

The UK culture denounces religious leaders who speak out against unjust laws, and who stand alongside the poor and the marginalised. They are accused of meddling in politics and told to attend to their proper sphere, religion. The one we seek to emulate, Jesus of Nazareth, told his followers that he came so that everyone would have fullness of life, to proclaim release to the captives and set at liberty those who are oppressed. His followers were enjoined to go and do likewise. They must be salt and light for the world; salt, which both preserves and heals, and light which is essential for life and growth and for seeing one's way. As well as loving God, Jesus' disciples are commanded to love their neighbour as themselves. Stone points our that "compassionate charity entails political commitment because oppression has to do with power, and politics - like it or not- is the realm where balances of power are fought for and decided".[12] Jeremiah writing to the Hebrews exiled in Babylon, enjoined them to "Promote the welfare of the city to which I have exiled you; pray for it to the Lord, for upon its welfare depends your own" (Jeremiah. 29:7).

As cells in the Body of Christ we must be concerned with our health and right function, because what affects one cell affects the whole. Our interconnectedness is not confined to the body of the church but to the whole of creation. Thus we are called to responsible stewardship of the resources of the world and the common good of all beings. This leads us to being involved in politics, which if defined in an Aristotelian way as adults coming together in a public space to talk about and take action for the common good, is not necessarily party politics.

The lay leader, whose task is to enable the communication of faith within and without the community, needs to have both charisma and authority. The talents needed are integrity, attentive openness and vision. The integrity called for is being genuinely oneself, not pretending to be other than one is, not pretending to believe other than what one believes. This links with the need for openness, which is a recognition that one's own stage in the journey of faith is one's own not everyone else's. The object is to journey alongside others where they are and not to try to lead or guide them to a place where we decide they should be. In that journeying both parties are affected and will most likely end up in a place not originally envisioned. In our faith we believe that the journey is under the guidance of God as Spirit, so that the place we arrive at is better that any we ourselves envision.

It is essential to have a vision, an end to which we can aim, for ourselves and our communities. This vision is generated and shaped by the teaching and ministry of Jesus which we feel called to emulate. A vision which is reshaped and renewed by the people we journey with, a vision which we share with, rather than seek to impose on those with whom we journey. The vision is that of the Kingdom of God translated and applied to the circumstances we live in today and as it applies to our various communities, local, national and international. This vision is forged in prayerful interpretation of scripture, not in isolation, but with groups within the community. Visions present an alternative to the status quo and are required from us as part of our share in the prophetic ministry of Jesus himself.

Lay leadership needs to spring from vocation, a genuine call which needs discernment by the individual and also by the parish community. A lay leader needs to emerge from the community because, it is living as a member of that particular community that their talents have been utilised and tested, and their vision shaped. Each parish community has its own faith journey and a leader, coming into it from elsewhere, would need a considerable amount of time to familiarise themselves with the community ethos and make themselves known to the community they enter. This is a situation familiar to the ordained minister, which has, up until the present day, been offset by the structural authority invested in the ordained.

Part of the above is in the sphere of our second requirement, the authority of the lay leader. The call to leadership needs the discernment of the institution and that of the community. The recommendation by the parish priest to the bishop, as leader of the particular church, is the most likely route to authorisation from the institution. Endorsement from the community, as a whole, needs to be structured. At present there is no formula in place for how to develop such authorisation and endorsement. The shortage of priests and the response of clustering parishes to form pastoral areas might generate a clarification of what is needed.

Lay ministers authorised firstly by the Bishop and endorsed by the community are well placed to communicate their own faith and enable the whole community to model what we believe to be our ultimate end, the Kingdom of God. The lay leader is given the time, which the busy parishioner has not, to plan and help execute ways that the community can reach out into the wider world.

In addition, it is helpful for a lay minister to be comfortable with failure. When a project does not achieve the desired and anticipated outcome it is easy to be discouraged and take the future stance of "we tried that and it did not work". This is an understandable attitude but not helpful. The realisation that nothing is wasted and that everything has effects which we cannot always categorise is essential. The work and effort put in can prepare the ground for a later initiative which will then achieve the desired outcome and be counted as successful. "Unless a grain of wheat falls into the earth and dies it remains alone; but if it dies, it bears much fruit" (John 12:24).

Communicating faith as a lay minister does not differ essentially from communicating faith as a baptised member of the community. Faith sharing by deed and word is a requirement of all the baptised. The differences are more of degree. A lay minister needs to have the necessary charisms and a sense of vocation, which is discerned and tested by the community leading to authorisation by the individual community and the institution. Acceptance of the position means that the time and effort needed to live the role are given a high priority. Training and formation develop the skills and vision necessary which are further developed through prayer, experience and sharing in the faith journey of the community.

## NOTES

1  James W. Fowler, *Stages of Faith. The Psychology of Human Development and the Quest for Meaning* (New York: Harper Collins Paperback Edition, 1995), p.5.
2  ibid., p.23.
3  ibid., p.31.
4  Wilfred Cantwell Smith, *The Meaning and End of Religion* (New York: Macmillan, 1963), chaps 6 & 7.
5  Fowler op. cit., p.23
6  Walter Brueggemann, *The Prophetic Imagination* (Minneapolis: Fortress Press, 2001).

7   Roy Oswald, *Power Analysis of an Organisation* (Washington DC: Alban Institute, 1981).

8   Evelyn Eaton Whitehead & James D. Whitehead, *The Promise of Partnership. A Model for Collaborative Ministry* (Lincoln NE: iUniverse.com, Inc, 2000).

9   *Lumen Gentium* n33 in *Vatican Council II: The Conciliar and Post-Conciliar Documents*, trans. Colman O Neill; edited by Austin Flannery (Dublin: Dominican Publications, 1975)

10  LG n 30

11  Evelyn Eaton Whitehead & James D. Whitehead, *The Promise of Partnership*, p.111

12  Bryan P. Stone, *Compassionate Ministry: Theological Foundations* (New York: Orbis Books, 1999).

# Chapter 7

# THE CHURCH AS A LEARNING COMMUNITY

*JOHN SULLIVAN*

In this chapter I comment first on learning in general, analysing its features, qualities and conditions, before turning my attention to learning about faith within the context of the Church. Then there is an exploration of three directions the Church faces in her diverse modes of learning: internally, as she draws upon living tradition in the formation of believers, most especially through liturgy and scripture; ecumenically, as she learns from Christians in other parts of the family of faith; and in dialogue with culture as she engages in the process of inculturation. In order to prevent the chapter from becoming too long, I will omit treatment of such key elements in learning the language of faith as preaching, catechesis, sacramental life, theology and the work of the magisterium.[1]

## 1. LEARNING

Learning requires openness and a capacity to receive, alongside humility (which alerts me to my inadequacies and limitations, and therefore my need to learn) and trust (which enables me to relate positively to potential 'teachers'). It calls for attentiveness, listening and reflection (a form of 'looking back' on what we are being offered). It relies on and extends our memory. There is a degree of risk-taking inherent in any endeavour of learning, for it is not guaranteed to succeed. The vulnerability that is integral to the process of learning (and that must also be associated with the path of discipleship) comes when we move out from comfortable places and positions, when we venture forth into some kind of unknown. Indeed Craig Dykstra suggests that "vulnerability is key to education."[2] He claims that one of the reasons that children are often readier to learn than adults is that they are vulnerable in a way that adults have learned to avoid. "Adults often learn slowly because we have, over a long period of time, built up our defences against anything that might be different from and threaten the way in which we understand things and react to things."[3] Sometimes this risk-taking is voluntary; at other times it seems demanded of us. Indeed, one principal task of a teacher is ascertaining when and how to put a person 'on the spot,' judging when and how to challenge without pressing too far and thereby frightening off the learner. In order for us to be willing to accept the risks that learning entails – of losing face, of becoming more confused, of failing in whatever we try to do – we need a sense of security and of self-confidence. None of us learn effectively or deeply while afraid and under threat.

Just as it helps in the process of dealing with illness if we feel treated as a whole person, where body, feelings, thoughts and context are considered as belonging together, not just as malfunctioning physical parts, so too in learning, it helps if we feel treated as more than containers for the deposit of someone's else's knowledge. In his insightful book *A Will to Learn*, Ronald Barnett says of university students (but his point applies to all learners) "her feelings, attitudes, worries, anxieties, hopes, understandings, priorities, values, capabilities and felt certainties, are all bound up in her being."[4] Teachers need to acknowledge the experiences and perspectives, the insights and wisdom of those they hope to teach; and this applies as much in the church as in any other arena of learning. Thus, Barnett's advice for university teachers is pertinent too for leaders within the church: "students have to be affirmed in their sense of themselves, such that their will to learn is gently warmed; students have to be encouraged to come forward with their offerings, so as to submit themselves for scrutiny."[5] Another way of putting this is to accept that learners are potentially also at the same time sources for the learning of others, including that of their teachers. Reciprocity and mutuality should be present – and evident – in exchanges of learning. I have found that three particular questions, put by teachers to learners - and indeed put by any professional or leader in relation to those he or she seeks to serve - can play a powerful part in fostering reciprocity: What am I doing that you do find helpful? What am I doing that you do not find helpful? What am I not doing that you would find helpful? Such an approach is a recipe for learning together, from one another, not simply alongside one another. Such learning calls for active involvement, not merely passive reception.

One aspect of this will be the facilitation of learners in taking the initiative – in what they study, as well as when and how. Another aspect of the active side of learning will be the asking of questions and the testing of what is being shared, probing for its weaknesses and inconsistencies, its lack of clarity, its implications, and noting whose experiences are not being drawn upon and the voices that remain unheard. The outcome of such probing is unlikely to be smooth and settled forms of knowledge, now permanently available for easy use. In much of the important areas of life we need to learn how to cope with ambiguity and uncertainty, with disagreement and conflict, with apparent contradiction and awkward (often temporary, holding and space-making) compromises.

There are many other features of and conditions for learning. It is often hard to distinguish which comes first and which are causes and which are effects. These often include excitement and enthusiasm, a sense of play, fun and the release of laughter, a lightness of touch, despite the effort and striving required. Learners need opportunities to rehearse what they are learning, to practice and receive feedback, a chance to make mistakes without being punished for trying. One detects in experienced teachers the skill of providing structure, while being flexible, of being sensitive to the sources of motivation and resistance, and of being inclusive of all by offering a diversity of approaches and by differentiating the material and tasks, thereby allowing people to engage with it in ways they feel comfortable with.

All the features of and conditions for learning described above apply equally to learning the language of faith within the context of the church. It is highly likely that our relationship to and resonance with the mission of the church will be mediated by our past and recent experiences of birth and bereavement, of sickness and recovery, of suffering and joy, of marriage and the breakdown of relationship, of success and failure in our endeavours, of friendship and betrayal, of recognition and isolation, of positive and negative encounter with the church. This requires great sensitivity on the part of those who aim to promote learning in matters of faith. They will need to attend to such factors as the cognitive ability of those being addressed, creating an atmosphere of affection and warmth, offering constant affirmation and encouragement and providing accessible and attractive models or examples. Then careful note should be taken of the possible bearing (on learning about faith) of age and level of maturity, of gender and sexual orientation and the particular features of personal spirituality that seem influential in someone's life. Also important as conditions for learning, there is clarity of explanation, a sense of freedom, a discipline that stems more from the material being studied than from the status of the teacher and awareness of the sources of (and obstacles to) motivation. If safe spaces for exploration are linked to appropriate types of challenge, there is a chance that commitment might be elicited, always more appropriate for effective engagement than mere compliance. In all cases, the troubling and significant questions facing people have a bearing on attempts to educate people in faith; these cannot be swept under the carpet just because they are embarrassing or difficult to address.

Among the key qualities for promoting Christian learning will be realism and hope, patience and courage, honesty and humility, invitation and hospitality, accompaniment and critical questioning, all surrounded by a prayerful environment that acknowledges God's Spirit is at work in ways beyond our reckoning. That regrettably neglected but most pastoral report on sacramental initiation, *On the Threshold,* underlines the importance of "listening to people without judging them; standing with them when faith is difficult and celebrating with them those joys they experience."[6] It asks "What do we find frightening about taking a very flexible approach to those at different stages of belonging?"[7] Such flexibility is integral to the adaptability shown in differentiating learning tasks in secular education and it should be equally on display in ecclesial learning. However, so often in the desire for tidiness and through fear of the accusation of inconsistency, the church displays a universalising tendency that rides roughshod over particularities in people and in pastoral situations. More bravery is needed. The difficulty is acknowledged in the report. "We live with the tension of being a custodian of the Church's riches and an explorer. Custodians tend to want to stand still and be protective, explorers want to move on and discover new avenues. These two are not mutually exclusive but keeping them in balance is not always easy."[8] If more emphasis was given to the notion of a pilgrim church, on the way, loved and sustained by God but still wounded, incomplete and in need of learning, and less emphasis on protecting a treasury fully possessed and safe, then the balance asked for in *On the Threshold* would be a step nearer.

This is not to argue that the church lacks a comprehensive and coherent 'syllabus' or 'curriculum.' There is indeed 'seed in the basket' for distribution. For example, over the centuries a minimal content to Christian teaching has included the Apostles Creed, the Ten Commandments, the two principal Gospel precepts (love God and love neighbour as oneself). It has also included the seven works of mercy (from Matthew 25): feed the hungry; give drink to the thirsty; clothe the naked; harbour the stranger; care for the sick; visit those in prison; bury the dead. These were threatened by the seven deadly sins: pride, envy, wrath (or hatred), sloth, avarice, gluttony and lust. In turn these can be resisted by the exercise of seven principal virtues: prudence, justice, temperance and fortitude; faith, hope and charity. Seven sacraments - baptism, confirmation, penance, eucharist, extreme unction, holy orders, matrimony – induct us into the ever-available grace of God. John Pecham, Archbishop of Canterbury, emphasised all the above in his 1281 guidance to clergy as to what their preaching should cover in the course of a year.[9] While this had long been standard teaching in the church it always remained a constant struggle to convey it in such a way that it became deeply rooted in people's lives.

The church has never lacked for content in her curriculum. However, if attention is to be paid to learning the language of faith, then in addition to the explicit curriculum, there needs to be awareness also of the church's implicit curriculum, the messages conveyed informally through her pattern of relationships, modes of communication and cultural practices. These can cumulatively reinforce what is taught in the explicit curriculum, but they can also contradict it, sowing confusion, eroding confidence and inviting cynicism. So too with the null curriculum, what is not taught, never mentioned, what does not reach the surface, the voices that are never heard, the subjects that do not receive attention, the questions that do not get asked. Perhaps the most powerful and pervasive assumptions of any community are those that do not (in some cases need not) get articulated; they are too obvious to be spelled out. It often requires an encounter with people who have quite different basic assumptions for us to become aware of some of our own underlying foundational views, values and expectations. Thus, healthy learning, in the context of the church, will take into account not only her explicit curriculum, but also what is implicit in her life and also those areas where silence currently prevails. A task of teachers is to listen to the heartbeats of the people they face and to hear them into speech, to look into their eyes and to love them into a more abundant life; so too in the church, this is our task.

## 2. HOW THE CHURCH LEARNS

I concur fully with James K A Smith's assertion that "Worship is the matrix of Christian faith, not its 'expression' or 'illustration.'"[10] I am going to treat the primary context for learning the language of faith as the Christian community's worship setting in the liturgy. "Before Christians had systematic theologies and worldviews, they were singing hymns and psalms, saying prayers, celebrating the Eucharist, sharing their property, and becoming a people marked by a desire for God's coming kingdom."[11] Yet too often liturgy is treated quite separately from the rest of theology, to the detriment of both the practice of worship and an understanding of theology. However, corporate worship is the integrating practice for Christians, one that "grounds, sharpens, and humbles the work the church does in every sphere of ministry."[12] In worship "our theology is shaped, our discipleship encouraged, and our spirits fed ... by word and sacrament."[13] It is a school for beginners in their faith journey but also essential for the most advanced of pilgrims. Liturgies, whether sacred or secular, have in common that they "prime us to approach the world in a certain way, to value certain things, to aim for certain goals, to pursue certain dreams, to work together on certain projects. In short, every liturgy constitutes a pedagogy that teaches us, in all sorts of precognitive ways, to be a certain kind of person."[14] In this pedagogy we learn how to read the world as creation and as gift; we learn the stance to adopt within this world where grace permeates all we meet and all we do; we rehearse the gestures that jointly comprise the life of discipleship, many of which are to be carried forward outside the worship context, into the wider community: love and gratitude, care and sharing, forgiveness and compassion, welcoming and blessing, healing and encouraging. As Brett Webb-Mitchell puts it, "worship is the place of education in the gestures of Christ's body."[15] We learn the actions in the liturgy, building up our sense of belonging to the community, gradually fostering within us a set of inchoate beliefs. Elsewhere (for example, in the home, at school, in the process of catechesis) we might reflect on these emerging beliefs, how they fit together, what their implications are and how they might be explained. But, in the order of knowing, beliefs follow from behaviour and belonging; they do not precede it.[16] The instructional and cognitive is not the primary language of faith. This is learned in the body as the site of an embedded spiritual intelligence, one that allows that God comes first and everything else second.

We do not engage in liturgy to alert God to our needs; we engage in liturgy to wake ourselves up to what God is already doing. We develop habits, through regular participation in the liturgy, that create in us a personal habitat, or environment, that is conducive to, that encourages us to, notice God at the heart of everything. The liturgy is a wake-up call for us. What is liturgy *for*? It is for the glorification of God and for the sanctification of humanity. "A major role of liturgy is to gather up, name, purify, intensify and celebrate every dimension of what we call ordinary, daily life," placing it in God's presence, as both gift and task.[17] But we need to be careful because, unless our liturgy sensitises us to the presence of Christ in the person of our neighbour, it can be a distracting activity. The true test of liturgy is how it forms and transforms us to live outside the liturgy.

The liturgy is an action, not a lecture. It awakens certain tendencies in us: trust, gratitude, obedience, contrition, reverence. It institutes or builds a community. It makes present for us a reality whose power we take into our own lives. It pulls together for us the story of God's reaching out to his people in the Old Testament, the earthly life of Christ, the offer to each individual of eternal life by responding to God's love, the task of the Church to carry the Gospel to all peoples and to put it into practice in the world, and our hopes for how God holds all this in harmony as part of his providential bringing creation to fulfilment in the heavenly kingdom. Through liturgy the church shapes the faith, the character and the consciousness of her members: what they believe, what they are like, and how they read the world.

Worship offers us an alternative to our normal way of experiencing time, memory, expectation, identity, belonging, meaning priorities and reality. It provides for us a different source of power, starting point, goal, orientation and sense of direction for life. It is both personal and communal; it is more concerned with 'we' than me. It is about the whole person – body, senses, feelings, mind, imagination, spirit. It opens up the possibility of spiritual knowledge linked with faith and obedience, love and humility. The kind of knowledge made possible via the liturgy is participatory knowledge. One does not grasp tradition by looking at it from a distance, any more than one comes to know a country by being a tourist; only full immersion is effective for true and deep knowledge in both cases. The liturgy gives us a chance to dwell in God's story. We learn, not by instruction, though there is, rightly, an element of instruction in the liturgy, but mainly by taking part in the action. We practice saying sorry and thank you; we ask for help; we experience being fed; we hear the words of forgiveness. It is more like hearing knowledge than seeing knowledge, though it is both; but it is even more like knowledge sensed in our body than knowledge achieved via our mind. In the liturgy we are not acquiring knowledge about God so much as acquiring knowledge of God. We participate in the liturgy so as to imprint what it has to teach us onto our personality and character, to inscribe it onto our body, so that we carry God's version of reality into all our encounters everywhere for all time. We might say that knowledge that is codified in doctrine is lived in the liturgy. It teaches us how to practice seeing, hearing, tasting, touching and smelling the divine presence all around us. It also rehearses in us how we should respond to that grace in all dimensions of our existence and with every person.

In the liturgy, we learn about our real needs. We also learn gratitude, love, receptivity, dependency, stillness, how to wait. Liturgy relativises and puts into another perspective what we thought we knew. Knowledge of God changes all other knowledge; it radically recontextualises it. Liturgy does not teach simplified lessons to unsophisticated people; it teaches the whole theological grammar to believers willing to undergo the discipline. It is in the liturgy that the sources of faith – the Bible and tradition – become a living reality. Without the liturgy, we cannot even begin to do theology.

What are the verbs that apply in liturgy? We repeat (although there is always newness too); we dwell in; we are assimilated. We practice who we are becoming. Other verbs that apply to the liturgy include both conform and change, participate and renew, reflect and reinforce, reveal and transform. These verbs lead us towards the possibility of growing from image to likeness, from the pattern of Christ's life to our own glory.

Outside the liturgy, as Debra Dean Murphy reminds us, we are being named and claimed, created and shaped by other languages and systems of meaning (such as consumerism, capitalism, nationalism, individualism): the world is not neutral.[18] Through the liturgy, we learn to dance to a different drummer; we allow ourselves to be made into a different kind of person, God-shaped and capable of reading the world with antennae oriented towards God and sensitised to recognise God's presence all around us. Through the Eucharist we are inducted into an alternative culture to those we meet in the world. Murphy speaks of the Eucharist as a kind of "counterpolitics to the cultural forces of consumerism, nationalism, narcissism, violence, oppression, and injustice."[19] Instead they learn how they are children of one God, brothers and sisters, all in need, all graced, all mutually dependent, all belonging together, all invited to eternal life.

A central and constitutive element in the liturgy is the word of scripture. Sacred scripture exerted its first influence in the context of worship. Its primary location, the setting in which it is best understood, remains that of worship, in the liturgy rather than in the library. Nevertheless, it has been and should be studied by individuals and groups outside the setting of worship. It provides essential elements for learning the language of faith. For two thousand years Christians have engaged the sacred text by hearing, reading, studying, memorising, applying, and meditating upon its words in countless settings. Scripture has been pondered in caves, cabins, cloisters, castles, and cathedrals. Its content has been studied in private, small groups, academies, schools, monasteries, and universities. Its meaning has been explained by prophets and popes, monks and missionaries, laypeople and clergy, scholars and the unlettered. Its teaching has been expressed in homilies, sermons, music, and art and formalised in councils, commentaries, creeds, and confessions. It has been used to support the status quo and motivate revolutionary behaviour. It has been translated into more languages than any other book, and it remains the best-selling non-fiction book of all time. It inspires and challenges, comforts and mystifies, transforms and instructs.

The Bible continues to be the world's best selling book. It has exerted the most enormous influence on world affairs, transforming the lives of millions of people across the centuries – and still does. The Bible has left its mark on our architecture and our laws, our morality and our history, our poetry and drama, our music and sculpture, our institutions and our habits. The Bible, really a collection of writings assembled over a period of more than a thousand years, tells us, not how the heavens go (science) but how to get to heaven (salvation is its business). It is aimed at spiritual growth, not intellectual knowledge. It is about meeting God in our life, realising we are God's children, in need of God's help; it invites us to share his life and love. We may begin a scriptural reading by saying something like "the letter of Paul to the Galatians", but we close by recognising what has been read as "the word of the Lord" – as God's communication to us, via the human author who has been inspired by God's spirit. None of the human writers involved could have had any idea of what would happen later to what they wrote, which became, in time, a biblical writing in company with a specific set of other witnesses.

It is only too easy to focus on parts of the Bible in isolation from the whole, and thereby to distort or misunderstand what the collection as a whole is about. Just as the verse takes shape in light of the chapter and the chapter in light of the book, so also the meanings expressed in the various biblical books took shape in light of the whole Bible. Although we can focus only on a small part at any one time, eventually we need to relate this small part to the whole picture being unfolded elsewhere in the Bible.

What we get out of it depends, to a large extent, on our state of spiritual maturity and readiness, our way of life, and this includes the company we keep, the practices we are engaged in, the disciplines we follow, the idols we are in hock to. A key document from Rome, *The Interpretation of the Bible in the Church* says, "As the reader matures in the life of the Spirit, so there grows also his or her capacity to understand the realities of which the Bible speaks."[20] It often works at different levels within us, touching our imagination, stirring our heart, pricking our conscience, calming our fear, building our hope, stimulating our understanding, and finds people at all levels of education and who have been through all types of experiences. We can sometimes encounter in scripture what the original writer meant us to, but often what we encounter in scripture could not have been foreseen by that writer. Both the original intention and our current experience can be embraced as operating within the providence of God. The Bible speaks to us in the present, just as it spoke to others in the past. Because of the state of our lives, individually and in society, it is likely that different aspects of the Bible speak to us in different ways. We won't all get the same things from it. However, there will also be continuity, both because of the consistent love of God for God's creation, and because human nature remains pretty much what it has always been, coming from God, owing existence to God, but resisting God, despite being in need of grace.

The Bible has inspired revolutions. It has turned lives upside down. It is difficult to read it and not face uncomfortable challenges. It is also a source of consolation and peace, because it tells us how much we are loved by God despite all our faults and failings. People have done dreadful things claiming the authority of the Bible for their actions. People have also endured great hardships, displayed great heroism, undertaken great projects and shared great love, also under the inspiration of the Bible. It has been an excuse to harden hearts that were already hard; but it has also softened hearts that seemed completely frozen when this seemed utterly impossible. Like the sacraments, it is not magic. Like the sacraments, it can be abused. Like the sacraments, it is charged with God's power. Like them, this power can be channelled into loving purposes. If we open ourselves to scripture properly we allow God to teach us how to live in the real world, which is, of course, God's world. It is not a book full of answers to all our questions, but it does give us a way of seeing, a light for our journey; it tunes us in to what God is communicating, it alerts us to God's presence; it offers us a share in God's love.

We believe that God has been active at all stages in the building of the Bible and in the way the Bible builds our lives into God's story of salvation: in the creation of the biblical books, in the way they were accepted as authoritative, in their transmission to many different people in every continent, and in the ongoing reading of the biblical texts. We have to hold together the meaning the original writers intended, the meaning the church decided was so important that the writings were included in the Bible, and how Christians across the ages have found meaning in the text, not make any one of these 'meanings' overriding. The particular preoccupations of any group of people, anywhere and at any precise moment, can colour what they find in scripture, predetermining and distorting the text. Reading 'with the church' means not only reading with the church now but across time. Reading with the church also means reading 'in the church' in the context of praise, of worship and adoration, of acknowledgement of our shortcomings and needs, within the practice of prayer. The best readings of scripture will be both intelligent (using the brains God has given us as best we can) and devout; it should be both critical and obedient. We will not come to understand the Bible properly if we do not seek to live it out, to put it into practice, to apply it to our particular circumstances, to read in its light the situations in which we find ourselves.

We should approach scripture with expectation, ready to stand under its light, to be instructed. We should treat it as food for our faith, in prayer, loving God, self and neighbour, with others, in the church and bringing our whole self, mindful of the world around us, and its needs. We should use the tools available to us for examining it, questioning and applying our minds, but all the while putting it into practice, relating it to our major decisions in life, and, wherever we can, reading, praying and applying it ecumenically.

## 3. ECUMENICAL LEARNING

In my lifetime ecumenical endeavour seems to have gone from being forbidden to being a compulsory dimension of the Church's life. As a Catholic growing up in the 1950s, I remember the time when entering a Protestant church or joining in prayer with Protestants was something that did not meet with approval. Gradually, over the years since the Second Vatican Council ended in 1965, engaging in ecumenical activity became more and more allowed, then accepted, followed by encouragement, until in 1995 it received the highest ecclesial level of advocacy as an essential element in living out the Catholic faith, without which one could not justifiably claim to be a Catholic. This was in John Paul II's papal encyclical, *Ut Unum Sint* (That They May Be One).[21] The commitment here to ecumenism is said to be irrevocable and unrelenting efforts are to be made to tackle the ignorance, misunderstandings, complacency and indifference exhibited within the Church as to other Christians.[22] "Ecumenism is an organic part of her [the Church's] life and work, and consequently must pervade all that she is and does."[23] Humble and respectful dialogue, sincere prayer together and joint action in solidarity in service to the world, as well as a genuine openness to the gifts offered by others will all form part of this ecumenical imperative.

The radical shift in emphasis underwritten by the pope in *Ut Unum Sint*, reversing a centuries-long stance towards other Christians, will require a sustained and extensive range of initiatives taken at many different levels, if it is to percolate right through the Church. Learning to cope with, then appreciate, then learn from and be enriched by diversity, matters as much in the church as in society. Until recently the Catholic Church has emphasised the value of the centre, of uniformity, of consistency and of order over scope for initiative at the level of the local, over diversity, of experiment and of freedom. Yet, in line with *Ut Unum Sint*, a follow-up guidance document from Rome acknowledges that "legitimate diversity is a dimension of the catholicity of the Church."[24] Certainly there is scope for much more to be done in terms of Christians learning from each other about how best to interpret, understand, express, celebrate, sustain and live out the faith that emerges in response to the grace of God and the promptings of God's Holy Spirit. In addition to upbringing in and learning about the specific tradition into which one is born, there need to be opportunities to engage in ecumenical learning, for the sake of better understanding the Gospel, for the health of mission, for healing wounds inflicted on each other by fellow Christians, for more effective service to the world. Ecumenical education is about fostering understanding of, commitment to and informed participation in the ecumenical process; it involves the transformation of relationships, understandings, attitudes and actions. This entails learning about, learning from and learning with other Christians.[25] There is much ground to be made up and ecumenical learning needs to take place in all sectors and agencies where the faith is taught, including the parish, in schools, colleges and universities, in seminaries, and in all kinds of group projects relating to study, prayer, and service to those in need.

Engaging in ecumenical learning, whether this be scriptural, spiritual, liturgical, doctrinal, social or pastoral will help Christians to "enter ever more deeply, ever more freely, more fully, more imaginatively, and more transparently into [the reality of the Trinity]." [26] Paul Murray, Director of the Centre for Catholic Studies at the University of Durham, and a leading light in the recently developed receptive ecumenism initiative, facilitating a real exchange of gifts between the churches, explains this new movement.

From the Roman Catholic perspective, this much-needed process of ecclesial growth, conversion, and maturing through receptive ecumenical learning is not a matter of becoming less Catholic but of becoming more Catholic precisely by becoming more appropriately Anglican, more appropriately Lutheran, more appropriately Methodist, more appropriately Orthodox, etc. ... [through receptive ecumenism, the hope is that] within each of our traditions, we become more sharply aware of our own lacks, needs, and sticking points and our inability to tend to them of our own resources without recourse to the particular gifts of other traditions. ... [It should] move us closer to finding ourselves in the other, the other in ourselves, and each in Christ.[27]

If openness and the capacity to receive, combined with humility and trust, are essential elements in learning, as was argued in Part 1 one of this chapter, then these qualities need to be displayed within the churches, if they are to learn from one another. The celebrated and wise canon lawyer, Ladislas Örsy describes what is needed if ecumenical learning is to occur:

> The receiving community must look inwards and be well established in a position of humility; it must believe – with faith divine – in its own limitations and incompleteness; otherwise it cannot conceive a desire for enrichment. ... The receiving community must look outwards; it must be alert to and observe the other community with the eyes of faith; it must believe - with faith divine – that they too are sustained by the gifts of the Spirit; it must consider the others' insights and practices with sympathy.[28]

There is much scope for joint witness to be given and for joint service to be offered by the churches in such areas as the pursuit of peace, respect for life, defending the sanctity of marriage, outreach to the poor, oppressed and most vulnerable, care for creation, interreligious dialogue and addressing the negative effects of materialism, as indicated by the archbishop of Canterbury in one of his talks in Rome.[29] However, such witness and service will be more coherent, clear and effective if it is underpinned by serious, sustained individual and corporate ecumenical learning, at local, regional, national and international levels. This learning needs to attend to and to nurture the same prerequisite conditions, features and qualities for learning as outlined in Part 1 of this chapter. Sometimes it happens that better attention to the conditions for effective learning in ecumenical endeavour – between the churches - shows what is possible (and necessary) in facilitating learning within a Catholic Church that has traditionally given more emphasis to promulgation and teaching than to reception and to learning. Certainly, so long as any particular church is operating in less than optimal conditions for learning within its own ranks, it will not be able to communicate the Gospel effectively, nor will it be able to derive full benefit from ecumenism. At the same, it may be that engaging in ecumenical learning will assist in the process of identifying inhibitors and blockages to learning internally that can be overcome with the wisdom gleaned from those in other parts of the Christian family.

## 4. CHURCH IN DIALOGUE WITH CULTURE

Some parts of culture are hospitable to religious faith; some parts are hostile; some parts seem indifferent to it, neither interested nor hostile. We need discernment – to avoid blanket acceptance or blind rejection of culture. If we run away from the surrounding culture, so as not to be contaminated by it, we slip into the ghetto, abdicate our responsibility to influence the world for the better and fail the people God wants us to touch; our purity becomes irrelevant to the world. On the other hand, if we throw ourselves into the world, we might soon find we have accepted too much of it on its own terms, and without realising it we could become assimilated and swallowed up by it and unable to bring to it the distinctive salt and light of faith. Can we learn to swim in our culture without drowning in it? In order to be relevant, we need to be rooted in culture and local needs. But, if we are to be adequately Christian, we also need to be able to transcend culture. Some aspects of a culture provide access to Christianity; some aspects of a culture are resistant to Christianity. Thus, at the same time, we have to be both at home in, familiar with and hospitable to our culture, but also, to some degree, also a stranger, unsettled and disturbing in it. We are called to be in the world, to love it towards God, yet also not of the world, fully accepting it as it is.

Christian activities include proclamation, witness, worship, service, nurture, liberation, nurture and dialogue. When the surrounding culture changes, these activities are understood and expressed differently in a new mixture and set of priorities. This is because the culture that we grow up in and in which we live affects our imagination, our sensitivity, our hopes, our fears, our expectations of others, our habits, our assumptions, our priorities and our relationships.

Within our modern culture we find some of the following notions operating in many people's lives, in different combinations and with varying kinds of emphasis: we have nothing to learn from the past; individual self-fulfilment is of supreme importance; there are no absolute truths or values; nobody has the right to tell anyone else what to do; humanity is the centre of the universe; the human mind is the measure of all truth. To these might be added such views as: no one can believe what s/he cannot fully understand; education will make us all better people; if something is pleasurable, it must be good; so long as we do not hurt anybody we are not doing wrong. Certainly, many people seem to get along quite well without God and for others there simply is no big picture, story or Meaning in life. For many, institutions are suspect, and, conscious of the abuse of power that accompanies any attempt to impose uniformity, it is believed that pluralism is unavoidable, that diversity is enrichment. In our culture, many prefer the term spiritual and shy away from any religious label or affiliation. Instead of recognising the authority of truth as the gateway to authentic living and thus real freedom, many take freedom as the necessary prerequisite before any truth might be found, if such is to be found at all. We have moved from the arrogance of authority to the arrogance of autonomy, with the claim that we are each of us is captain of our own self (since the soul is disavowed). Religion for many is on a par with other forms of self-creation and is reduced for some people to a form of interior decorating. There is a loss of sense of the transcendent. Rights rather than souls form the focus of our efforts. In their openness to everything, it appears that many people are unable to commit to or to embrace anything in any irrevocable sense.[30]

I have painted in the last paragraph a rather negative view of contemporary culture. This cannot be the final word, since it ignores the presence of God's grace effectively at work in the lives of vast numbers of people, bringing out goodness, beauty and truth in what they do. A purely negative approach to culture would surely undermine efforts to relate the Gospel to our world and its cultures. Inculturation is the process of relating the gospel to a particular time, place and way of life. The Gospel should affect our "criteria of judgement, values, points of interest, lines of thought, sources of inspiration and models of life."[31] It is not simply the icing on a cake already baked; it must radically change the cake from the middle outwards. Our Christian faith does not belong in church; or at least, it is not meant to be kept safe there; going to church is meant to reinforce our willingness and capacity to take faith outside the church and into the world. While the faith is kept in a church box, it cannot become fully operational in our lives, it will not be properly thought out; it cannot change our world; it will not be lived out in every dimension of our actions, desires, decisions and viewpoints. Every aspect of human life and activity need to be brought into contact with the gospel; otherwise only part of life will be saved. The gospel is not just about saving our religious life, but the whole of our life, every single aspect of it: the way we think, the way we decide things, the way we value things, our getting and spending, our voting and volunteering; our hopes and fears; what and who we love; whatever we give our energies to. "The inculturation of faith and the evangelisation of culture go together as an inseparable pair."[32] An inculturated evangelisation enables the Christian community to receive, celebrate, live and translate its faith into its own culture.

Inculturation is a two-way process. Just as the gospel casts new light on each human situation, those situations in turn can bring different dimensions of the gospel into new life. Throughout history, from the beginning of the church until now, each generation has had to read, receive and respond to the gospel in ways made possible by, but also in ways restricted by, the rest of their life in the world and all the patterns of behaviour and action associated with that life in the world. The gospel always has to take roots, to touch down in flesh and blood people, in concrete circumstances. Inevitably, in doing so, it changes colour, depending on the light around it, what is already lighting up the lives of the people and what is darkening these same lives. Some might fear that the adaptation and creativity implied by the process of inculturation might put in jeopardy the permanence of faith and the stability of tradition. However, just as there are some goods that cannot be retained unless they are given away,[33] so a living faith cries out to speak to and to be expressed in the cultures it meets, since part of being human is to be a being of culture. We should remember that "inculturation and tradition are not opposites, but "two sides of the same coin". For tradition is "the record of inculturation past, a storehouse of models and resources for inculturations today, which in turn will generate the traditions of the future".[34] Inculturation then is our duty, our challenge and our opportunity to make the faith come alive in our time.

The Council of Chalcedon said of the humanity and divinity of Christ that one is not to be confused with another; one is not to be changed into the other; they are not to be divided off from one another; they are not to be separated from one another.[35] The same can also be said of how faith relates to culture. "It is their individual integrity that allows for them to be united rather than identified."[36] It is interesting to note that this is rather like what should happen in the relationship between a man and a woman in a marriage. Their previous identities are not swallowed up and lost; they remain separate individuals; however, they now become a new, united body in their relationship; their being is taken up with each other, though they should not turn inwards in an egoism à deux; rather it should be a source, a stimulus and a springboard for creative outgoing love, overflowing to others.

## 5. CONCLUSION

Being in the truth is not about accumulating more information; it is about appreciating, indwelling and realising (making real in your life) what you know already. I will take the risk here of claiming that many a child knows as much as is necessary, in terms of faith: God loves us and invites us to share this love with others. However, it takes a lifetime, as long as we are given, to unpack what this means. Learning the language of faith is about unpacking the treasure contained in the simple formula I have just used. Learning how to surrender our whole selves entails having a self to offer. Learning the language of faith requires an unending process of gradual attunement to the will of God, as philosopher Paul Moser says, a (probably lengthy) process of dying to self and of letting go of idols such as "success, happiness, comfort, health, wealth, honour, and self-approval."[37] In contrast, then, to modes of learning encouraged outside the church, learning the language of faith is less about mastery and more about letting go.

Letting go is not easily learned in the context of people concerned about maintaining control. The freedom offered in the gospel and the freedom where the Spirit moves is experienced with difficulty when faith is associated with power, even when this power is used in the defence of orthodoxy. While learning benefits from the stability of order, it flourishes best in an atmosphere that fosters all the features and conditions for learning identified in Part 1, above. It models the capacity to let go and let God be God and trust that God's purposes are being worked out in ways we cannot fathom and certainly cannot control. How might this attitude be demonstrated in a church learning context? The philosopher Stephen Law, not himself a religious believer, offers an approach that I think could well be applied beyond the setting he has in mind when he says,

A religious school might say to its pupils, 'We believe this text is the word of God. We believe that the moral code it presents is the one we should follow. But we don't want you unquestioningly and uncritically to accept this. We will explain why we think you should believe what we believe. But the decision whether or not to believe is ultimately yours, not ours, to make. It's a decision we want you to make only after careful, critical reflection.'[38]

Learning the language of faith in the church might benefit from such an approach. It would foster a greater sense of ownership and responsibility, at the same time as it reduced the guilt (and therefore resistance) associated with doubt and the critical questions that sometimes can arise in the face of an apparent mismatch between life's problems and the church's teachings.

The three kinds of learning analysed in this chapter, learning within the church, learning ecumenically and learning from dialogue with the world in the process of inculturation, would be enhanced if the principles advocated by Mary Hess were adopted. She describes what she calls features of deconstructive criticism. While I do not like the term itself, the ten attitudes she describes seem to me to be likely to assist learning, sharing and communication in matters of faith, as in other spheres of learning:

1. There is probable merit to my perspective.

2. My perspective may not be accurate.

3. There is some coherence, if not merit, to the other person's perspective.

4. There may be more than one legitimate interpretation.

5. The other person's view of my viewpoint is important information in assessing whether I am right or identifying what merit there is to my view.

6. Our conflict may be the result of the separate commitments each of us holds, including commitments we are not always aware that we hold.

7. Both of us have something to learn from the conversation.

8. We need to have two-way conversations to learn from each other.

9. If contradictions can be a source of learning, then we can come to engage not only internal contradictions as a source of meaning, but interpersonal contradictions (i.e., "conflict") as well.

10. The goal of our conversation is for each of us to learn more about ourself and the other as meaning makers.[39]

Hess comments: "These propositions shift us from the mode of being the owners of truth to being seekers of truth … we rely on our faith that there is, indeed, truth to be discovered – but our very faith shapes the humility of our search for truth.[40] What she is preserving here are the conditions that sustain and enable genuine openness, real learning and fruitful communication. The attitudes that she lists cumulatively put into practice the virtues of humility and charity that open us up to learn, about faith as about other matters. Here St Vincent de Paul wisely sums up:

> Humility and charity are the two master-chords: one, the lowest; the other, the highest; all the others are dependent on them. Therefore it is necessary, above all, to maintain ourselves in these two virtues; for observe well that the preservation of the whole edifice depends on the foundation and the roof.[41]

Combined, these two virtues will help us to learn to be faithful and to learn from life; they give us the capacity to receive that is integral to learning: "There is no knowledge of the other that is not ultimately a gracious gift of the other, which we must be glad to receive."[42]

This capacity to receive, in humility and charity, should be a feature not only of individual members of the church, but of the church as an institution. Here a major task remains for the twenty-first century: learning how to listen more attentively to the sense of the faithful and to integrate better this ecclesial source into the partnership and dialogue between scripture, tradition, theologians and the magisterium.[43]

## NOTES

1   On Christian teaching via preaching see Michael Pasquarello, *Sacred Rhetoric* (Grand Rapids, MI: Eerdmans, 2005). For catechesis, see William Harmless, *Augustine and the Catechumenate*, (Collegeville, MN: Liturgical Press, 1995); Petroc Willey, Pierre de Cointet & Barbara Morgan, *The Catechism of the Catholic Church and the Craft of Catechesis* (San Francisco : Ignatius Press, 2008); Congregation for the Clergy, *General Directory for Catechesis* (London: Catholic Truth Society, 1997). On sacraments, see Joseph Martos, *The Sacraments* (Collegeville, MN: Liturgical Press, 2009). On theology, see Fergus Kerr, *Twentieth Century Catholic Theologians* (Oxford: Blackwell, 2007). As an authoritative magisterial compendium, see *Catechism of the Catholic Church* (London: Geoffrey Chapman, 1994). For an overview of the Catholic tradition, combining history, doctrine and spirituality, see Gerald O'Collins and Mario Farrugia, *Catholicism* (Oxford: Oxford University Press, 2003).

2   Craig Dykstra, *Growing in the Life of Faith* (Louisville, Kentucky: Geneva Press, 1999, p.160.

3   Ibid. He adds, with regard to our discipleship, "we cannot be sent ones unless we are willing to be vulnerable to the ones to whom we are sent." Nor will we adequately understand our faith and the sources by which it comes to us, if we are hardened against or have protected ourselves against vulnerability. Thus Dykstra (p.161) claims, "The stories of the Bible, the history of the church, discussion of theological and social issues, the experience of Christian fellowship, participation in worship mean nothing to people who are not going into the world vulnerable."

4   Ronald Barnett, *A Will to Learn* (Maidenhead: Open University Press, 2007), p.28.

5   Ibid., p.87.

6   *On the Threshold,* Report of the (RC) Bishops' Conference Working Party on Sacramental Initiation (Chelmsford: Matthew James Publishing, 2000), p.17.

7   Ibid., p.30.

8   Ibid., p.37.

9   Joseph Goering, 'The Thirteenth Century English Parish' in *Educating People of Faith,* edited by John Van Engen (Grand Rapids, MI: Eerdmans, 2004), p.212. Around the same time Bonaventure instructed his Franciscan brothers on another long-reflected theme in church teaching, the seven gifts of the Holy Spirit, as an essential element in the armoury of a Christian: fear of the Lord, piety, knowledge, fortitude, counsel, understanding and wisdom. See *Works of St Bonaventure Volume XIV, Collations on the Seven Gifts of the Holy Spirit,* introduction and translation by Zachary Hayes, O.F.M. (New York: Franciscan Institute Publications, 2008). Right from the beginning great care was taken to preserve the teaching essential for salvific knowledge. For example, see *The Didache*, text, translation and commentary by Aaron Milavec (Collegeville, MN: Liturgical Press, 2003).

10  James K. A. Smith, *Desiring the Kingdom* (Grand Rapids, MI: Eerdmans, 2009), p.138.

11  Ibid., p.139.

12  *A More Profound Alleluia. Theology and Worship in Harmony*, edited by Leanne Van Dyk (Grand Rapids, MI: Eerdmans, 2005), p. ix.

13  Ibid., p.15.

14  Smith, op. cit., p.25.

15  Brett Webb-Mitchell, *Christly Gestures. Learning to be Members of the Body of Christ*, (Grand Rapids, MI: Eerdmans, 2003), p .118.

16  Ibid. p.158.

17  Daniel O'Leary, *Begin with the Heart* (Dublin: The Columba Press, 2008), p.38.

18  Debra Dean Murphy, *Teaching That Transforms. Worship as the Heart of Christian Education* (Grand Rapids, MI: Brazos Press, 2004), p.15.

19  Ibid., p.188.

20  The Pontifical Biblical Commission, *The Interpretation of the Bible in the Church* (Quebec: Editions Paulines, 1993), p.77.

21  John Paul II, *Ut Unum Sint* [encyclical letter on commitment to ecumenism] (London: Catholic Truth Society, 1995).

22  Ibid., p.5.

23  Ibid., p.26.

24 Pontifical Council for Christian Unity, *The Ecumenical Dimension in the Formation of Those Engaged in Pastoral Work* (Boston: Pauline, 1998), p.20.

25 Simon Oxley, *Creative Ecumenical Education* ( Geneva: World Council of Churches, 2002).

26 Paul Murray, ed., 'Establishing the Agenda' in *Receptive Ecumenism and the Call to Catholic Learning* (Oxford: Oxford University Press, 2008), p.6.

27 Ibid., p.16.

28 Ladislas Örsy, 'A Search for Criteria' in Murray, op. cit., p.45.

29 Rowan Williams, November 2006, cited by Robert Mickens, 'Bittersweet in the Eternal City', *The Tablet*, 2nd December 2006, p.10.

30 For an alternative, but not dissimilar, analysis of contemporary culture, see Matthew Fforde, *Desocialisation* (Manchester: Gabriel, 2009).

31 Pontifical Council for Culture, *Toward a Pastoral Approach to Culture*, (Boston, MA: Pauline, 1999), p.17 [# 4]).

32 Ibid., p.20 [#5].

33 Augustine (edited by R.P.H.Green) *On Christian Teaching* (Oxford: Oxford University Press, 1997), p.8.

34 Peter Jeffrey, 'The challenge of language', *The Tablet*, 22nd January 2005, p.15.

35 Michael Buckley, *The Catholic University as Promise and Project* (Washington, DC: Georgetown University Press, 1998), p.18.

36 Ibid

37 Paul Moser, *The Elusive God* (Cambridge: Cambridge University Press, 2008), p.104.

38 Stephen Law, *The War for Children's Minds* (London: Routledge, 2006), pp.60 – 61.

39 Mary Hess, 'Go and Make Learners! Supporting Transformation in Education and Evangelism' [summarising Robert Kegan and Lisa Lahey, *How the Way We Talk Can Change the Way We Work*, San Francisco: Jossey-Bass, 2002, p.141] in *Christian Education as Evangelism* edited by Norma Cook Everist, (Minneapolis: Fortress Press, 2007), p.106.

40 Ibid

41 Quoted by the column The living Spirit in *The Tablet* 22nd December 2007, p.18 from St Vincent de Paul (1581 – 1660).

42 Phillip Cary, *Outward Signs* (Oxford University Press, 2008), p.150.

43 For an extremely valuable study on the sense of the faithful and the Church's reception of revelation, see Ormond Rush, *The Eyes of Faith* (Washington, DC: Catholic University of America Press, 2009).

# Part Three:
# School and University

# Chapter 8

# COMMUNICATING FAITH IN CHURCH SCHOOLS

*PETER SHEPHERD*

This chapter title, with its implicit assumption that it is appropriate for state schools[1] to pursue frankly evangelistic aims, begs a fundamental question. So does 'communicating faith' have educational validity? If not, it surely has no place in a nationally-funded education system. Examining the relevant issues, I consider in part one of this chapter the nature of the (inevitably 'captive') audience: should church schools, essentially communities of faith *and* of a particular Faith,[2] be open to all; or does a 'church school education' make sense only for children of the Faith? Then, in part two, I argue that it is coherent to speak of 'Christian Education' and that 'Christian Nurture' (or nurture in any Faith/philosophy) may justifiably be an element of the educational enterprise, provided that commitment to a particular philosophical or religious position does not prevent the educator being open to the insights of others and encouraging such openness in pupils. Conversely, in part three, it is argued that claiming neutrality on any matter of human significance is erroneous. Nevertheless, indoctrination (literally 'imparting doctrine', an intrinsic aspect of faith communication) is potentially destructive of the educative process, and a case must, therefore, be made for the mutual compatibility of (some kind of) evangelism and education. This is the task of part four. I conclude, in part five, that the communication of faith through church schools is defensible, but only when the target audience is already part of the Faith community.

What follows will focus particularly on the role of Church of England schools within the state system, although many issues will be relevant to other Christian (particularly Roman Catholic) schools and, more broadly, to any school contextualised by and within a religious Faith. The British Education Act of 1944 introduced a daily act of worship and compulsory Religious Education for all pupils in state schools, and also formalised the school category previously known as 'Voluntary' (those schools which, in the main, had been provided by the Churches). From 1944 - 1998 there were three types of State-funded 'voluntary' school: voluntary controlled, voluntary aided and special agreement. In general the Controlled School has a limited connection with the church. Their providers were not able, either at the time of the 1944 Act, or later, to meet their share of the cost of bringing the premises up to the required standard and/or of the continuing external repair. Generally, school buildings are owned by the voluntary body, but the Local Authority, which also employs the staff, meets all costs. In terms of Christian ethos there is wide variation, from those schools which have virtually ignored their church status (now much more difficult with the sharpening up of 'denominational' inspection), to those which are almost indistinguishable from VA schools. In Aided Schools the establishing body, the Foundation, has a majority on the Governing Body, which is the legal employer of staff, has ownership of land and buildings, and control over admissions. The Governing Body is also responsible for the provision of buildings and their external maintenance. They now meet 10% (originally 50%, and for many years 15%) of the capital cost of any improvement or enlargement of the buildings. Running costs are provided through the Local Authority. Only around 150 Special Agreement Schools (both primary and secondary) were ever established. The powers of Governors of SA Schools were greater than those in Controlled schools, but more limited than those of Governors in Aided schools, in certain respects. The main difference was that the LEA was the employer of staff. 'Special Agreement' status was ended by the 1998 School Standards and Framework Act, and all SA CE Schools became Voluntary Aided, with their Governing Bodies becoming the employers of staff. Following the 1998 Act, there were three categories of state school in England and Wales (Scotland has a separate system): Community (ex-'County Schools' i.e. those schools 'owned' by the Local Authority), Voluntary (both Aided and Controlled as previously, including the bulk of former Grant-Maintained schools[3] which had been Voluntary Schools), and Foundation (mainly ex-Grant Maintained Schools). Since September 2000 a new school category has emerged – the Academy. Academies are all-ability, state-funded schools established and managed by sponsors from a wide range of backgrounds and contexts. The Church of England is sponsor or co-sponsor of several such projects. In 2009 around 25% of all primary schools in England and Wales are CE/CW schools; around 6% of all secondary schools in England are CE schools; Wales has a very small number of church secondary schools.

## 1. INCLUSION AND/OR EXCLUSION

The Church of England has traditionally understood its schools to have a 'twin focus', and although some have argued more strongly for one rather than the other, each focus or function has generally been considered equally valid. 'Service to the children of the nation' itself reflects a twin rationale:

(i) ecclesiological - the Church of England, despite a relatively small active membership, still regards itself (and is Established) as the 'National Church', with anyone entitled to its services, used now by a decreasing number for rites of passage;

(ii) theological - the Church as Servant reflects the Servanthood of Christ and practices William Temple's aphorism that the vocation of the Church is to serve those who are not its members.

This particular focus was termed 'general' by the Durham Report[4] (reflecting the ecclesiological emphasis) and 'service' by the (so-called) Dearing Report[5] (embracing the theological imperative); in the political language of modern Britain it would be called 'inclusive'.

The other focus has been termed (respectively, as above) 'domestic' and 'nurture'. These two words connote a more exclusive, inward-looking role: serving the 'children of the Church' or 'Christian families' (some CE schools have admitted only Christian children, either treating all Christian denominations equally or giving priority to Anglicans).[6] The traditional understanding of the Roman Catholic school is very much a 'nurture' model: "Every Catholic child from a Catholic home, taught by Catholic teachers in a Catholic school."[7] The late Cardinal Hume expressed the same principle slightly differently: "There should be a place at a Catholic school for every Catholic child."[8] But for Catholic children only? Writing back in 1987, Patrick Kelly, then Bishop of Salford, had strong reservations: "To open our schools to those who are not Roman Catholics, besides being deeply incompatible without massive resourcing to our claimed philosophy of education, runs the risk of undermining their character."[9] Despite reaffirmations of this view by commentators such as Haldane,[10] other Catholic voices have urged an approach similar in theological intention to the CE's 'general'/'service' model:

> Unless Catholics can show that their desire for a distinctive form of education is not vulnerable to accusations of being inward-looking, isolationist and unconcerned about the common good, their schools will neither deserve nor attract the support of a wider society.[11]

Hypher supports this more inclusive view, finding in the traditional model of the Catholic school:

> ....a somewhat stunted understanding of Catholicism leading to a loss of a true understanding of the *need for evangelism*, and also narrow-mindedness or even unconscious racism.[12]

There has been a similar shift of emphasis within a Church of England previously content that the 'twin focus' was effected within the *system* of CE schools: some schools would balance these two intentions, whilst others would be more (or even exclusively) 'service schools' or 'nurture schools' (usually, but not always, primary in the former category and secondary in the latter). Since a statement by the House of Bishops in 2002[13] the Church of England's policy has been that the 'twin focus' be reflected in the admissions policies of *all* its schools. It is a matter of judgement as to how well this policy was thought through and what will be gained or lost by its implementation[14] but, as for the inclusive Catholic school, one thing is certain: it makes the matter of communicating faith much more complex. Even if it were acceptable to seek to use the school system to communicate faith to those who are already in membership, active or even nominal, of that Faith; it is quite another matter to seek to do so with those who have no religious commitment whatsoever (many secular parents want their children to attend church schools simply because they perceive them to be good schools) and particularly with those who are already members of another Faith (such parents often prefer a Faith to a secular school because they believe them to be places where religious faith is taken most seriously[15]).

Following publication of a Consultation Document early in 2001 by the Church of England's 'Church Schools Review Group' (CSRG), the Times Educational Supplement (*TES*) ran a front page headline: "God Help Us: But is it the church's place to run state schools?";[16] the article itself was headlined: "Backlash against church schools drive".[17] Richard Dawkins argued that "sectarian religious schools serve only to promote prejudice, confusion and division"[18] as did Anthony Grayling:

> Given the harm that religions do....in the way of conflict, war, persecution and oppression and preventing the growth of science and freedom of thought, I object profoundly to my taxes being used to this end. [19]

Even some Anglican clergy attacked the emerging proposal to double the number of CE secondary schools.[20]

Such secular concerns are even more understandable in the light of the Church of England's policy shift which signals that all children in CE schools, whether they are Anglican, members of another Christian denomination or another Faith community, or from a non-religious family, are considered 'fair game' to have the Christian, if not the Anglican, Faith 'communicated' to them. Presumably to pre-empt criticism, the CSRG sought to distinguish between evangelisation and proselytisation: church schools "are not, and should not be, agents of proselytism where pupils are *expected* to make a Christian commitment", it was asserted.[21] Yet the Report also made it clear that evangelism was not only appropriate, but was an essential task (as indeed it still was in the 'reformed' Catholic view espoused by Hypher), albeit light-touch and unthreatening: church schools might simply proclaim the faith by which they live and provide opportunities for pupils to find out more. They would be places where other Faiths are respected (ignoring a fundamental theological problem for those Christians who, based on such Biblical texts as Acts 4: 12 and John 14: 6, claim an 'exclusive' revelation and soteriology) and where faith would be offered "as a gift to be experienced...."[22]

However, the actual rationale for church schools provided by the CSRG seems at odds with such reassurances:

> The church has a major problem in attracting young people to its services as a means of discharging its mission, and one that causes much concern. This bears directly on the future of the church.

In short: the church is failing to attract youngsters and, because the popularity of church schools provides a "reverse image of attendance at church services",[23] it is now for church schools to undertake this 'missionary' task. Churches are unpopular; church schools are extremely popular and the evangelistic opportunity is just too good to ignore,[24] not least because children "provide access to parents, very many of whom would otherwise have no contact with the church."[25] Introducing young people to church is

> ....[a] measure of effectiveness of church schools....whether they come into church or not, church schools are giving them the opportunity to know Christ.....[and] it may well be that the Christian grounding at school will bring them into church when they have families of their own. *The justification for church schools lies in offering children and young people an opportunity to experience the meaning of the Christian faith.*[26]

It is clear that, for 'Dearing', the single rationale for church schools was their role as vehicles for communicating faith (or 'the Faith'): "...if the children are not coming to us we must go to them."[27] Interestingly, in claiming that church schools should "provide a foundation of experience of the Christian life and a body of knowledge of the Christian faith that can sustain their pupils throughout their lives,"[28] it never seems to have occurred to the Review Group to enquire just how successful church schools had so far been in pursuing this kind of aim. Studies examined by Kay and Francis suggest not much success at all in developing positive attitudes towards the Christian Faith.[29] But, regardless of whether it actually works, is evangelism educationally justifiable when the move to more inclusive admissions policies (formally in the CE, less formally within the RC Church[30]) means that an increasing number of pupils are either not of that particular Faith or have no religious faith at all? Furthermore, when a school is oversubscribed and no expansion is possible, then places offered to non-Faith children will inevitably reduce those available to children of the Faith[31] who, it may be argued,[32] are its proper focus.

Today church schools continue to have a significant role in the provision of State education: just over 22% of all schools in England are Anglican (25.5% of primaries and 6% of secondaries) with almost 10% RC; just under 19% of primary pupils in England attend CE schools (just under 10% RC); just over 5% of secondary pupils attend CE schools (just under 10% RC).[33] Anglican secondary provision, currently around half of RC provision, has been quite sparse in some areas of the country, but the Dearing proposal for the creation of 100 new secondary schools over ten years – particularly with involvement in the Government's Academies program – looks like being easily achieved.[34] Church schools operate in most respects as any other school e.g. teach the National Curriculum and provide teachers with the same pay and conditions of service. On the other hand it is an expectation that they should be distinctive in their religious life and worship, in the provision of Religious Education (RE), in the 'hidden curriculum' and ethos, and also in their approach to the curriculum.

This distinctiveness is formally inspected. The Statutory Inspection of Anglican Schools (SIAS) framework requires inspectors to report on

(i)   how the distinctive Christian character of the school meets the needs of learners;

(ii)  the quality of school worship;

(iii) the quality of RE;[35]

(iv) the effectiveness of the leadership and management of the school "as a church school".

An overall judgement is made on the "distinctiveness and effectiveness" of the school "as a church school". It is possible that the judgements will vary (one way or the other) with OFSTED's judgements about the school as an educational institution measured against purely secular criteria. It is clear, therefore, that the nature of the education provided by the church school is expected to be different from that of a purely secular (i.e. community) school, and what is different is that it is providing *Christian* as opposed to any other form of education. Christianity is the lens through which the education is focused; it is the context in which the whole activity of the school is framed.

## 2. CHRISTIAN EDUCATION AND/OR CHRISTIAN NURTURE

The core function of any school is to educate, but are education and faith compatible? Even if secularists accepted both the historical fact and the current parental demand for Faith schools, they may still be concerned that an evangelical or allegedly indoctrinational agenda might take priority over the (equally allegedly) 'neutral' educational task. 'Christian education' embraces what the school has to offer as a distinctive religious community engaged in education and indicates how the process of education is mediated through a Christian, as opposed to a secular, world-view. However, is the concept coherent?' Is it not (as Hirst argued[36]) a contradiction in terms? Or, at least, as Miranda urged, is there not still work to be done in "explicating [the meaning of 'Christian Education'] and arguing for its acceptance in the light of current understanding about education and the transmission of knowledge"?[37]

Education is the process by which we are provided with the tools to enable us to become what we have it in us to be; it provides the maps and guidebooks for life's pilgrimage (to use a religious image). The process may be understood (taking some liberties with the Latin root) to be all about *'leading out'*:[38] leading the child out onto the road to authentic, autonomous and responsible adulthood. Once it is recognised that there is no value or belief-free environment in which education is delivered, that the secular is just as potentially biased as is the religious, and that there is never any truly neutral perspective, then it would seem incontrovertible that within a democratic society education should be available from a variety of providers and based in a variety of world-views. This meets a fundamental principle that the values and beliefs context in which children are educated should, so far as it is possible, reflect, rather than contradict, those of the home. After all, the education system should normally work in partnership with parents, not against them. This would logically require that children who are admitted to church schools come from Christian families, because if they do not, then not only is the parental values principle voided, but the criticisms of those who see the whole purpose of church schools to evangelise children of no faith or of other Faiths would, in the light of the Dearing rationale and similar Catholic statements,[39] be difficult to refute. There is also the issue, raised by Bishop Kelly, as to whether distinctiveness is inevitably diluted by inclusion.[40]

Christian nurture is undoubtedly a faith (and Faith)-centred activity. Some will argue, for that reason alone, it should have no place within a state-funded educational system, and there are evident problems, practical and philosophical, in engaging in religious nurture with children who are not of the Faith; indeed, the concept of religious nurture itself only makes sense in relation to children of the Faith. But to deny *those* children that process within their church school would be to take a very narrow view of education. If the whole point of educating children is to support them in their human growth, physical, spiritual and moral, then to place a *cordon sanitaire* around religion is as restrictive as placing it around music or any other potentially enriching life-experience or locus of meaning. That is why

Christian nurture must remain a crucial constituent of the provision of church schools. For those children whose families do profess membership of the 'household of faith', it would seem both uncontroversial and axiomatic that they might be nourished, supported, and brought to maturity[41] in the Faith as part of the process of education within a religious context. Indeed, it would seem odd if this did not occur. This is because the process of education never operates in a values vacuum, and values inevitably imply some kind of belief, religious or secular. That may be seen to be one of the advantages of schools with a religious foundation. Their contribution is at least based on a coherent and tested world view and values system, which may not always be accessible in a system based on more transient political trends or the domination of particular social groups.

While 'Christian Education' is education contextualised in (Christian) Faith, in contrast to that embedded in a secular world-view, 'nurture' connotes a more inward journey. But does the guide necessarily take a much more positive and possibly protective, or even dominating, role in the process, and is the destination assumed? Thiessen concludes that 'it is logically possible for Christian nurture to satisfy the ideas of a defensible form of liberal education.'[42] Problems only arise when 'religious schools' (Thiessen writes from an American context) become "breeding grounds for fanaticism and intolerance" rather than exhibiting "healthy commitment", which should be the goal of all proper education.[43] Of course,

> teaching for commitment can foster these perversions, but it need not. And we must not let the fear of such perversions make us miss out on the benefits of healthy commitment. Love has its perversions too, but we do not let this stop us from praising the virtues of love.[44]

The alternative of teaching for commitment is, actually, "the hell of non-commitment" from which children deserve to be spared.[45]

## 3. COMMITMENT AND/OR NEUTRALITY

The late John Macquarrie, reflecting on the apparent contradiction between openness and commitment, believed it to be entirely possible to have a commitment to something or someone, yet still be open to others, valuing their priorities and their insights.[46] Macquarrie argued that it is not contradictory to hold to what we believe to be true, whilst accepting the challenge that we may learn things which might not only enhance our beliefs, but may even cause us to reconsider them. The educational problem arises when the teacher or pupil is so sure s/he has the whole truth, that s/he is unwilling to entertain the possibility of error. But this is not simply a religious problem; the 'secular' educationalist who is never open to the possibility of being wrong and intolerant of those with whom s/he disagrees is as guilty of failing his/her students as any religious dogmatist. This is implicit in the essential nature of our humanity: we cannot know anything with absolute certainty, although that doesn't prevent us making reasonable judgements on such evidence as we believe we have, and entering into appropriate commitments, rather than wallowing in an epistemological agnosticism.

So human knowledge is inevitably limited and neutrality in any teaching or learning enterprise is impossible. Let us examine these assertions. Stephen Hawking, making reference to the scientific quest for "the unification of physics",[47] claimed that while "it would be very difficult to construct a complete unified theory of everything *in the universe* all at one go" (my italics), this is still the ultimate scientific aim. He offered three alternative scenarios:

(i)   there is such a theory and one day ("if we are smart enough") it will be found;

(ii)  it will never be possible to construct an ultimate theory, only partial ones;

(iii) there is no theory ('out there') to be had.

Even if we did discover an ultimate theory "we could never be sure that we had indeed found the correct theory, since theories can't be proved";[48] furthermore, we could not use it to predict anything. So the 'ultimate quest' is only "the first step" to another goal: "a complete understanding of the events around us, and of our own existence".[49] If we achieved that goal "it would be the ultimate triumph of human reason – for then we would know the mind of God".[50] But would we? Hawking had argued that it would be wrong to imagine "God as a being existing in time".[51] If a unified theory could only encompass "everything *in the universe*", then it follows that any ultimate theory will still be limited to the created order and not have anything to say about any transcendent dimension(s). It may tell us something about the mind of God, but not everything. Human knowledge can never (unaided by revelation) pierce beyond the universe in which we are 'trapped' by time and space; and we still seem some distance away from fully understanding the nature of that.

The search for neutrality is similarly elusive. Each one of us is grounded in a complex of 'knowledge networks'. Leaving aside the traditional philosophical problems posed by epistemology, it is reasonably clear that we come to know things (assuming we can actually know anything) in a variety of ways and from a variety of sources. Apart from the bare facts of the world: that it exists, that we experience (or appear to) certain physical phenomena, most of the 'facts' with which we deal are nothing of the kind. It follows that so far as most knowledge and experience goes, we take a perspective. We approach our ideas and beliefs from 'where we are'. Astley refers to Runzo's understanding of 'conceptual relativism' i.e. that there are

> no "neutral" facts, independent of minds, that can be read off the world. All perceiving is "theory-laden". Further there is no single correct set of facts representing the facts, for facts about reality are relative to the conceptual schemes of different perceivers.[52]

This may seem dangerously relativistic, implying that the only truth is 'my truth' or 'your truth', and many, religious or not, would not wish to go that far. Nevertheless, it illustrates how important it is to recognise that everyone who passes on knowledge or ideas does so from a position of partiality. Indeed, if education were to be limited to indisputable facts, then it would not only be extremely tedious; we would wonder what the point was, apart from playing Trivial Pursuits! The only real facts are, virtually by definition, quite mundane. On the other hand claiming to have certain knowledge of that which goes beyond the mundane is not only astonishingly arrogant, but is intrinsically inimical to the delivery of education. It is never the teacher's, nor even the parent's role to do the learner's thinking for her. As Astley warns:

> In the case of those students who are capable of reflection, and whose fulfillment lies in its exercise, to encourage the development of an intellectual position that remains at a precritical level of consciousness is to have failed educationally.[53]

If all a teacher aims to do is transfer his own beliefs, perspectives and worldview uncriticised and undigested into the heads of the students, then that not only represents a failure to understand the finitude of our human condition, it is an abrogation of the fundamental duty of an educator.

This is particularly the case regarding matters of faith. Many seem to assume that faith is belief: assenting to a particular proposition. Great faith is then portrayed as the ability to believe things that are very difficult to believe (like the White Queen in Lewis Carroll's *Through the Looking Glass* who practiced believing six impossible things before breakfast!). Clearly belief has an important role in the Christian Faith, but the problem with 'faith as belief' is that it lays the emphasis in the wrong place; faith as trust and fidelity – the form of a relationship rather than a form of knowledge - is of much greater significance for the religious person. Nevertheless, faith is presumably based on something which is at least analogous to knowledge, even if it is not knowledge *per se*. We might say that faith is a way of apprehending the world and our place in it. Nevertheless, although we may be "always confident" in what we believe, we "walk by faith, not by sight".[54] As Macquarrie rightly asserts:

> Neither the man of faith nor the man of unfaith….has certitude. This is part of our finitude. We are thrown into a world and so we see it only from within. If we were to know with certitude the why and wherefore of our existence, whether we belong within some meaningful pattern or are absurd items flung up in a meaningless process, we would have to step outside of our world and see the whole range of being. But this is impossible.[55]

The teacher is as vulnerable to the possibility of being mistaken as the student. That is why the teacher must always be a learner.

So in the light of our twin proposals: the impossibility of neutrality and the equal and linked possibility of a committed openness, perhaps education and nurture are not so different as they appear? Mention was made above of the contrast between *educare* and *educere*. That distinction has been debated hotly in terms of the proper business of schools. Is the function of the school to educate or to train? Put this way the distinction is between what has often been termed 'education for life' (education in the broadest sense) and 'education for work' (training or vocational education, seen as rather more narrow). Despite such differing emphases it is generally recognised (not least as life includes work) that young people are entitled to an education which combines both, although perhaps to varying degrees.

But the idea of preparing for life is itself such an all-embracing endeavour that it must necessarily (as *educere*) involve an element of nurture. Astley's suggestion is that any distinction between education and nurture should be more nuanced:

> The nature of feeling…and the way in which it is known – which includes a partly private, introspective element – should give us pause before drawing too sharply the lines of demarcation.[56]

So 'Christian education', neither incoherent nor self-contradictory, is inextricably linked with nurture. However, we must recognise, as Francis pointed out in his specific consideration of the "tension between mission and nurture",[57] that both are capable of being abused. But it is their combined impact on both the curriculum and the 'hidden curriculum' which makes church schools distinctive.

## 4. INDOCTRINATION AND/OR LIBERAL EDUCATION

The concept of a hidden curriculum has been helpfully explored by Astley,[58] who describes it as "a set of learning experiences that are tacit, implicit, informal and (usually) unstructured".[59] Astley quotes John Westerhoff with evident approbation: "My conviction is that this hidden curriculum, this unconscious learning, is so important we cannot afford to let it remain unconscious".[60] This is the part of the iceberg which lies under the water, one which (to continue the metaphor) if ignored will do the most damage. Although this curriculum has not been deliberately hidden, it is important to search it out. It is particularly important for teachers, because they need to know what they are doing; it is, Astley claims, less important for pupils to be able to recognise it. Indeed, it may actually be undesirable, because there may be "certain learning situations where an insistence on explicit articulation of all learning can only disable it."[61] A similar danger is to be found in the analysis of certain types of religious discourse, particularly myth, where critical scrutiny can destroy the power of the myth to communicate its meaning. There is a sense in which one has to live the myth in order to be able to properly (i.e. existentially) comprehend it. Similarly, there are aspects of the hidden curriculum which can only be lived. Astley points here to Polanyi's notion of "tacit knowledge", where "there are things of which we are focally aware only through our subsidiary awareness of other things."[62] Those who argue for the pupil's rational autonomy (the 'educational liberals') need, urges Astley, be cautious, for rational autonomy is only one among many elements in the life of a properly educated, and particularly the properly religiously educated, person. 'Unbridled lucidity' is not an unqualified educational virtue, at least not in Christian education.[63]

But is this not to allow indoctrination to infect the life of the school, just as all religious education used to be confessional? One need only read some of the Agreed Syllabuses which appeared during the 1940s, '50s and '60s (the West Riding Syllabus[64] became the classic[65] and much copied example) to recognise that.[66] Furthermore, a huge proportion of RE teaching was dedicated to the study of the Bible. Indeed, back in those days there was a general expectation that all schools[67] would deliver a Christian (based) education. Michell has described the years up to 1960s as "the era of educational evangelism",[68] and as Cox notes:

> There was a time when a teacher would have been proud to be described as a good indoctrinator…For an indoctrinator was originally one who imparted doctrine, and doctrine, when used in the meaning implied by its classical roots, is only another word for teaching. So to be an indoctrinator was to be a successful teacher. It was, however, taken for granted that the doctrine was true, and that the teacher was not trying to impart ideas that were false.[69]

Thiessen reminds us that the term 'indoctrination', originally used virtually as a synonym for education, became strongly negative for educators; indeed, it came to represent everything that was antithetical to a liberal education which had as its core values individuality, freedom, autonomy, rationality, and tolerance.[70] However, he subjects the related concepts of indoctrination and liberal education to a detailed critique, proposing a

'more holistic and developmental concept of liberal education [which] will lead to a rather different definition of 'indoctrination'.[71] Taking the "core idea" of indoctrination to refer to "the curtailment of a person's growth towards normal rational autonomy", he argues because 'normal' rationality is neither "complete independence [n]or perfect rationality", then

> ….initiation into the present and the particular is a necessary phase of a person's growth towards rational autonomy and therefore the charge of indoctrination is not applicable to this stage of development.[72]

In other words, the traditional liberal view fails to take account of the developmental process and assumes that the provision of a liberal education is a pure activity, unsullied by any transmission of pre-formed beliefs or values. This assumption replicates the mistake of those engaged in 1960s &1970s educational thinking and which became quite a strong thread in the School Council's Humanities projects which proposed the teacher as neutral provider of education and which counselled teachers against expressing their own opinions to pupils. But "if neutrality is too studiously applied...it can easily pass from being an instrument of method to being a fixed commitment in its own right, where the cultivation of impartiality becomes an end in itself".[73] Commenting on this phenomenon, Ninian Smart pointed out that

> history teaching is vastly more than telling people when and how things happened. It should issue in the capacity to do history – to think historically, to judge about historical issues, [and] to understand some of the forces at work in major historical events....[equally] religious education could be designed to give people the capacity to understand religious phenomena, to discuss sensitively religious claims, [and] to see the interrelations between religion and society.[74]

The solution is what Smart called 'transcending the informative'; recognising that the educational enterprise has to do with much more than passing on information in some kind of objective manner. The problem is that the child has too often been seen as a blank template ready to soak up neutral facts, about which she would then make up her own mind. This very idea has been used by parents to justify their 'non-interference' in their child's religious upbringing (such parents are, Thiessen argues, actually indoctrinating).[75] Some years ago a parent told me that she didn't take her child to church because she wanted him 'to be able to make up his own mind'. Apart from how we can make up our minds about an experience we haven't had, we may wonder whether the parent would allow the child to make up his own mind about sex and drugs! For Smart, as Macquarrie,

> commitment does not, by itself...imply the bad sort of prejudice: it does not involve distortion: it does not involve lack of sympathy for other positions. It is not that crass evangelicalism which wants to find fault in those who do not agree. Real commitment...is secure; and as secure, it belongs to the world of dialogue rather than to the sphere of judgement. It is as willing to listen as it is to speak.[76]

The truth is that values/beliefs intervention in the child's developmental process (Thiessen describes this as the "initiation/socialisation/transmission component") is a proper role for parents and, we might add, the Faith community and the Faith school.

Having developed this concept of 'normal rational autonomy', Thiessen argues for active Christian nurture which will not undermine personal autonomy. Firstly, he urges: "initiate boldly. Christian parents should not sell the Christian birth-right of their children for a mess of liberal pottage."[77] In particular Christian schools and colleges will be places which support the development of faith and where there must be "a systematic, serious and orderly initiation into the study of the Christian tradition".[78] This is no different from the normal educative process into "the human inheritance", for neither can, nor should be, a neutral process. So far as specifically Christian nurture is concerned, the goal must still be to maintain "normal autonomy". Parents (church, church school) may hope that the outcome is a choice for faith, but this must not be forced – that would be indoctrination. So,

> although their children ...are brought up within a context of Christian commitment, they will be taught and nurtured towards an eventual 'independent' choice for or against Christian commitment.[79]

This involves the child being encouraged to take steps towards an autonomous faith commitment. The time will come when she will have to make up her mind for herself. Thiessen remarks that this principle "calls into question the continuing practice of infant baptism in many Christian churches". If baptism is to be the true (and single) mark of commitment and initiation, then children "need to mature towards normal rational autonomy before they make any *firm* commitments". The Church of England continues to place its faith in confirmation as a public declaration of personal commitment, but it is clear that many young people (and their parents) see confirmation as little more than a graduation ceremony, thus treating it with as little seriousness as they treated baptism.

Indeed, the Christian nurture of children is a joint responsibility of the family and the Christian community (represented by the local church and the church school). But the primary educator/provider of nurture is the parent:

> Education is much more than schooling, and parents cannot delegate their own role to the school....[Furthermore]...no Catholic [we could add 'or Anglican'] school, however strong a caring community it is, can substitute for a loving home....Schools cannot be expected to inculcate what is ignored or denied in the home".[80]

Without the active involvement and support of the parent (whose own actions or inactions may send the child negative signals) it is likely that any other participant will fail. If, for example, a child is sent to Sunday School, whilst the parent stays at home, then the child will learn that church attendance is unimportant. If, however, the parent genuinely wishes their child to be nurtured in the Faith, then both the local church community and the church school can be invaluable partners in the process. The church community can teach the child what the life of Christian discipleship is about – the centrality of worship, caring for those in need, and participating in a community which sees itself as the Body of Christ. The church school, too, will enable the child to participate in worship, to pray and so to recognise the presence of God in their lives. Taking RE particularly seriously, it will provide appropriate opportunities for the child to learn not only about religion, but from the religious experience of others. In a community which seeks to put Christian values into practice, the child will be enabled to grow spiritually and come to understand 'from inside out' what it is to live a Christian life. All that will initiate the child into Christian doctrine (in-doctrinate) in its broadest sense of the word.

But this process is not indoctrinational in the pejorative sense, for it need not endanger normal rational autonomy, nor should it prevent cognitive growth; indeed, it allows a proper balance to be maintained between cognitive and affective development. More specifically, it allows the fostering of "honest and serious grappling with doubts, questions and objections to Christian convictions".[81] It should also involve positive consideration of alternative religious and world views. However, the general education provided by a Christian school or college

> should not be thought of as precluding the interpretation of these forms of knowledge as a revelation of God's truth. For the Christian, all truth is God's truth and needs to be taught as such.[82]

This is just another reminder that education is never delivered in a values or beliefs vacuum; that all knowledge is interpretation and, as Astley reminds us:

Christian education does not pass on a ready-made Christian culture, belief-system or lifestyle, for that would be to pass on a second-hand, inherited Christianity that would not necessarily suit the needs of the next generation of Christians.[83]

## 5. EVANGELISM AND/OR EDUCATION

This brings us, appropriately, back to the fundamental question: is it right for the church school to engage in 'communicating faith'? Astley has urged that there should be

some overt proclamation and invitation must somehow be presented to and heard by the pupils within the school, and perhaps also their parents and families and the community that the school serves. But that 'community' may itself be understood in two ways: as the church community ('the gathered church'?) or as the non-ecclesial neighbourhood.[84]

He therefore distinguishes between the approach to mission in a general/service school and in a domestic/nurture school. Astley correctly notes elsewhere that 'Dearing' 'appears to allow for a role of explicit mission in the rationale and practice of church schools. This would be a controversial position to take.'[85] Indeed it is. I have argued that it is difficult to justify 'evangelism on the rates' and Astley explicitly recognised that difficulty.[86] Nevertheless, he also argued that "we need not be quite so mealy-mouthed about evangelism" and set out to "explore with more sympathy the appropriateness of the language of evangelism and conversion in church schooling, and even in general schooling."[87] In the church school, if Christian formation is an appropriate activity (as he believes it is) then that can be complemented by evangelism. Christian pupils and staff 'need constantly to be challenged to new and renewed commitment, and to multiple conversions in different dimensions of their Christian life.'[88]

Referring to the eschewing by most RE professionals of a confessional approach to the subject, Astley offers the important insight that even secular educators are evangelists of a kind. They

engage daily in what we may surely think of as a form of implicit (general) evangelism, through teaching that leads to the adoption of particular attitudes, values and dispositions – and, of course, beliefs. Education is always in the business of changing belief: not only beliefs-that about the natural and human world, but also the 'beliefs-in' that express the trust,

141

commitment and engagement that are essential to both academic pursuits and everyday life.[89]

Indeed, if teachers did not alter attitudes and inspire children to consider their values, then they would not be engaged in education at all. Astley also wishes to define evangelism is very broad terms, so that it is not so far distant from education, and well away from the "anti-rational, wholly heteronomous and negatively indoctrinatory"[90] activities of some. So evangelical activity (so defined) in church schools is not simply acceptable, it is proper; and it may be quite explicit and specific. It must have "something to do with Christ", and there must be

> some patent, definite focus on the tradition of Jesus within the school, as a touchstone for all its forms of Christian education, so as to ensure that it is his concrete life, teaching, character, death and spirit that children are faced by and formed in.[91]

I find myself in agreement with Astley, but only to a degree. Although Astley's definition of evangelism is broad, and

> consistent with good education [in that it helps] learners identify and evaluate what they believe, and the grounds and implications of those beliefs, thus developing their ability to think for themselves,[92]

there still remains an intention to engage in some positive Christian formation, which should also be a liberating activity, one by which youngsters can work out their own beliefs and values, but which is fundamentally about nurturing a child within the family of the church. Elsewhere, Astley expresses disappointment at an evangelism which is so implicit, it is almost unrecognisable: it is not just about being good and polite, or even environmentally aware,[93] it should be about Jesus Christ.[94] Indeed, 'Churches need children in order to learn how to be themselves, how to be really human and how to be Christian. Church schools can only help in that learning.[95]

But what if the child in the church school is a Muslim; or what if her family is committed to its membership of the British Humanist Association (perhaps the church primary school is the only local school)? Does the fact that they are in a church school mean that they should be subjected to what is, fundamentally, a programme of Christian formation? What if the family is not particularly religious, but might still designate itself 'Christian'? Such families will often resent any attempt to 'convert' their children: religion, for them, is often such a private matter, that they themselves have no wish to discuss it with their children: 'let them make up their own minds'. Would it be considered acceptable for a Muslim voluntary aided school to adopt the same approach to nurture, if it happened that non-Muslim children attended the school? What if a secular school head teacher decided that she wanted to 'spread the gospel' of secular humanism? However widely evangelism is defined, if it is to retain any element of its original meaning (i.e. preaching the *euangelion*), its place can only appropriately be in a school which makes it clear that it is committed to Christian nurture. That is the only context in which 'communicating faith' can possess educational justification.

## NOTES

1 Despite those who make a distinction between 'church' schools and 'state' schools, the majority of church schools in England and Wales are state, as opposed to private/'public' schools.

2 I use 'Faith' when referring to a particular religious tradition, and 'faith' for all other usages.

3 A category of State-funded 'independent' schools introduced by a Conservative Government in 1988 and abolished by a Labour Government in 1998

4 Durham Commission on Religious Education in Schools, *The Fourth 'R'* (London: National Society/SPCK, 1970). *Passim.*

5 Church Schools Review Group [Chaired by Lord Dearing]. 2001. *The Way Ahead: Church of England schools in the new millennium.* (London: Church House Publishing). *Passim.*

6 For a discussion of the historical, theological and ecclesiological issues and a critical examination of both models see Peter Shepherd, *Who are church schools for? Towards an ecclesiology for Church of England Voluntary Aided Secondary Schools.* Unpublished PhD Thesis. (Milton Keynes: The Open University, 2004).

7 Quoted by William Kay and Leslie Francis, *Drift from the Churches: attitudes towards Christianity during childhood and adolescence.* (Cardiff: University of Wales Press, 1996). 48, but originally from Pope Pius XI's encyclical letter of 1929: *Divini Illius Magistri.*

8 Basil Hume, "Education since the 1944 Act' in Bishops' Conference of England and Wales," in *Partners in Mission: A collection of talks by Bishops on issues affecting Catholic education.* (London: Catholic Education Service, 1997), p.118.

9 Quoted by Bernadette O'Keeffe, "Fidelity and Openness," *International Journal of Education and Religion* Vol 1.1 (2000): p.132.

10 "The primary function of Catholic schools is to transmit Catholic truths and Catholic values. Everything else, no matter how important, is secondary to

this." John Haldane, "Catholic Education and Catholic Identity". In *The Contemporary Catholic School: context, identity and diversity,* edited by Terence H McLaughlin, Joseph O'Keefe and Bernadette O'Keeffe, p.135. (London & Washington DC: Falmer, 1996).

11 John Sullivan, *Catholic Education: distinctive and inclusive* (Dordrecht: Kluwer, 2001), 176.

12 Paul Hypher, "Catholic Schools and Other Faiths". In *The Contemporary Catholic School: context, identity and diversity,* edited by Terence H McLaughlin, Joseph O'Keefe and Bernadette O'Keeffe, p.224. London & Washington, DC: Falmer, 1996). My italics.

13 *House of Bishops Statement* released 15/1/02: "Through each of its 4,700 schools, the Church of England is strongly committed to serving the whole community from a distinctively Christian standpoint. Church schools must be distinctively Christian institutions rooted in the life of the parishes and open to the diverse communities they serve. Historically, Church of England schools have been a service to the nation's children and this requires them to be inclusive in admissions, as most already are. We are committed to ensuring that all Church of England schools should seek to offer places to children of other faiths and of no faith in their local community."

14 See Peter Shepherd, "From Facilitation to 'Diktat': a brief survey of recent CE policy on church schools", *The Journal of the Association of Anglican Secondary School Heads,* Issue 15, (2005), pp.10 – 23 and Peter Shepherd, "'So she can't actually do anything?'" *The Journal of the Association of Anglican Secondary School Heads,* Issue 17, (2006), pp.7 – 16.

15 But it is also clear that many would prefer their own Faith schools: "The silent majority of Muslim parents would like to see their children attending Muslim schools." Letter from Iftikhar Ahmad of the London School of Islamic Trusts. *Times Educational Supplement* 2.8.02, p.14.

16 *Times Educational Supplement.* 23.2.01.

17 *Times Educational Supplement* 23.2.01, p.3.

18 *Times Educational Supplement* "No faith in the absurd". 23/2/01, p.17.

19 *Times Educational Supplement* 23.2.01, p.13.

20 Letter from the Revd David Jennings: "I am not sure we need church schools in the society we live in at the moment. Churches run the risk in a multicultural and predominantly secular society of establishing something that is not entirely real and, at worst, quite divisive." *Times Educational Supplement* 23/2/01

21 Church Schools Review Group [Chaired by Lord Dearing]. 2001. *The Way Ahead: Church of England schools in the new millennium.* London: Church House Publishing. para 3.12: 12. Their italics.

22 Ibid: para 3.25, p.15.

23 Ibid: para 3.5, p.10.

24 Ibid: paras 3.3 & 3.4, p9.

25 Ibid: para 3.8: 10.

26 Ibid: para 3.9: 10 – 11. My italics.

27 Ibid: para. 3.14: 12.

28 Ibid: para 4.8: 21.

29 William Kay and Leslie Francis, *op cit*, pp.57 – 58, 152 – 154. The authors conclude that Roman Catholic schools tend to be most successful, with some secular school pupils actually displaying more positive attitudes towards Christianity than their CE counterparts. They comment: "To the outsider it may seem somewhat puzzling that a denomination should wish to finance an educational system which actively undermines its *raison d'être*." p.58

30 *Times Educational Supplement* 8.2.02. Article by Clare Dean: "We're too poor to be inclusive". This suggested that to offer places to non-Catholics would mean building more schools and claimed that there were no funds to do this.

31 Ibid. The Director of the Catholic Education Service, Oona Stannard, was quoted: "Rejecting even more Catholics from the places they have funded and nurtured over so many years would cause considerable pain."

32 See Peter Shepherd, "Our Nature is to Nurture," *Journal of the Association of Anglican Secondary School Heads.* Issue 10, (April 2002), pp.21 - 23.

33 Figures for January 2006 taken from the (then) Department for Education and Skills' statistics and provided by the Culham Institute: *www.culham.ac.uk/CS_stud/stats/2006/cs_stats_schools.html* [accessed 24.8.07]

34 Whether there will be sufficient Christian senior managers available to staff them is a matter of current concern to the Church. See article by Adrian Pritchard: "Progress on new academies", *National Society News.* Issue 29, March 2007, p.4.

35 In Voluntary Aided schools; RE in Voluntary Controlled schools is usually inspected by OFSTED (The Office for Standards in Education).

36 Paul Hirst, 'Christian education: a contradiction in terms', Learning for Living, 11, 4 (1972), pp.6 – 11. For a full discussion and response to Hirst's challenge see Leslie Francis, "The logic of education, theology, and the church school," in Christian Perspectives for Education: a reader in the theology of education. Edited by Leslie Francis & Adrian Thatcher , (Leominster: Gracewing Fowler Wright, 1990), pp.20 – 35 and Elmer J Thiessen, "In defense of a distinctively Christian curriculum", Ibid. (1985), pp.83 – 92, at p.87, where the underlying problem is seen to be "showing exactly how religion can be integrated with other forms of knowledge."

37 E. O. Miranda, "Some Problems with the Expression 'Christian Education," *British Journal of Religious Education.* Vol. 8.2 (1986), p.101.

38 'Education' strictly derives from the supine of the Latin verb *educare,* which, linked to the idea of assisting at a birth, carries the meaning of 'bringing up' or 'rearing' a child, normally referring to the more limited idea of bodily nurture/support; however, the Latin *educere,* meaning 'to lead out', 'to bring out', can also carry the meaning 'to bring up' and may be thought to represent a richer

and more creative understanding of the educational process.

39 For example: "The activity of a Catholic school is, above all else, an activity that shares in the evangelising mission of the church". Congregation for Catholic Education, *The Religious Dimension of Catholic Education,* (Rome, 1988) para.101.

40 A warning was also given by Anglican education researcher Leslie Francis: "....at key points sharp conflict may emerge between the practical implications and expressions of the theology of nurture on the one hand and a theology of service on the other. The very values represented by the development of a network of ecumenical and distinctively Christian schools may well not only contradict the values most cherished by schools committed to radical Christian service to the community, but also conflict with certain Christian expectations and hopes for the state maintained system of education as a whole". Leslie Francis, "Theology of Education". *The British Journal of Educational Studies* Volume XXXVIII, No. 4 (1990), p.360. We might compare the cautionary words of RC Bishop Konstant: "...it is not possible to determine, in any realistic way, what is the maximum proportion of non-Catholic pupils that can be accepted into a Catholic school without changing the religious nature of the school; there can be no hard and fast rule". Quoted in James Arthur, 1995. *The Ebbing Tide: Policy and Principles of Catholic Education* (Leominster: Gracewing, 1995), p.213.

41 Elmer J Thiessen, *Teaching for Commitment: Liberal Education, Indoctrination and Christian Nurture* (Leominster: Gracewing, 1993), p.26.

42 Ibid, p.207.

43 Ibid, p.277.

44 Ibid, p.276.

45 Ibid, p.277. Here Thiessen quotes Smedes' "Care and Commitment".

46 John Macquarrie, *Theology, Church and Ministry* (London: SCM Press, 1986), p.148 – 9.

47 Stephen Hawking, (2nd Edition). *A Brief History of Time: From the Big Bang to Black Holes* (London: Transworld Pub, 1998), p.187.

48 Ibid, p.203.

49 Ibid, p.204.

50 Ibid, p.210.

51 Ibid, p.201.

52 Jeff Astley, *The Philosophy of Christian Religious Education* (Birmingham Alabama: Religious Education Press, 1994), p.269.

53 Ibid, p.289.

54 2 Corinthians 5: 7.

55 John Macquarrie, (2nd Ed.). *Principles of Christian Theology*. London: SCM Press, 1977), 81. Macquarrie, in using the term 'unfaith', adds the qualification: "if I may use that expression"; he is using 'faith' here with religious connotation i.e. 'faith in God'; so 'unfaith' in this context represents

atheism. But, as Richard Dawkins has so clearly demonstrated, the atheist can be as passionate and 'evangelical' about his 'faith' as the theist.

56 Jeff Astley, "The place of understanding in Christian education and education about Christianity". *British Journal of Religious Education.* Vol. 16.2 (1994), p96.

57 *International Journal of Education and Religion.* Vol 1. (2000), pp.116-117.

58 Jeff Astley, "Christian Worship and the Hidden Curriculum of Christian Learning," in *The Contours of Christian Education,* edited by Jeff Astley & David Day, pp.141 – 152, (Great Wakering: McCrimmons, 1992).

59 Ibid, p.141.

60 Ibid, p.142.

61 Ibid, p.146.

62 Ibid, pp.146 – 147.

63 Ibid, p.147.

64 1966: [for children aged 4 – 7 years] "The school will introduce children to beautiful things, growing things and living things, thus helping them to be aware of the wonder of life and to worship its Creator.". p.8.

65 John M Hull, "Agreed syllabuses, past, present and future," in *New Movements in Religious Education* edited by Ninian Smart & Donald Horder, p.101 (London: Temple Smith, 1975).

66 So, for example, the Cornwall Agreed Syllabus for Religious Education (i.e. that of a secular Education Authority) tells teachers that the effect of their teaching might "only be gauged by the love of God, which is inculcated, together with its corollary, love to our neighbors". Cornwall Education Committee. 1944. *Supplement to the Cornish Syllabus of Religious Education,* p.8.

67 M. Levitt, "'The church is very important to me.' A consideration of the relevance of Francis' attitude towards Christianity scale for the aims of Church of England aided schools," *British Journal of Religious Education.* Vol 17. (1995), p.101.

68 C. Michell, "Some themes in Christian Education c. 1935 – 60," *British Journal of Religious Education.* Vol 6.2 (1984), p.82.

69 Edwin Cox, *Problems and Possibilities for Religious Education* (London: Hodder and Stoughton, 1983), p.101.

70 Elmer J Thiessen, "Christian Nurture, Indoctrination and Liberal Education," in *The Contours of Christian Education,* edited by Jeff Astley & David Day, p.67 (Great Wakering: McCrimmons, 1992). For Hull, "indoctrination and education are mutually exclusive". "Indoctrination," in *A Dictionary of Religious Education,* edited by Sutcliffe JM. pp.166 – 168. (London: SCM Press, 1984).

71 Ibid, p.76.

72 Ibid, p.77.

73 Edward Hulmes, "Neutrality," in *A Dictionary of Religious Education,* edited by Sutcliffe JM. p.243. (London: SCM Press, 1984).

74 Ninian Smart, *Secular Education and the Logic of Religion* (London: Faber, 1968), pp.95 – 6.

75 Elmer Thiessen, 1991. "Christian Nurture, Indoctrination and Liberal Education". In *The Contours of Christian Education*, edited by Jeff Astley & David Day, p.81 (Great Wakering: McCrimmons, 1992). Conversely McLaughlin argues that there is "a non-indoctrinatory form of religious upbringing which a liberal can in good conscience claim a right to offer to his or her child." Terence McLaughlin, "Parental rights and the religious upbringing of children, " in *Critical Perspectives on Christian Education: a reader on the aims, principles and philosophy of Christian education*, edited by Jeff Astley and Leslie Francis, p.181 (Leominster: Gracewing Fowler Wright, 1994).

76 *Op cit,* p.98.

77 Ibid, p.79.

78 Ibid, p.80.

79 Ibid, p.81.

80 Basil Hume, "The Church's Mission in Education", in Bishops' Conference of England and Wales. *Partners in Mission, (1997),* p.27, p.28.

81 Ibid, p.82.

82 Ibid, p.83.

83 Jeff Astley, "Tradition and Experience: Conservative and Liberal Models for Christian Education," in *The Contours of Christian Education*, edited by Astley & Day, p.42 (Great Wakering: McCrimmons, 1992).

84 Jeff Astley, "What is the church's mission to the nation, and what part do church schools play?" *Journal of the Association of Anglican Secondary School Heads.* Issue 8 (2001), p.7.

85 Jeff Astley, "Evangelism in Education: Impossibility, Travesty or Necessity?" *International Journal of Education and Religion.* 3.2 (2002), p.180.

86 Astley, 2001. *Op cit,* p.8.

87 Astley, 2002. *Op cit,* p.181.

88 Ibid, p.181.

89 Ibid, p.186.

90 Ibid, p.190.

91 Ibid, p.191.

92 Ibid, p.190.

93 Jeff Astley, "Church Schools and the Theology of Christian Education," *Journal of the Association of Anglican Secondary School Heads.* Issue 10. (April 2002), p.8.

94 Ibid, p.9.

95 Ibid, p.14.

# Chapter 9

# THE WORK OF A DIOCESE IN SUPPORTING SCHOOLS

*IAN TERRY*

## INTRODUCTION:
## THE BIG PICTURE — STRATEGY AND SUPPORT

The diocesan perspective on communicating faith is about strategy and support. Diocesan officers see the big picture of diocesan life and relate it both ways to local and national initiatives. This big picture enables strategies to be developed so that the Church can be pro-active in communicating its faith at all levels. The strategies will support the very many ways in which faith is already being shared.

I shall set the general scene of what it is to be an Anglican diocesan officer, specifically, in the Church of England, a Diocesan Director of Education, or in the Episcopal Church a Superintendent. All Church Schools Officers are concerned with communicating faith in Anglican Schools. I shall then explain my personal context, which will have formed my views. Faith schools and social cohesion is a topic of current debate in educational and political circles in Britain and I shall explain how I believe Anglican schools make a significant positive contribution to social cohesion throughout that country but this will also apply to such schools in the USA. This leads naturally into a consideration of what I have called the touchstones and pressure points in Anglican schools; for example, the quality of candidates for headship is critical in determining the school's success in promoting an attractive Christian vision of education for fullness of life so I shall describe how Diocesan Directors spend much time on both appointments and succession-planning. Equally, I shall touch on training and supporting Foundation Governors, specific Clergy training, school inspection, links with local universities and the importance of more Christians coming to see teaching as a personal vocation. Other touchstones and pressure points in Britain are in a most welcome increasing demand for Further Education College Chaplaincy, the 'hot potatoes' of admissions criteria and rural primary school viability and the implications of all these proper demands upon the capacity of Diocesan Boards of Education to adequately meet them and to have the space, vision and energy to lead proactively in a time of great opportunity. Finally, as an opportunity which is unparalleled in Britain in both its positive potential for faith sharing and its extreme demands on diocesan capacity, I shall mention Academies as a category in their own right.

## 1. COMMUNICATING FAITH IN ANGLICAN SCHOOLS: A PROFESSIONAL AND PERSONAL CONTEXT

Faith is already being shared in parishes and schools, seen from the particular perspective of a Diocesan Director of Education, and so that is where our Diocesan Board of Education (DBE) strategies must have supportive impact. An evaluation of that impact is fundamental to our accountability as diocesan officers. We are mutually accountable because we share Christian vocation. We are accountable, also, because in England voluntary financial contributions from parishioners pay for much of our work and because voluntary contributions of time and commitment by vast numbers of Foundation Governors keep our schools viable ~ and enviable ~ as Christian places of teaching and learning. This accountability keeps all diocesan officers grounded. In Hereford Diocese many of these officers are designated as Support Ministers and that title gives the work focus in support.

The work of a Diocesan Director of Education also has a statutory focus for the Director is also a statutory office-holder, looking to the English Parliament's 1991 Diocesan Boards Measure for the statutory responsibility the Director has for directing the work of the Board in schools and educational institutions. In this statutory work the Director is accountable to the Diocesan Board of Education, in turn, accountable to both Diocesan Synod (of which it is one of only two statutory Boards ~ the other is the Diocesan Board of Finance) and to the Department for Children, Schools and Families. These accountabilities are the framework within which faith can be communicated. They can be seen as a scaffolding of opportunities ~ never to be taken lightly but, rather, cherished and nurtured for many of these opportunities for communicating faith would be out of reach without the scaffolding.

As diocesan officers we scale the scaffolding in mutually supportive teams with each dependent upon the expertise and inspiration of the others. In providing diocesan strategy and support for work with children and young people our Children's Work Adviser and Youth Officer are central team players, as is our Diocesan Further Education Adviser. Most English Diocesan Boards employ at least one School Buildings Officer and, similarly, a Schools Curriculum Adviser, who organises the team that inspects Church Schools as the Statutory Inspection of Anglican Schools (under Section 48 of the English Parliament's 2004 Education Act). The Chairman of our Board works closely with the Director to achieve coherency in the strategic leadership and support given by our team of diocesan education officers. Much invaluable support is also given to this work by a wide range of Board members and other volunteers. All are committed to working with the government's "Every Child Matters"[1] initiative, in partnership with Local Authorities and voluntary organisations, so that we communicate faith, within all the above range of accountabilities, always ensuring that the needs of the child and young person are paramount.

All good schools throughout the world are 'safe spaces' in which the needs of the child are paramount. My particular experience of Church of England primary schools as a Diocesan Director has been that they are full of hope and energy. The children and the staff are over-flowing with hope for all that the future holds. The future will be different for each child and each school. Their abundant energy will fulfill the hope in a multitude of different ways. They will be different in the future because they are different now. There are no two children or schools the same. And that diversity is what we are privileged to explore and celebrate. It is the fundamentally child-centred context in which we can communicate faith.

It might be asked how I know, with such positive feeling, about that diversity. How have I become convinced that it is worth exploring and celebrating? I know from an exhausting but exhilarating four months of visiting all the eighty-four primary schools in the Anglican diocese of Hereford. I became convinced as I visited an average of two or three a day, map beside me in the car, frequently in glorious sunshine but sometimes slithering around muddy and icy country lanes; even, on one occasion, in a raging snow-storm. Whatever the weather, it became clear that surprise and delight awaited me just inside each school door. It was an awesome experience of different smiling faces showing that hope and energy day after day.

I had experienced Church of England primary schools before; though never with that daily intensity of focus on such a large scale. For ten years, as an Anglican parish priest, I had visited, week by week, the two C. of E. primary schools in my parish. Many 'assemblies', teaching Religious Education (RE), long governors' meetings, sports-days and nativity plays, so many conversations, particularly supporting the heads, and all this took on another dimension when three of our children became pupils. So I learned about the close detail of those two schools and was part of it all. It was not hard to see that there weren't many similarities between those two schools, even though they both lived by the same Christian gospel and supported the same local churches. Other experiences of Anglican primary school diversity came through inspecting and, when I was in secondary teaching, from visiting the feeder schools. And then, of course, there was St John the Evangelist Church of England primary school, just outside of Reading, where I learned what it was to be a pupil in one of these happy and wonderful places.

My experiences in those happy and wonderful Anglican Primary Schools were reinforced when I taught R.E. in three Anglican Secondary Schools, (one in Lesotho, Southern Africa, one on the beautiful island of Guernsey ~ where the Anglican Church has very close links with Normandy, in France, and one in Surrey, in England). It has been my delight since then to work closely with the Bishop of Hereford's Bluecoat School (Voluntary Aided Secondary) and with Ludlow (Voluntary Controlled) High School. The Anglican Schools aspiration which I now want to draw out is grounded also in these positive and inspirational experiences of the Anglican Church's active presence in communicating faith and contributing to social cohesion with young people in secondary schools in different parts of the world.

## 2. FAITH SCHOOLS AND SOCIAL COHESION

The Anglican schools' aspiration is that, in England, we want to build on our long history of two hundred years of provision of schooling for children and young people throughout England by consciously finding more and more effective ways of enriching the social cohesion of the nation. Our vision is of "fullness of life for all" ~ not just Christians, nor only bright and able pupils, and certainly not only white middle-class students ~ and we are aware that we live in a fast-changing society which demands ever more imaginative efforts to reduce social disintegration and help to create in each place a harmonious society based in mutual respect and celebration of diversity. I suspect that many of these challenges are also common to social culture in the USA.

At a local level, in England, this means encouraging links with inner-city schools to broaden children's multi-cultural experiences and using possibilities afforded by the extended schools initiative to embed the learning culture of the school more deeply in its local community and create expectations of life-long learning. Not only does every child matter but also every community matters. Believing this, the Church of England wants to use its schools to work in partnerships that are socially enriching with all in each local area. We will promote inclusion from the viewpoint of our own Christian distinctiveness with those of all faiths and none.

25.3% of all state primary schools in England are Church of England schools ~ that is 4,470 schools.
5.8% of all state secondary schools in England are Church of England schools ~ that is 220 schools.
Thus, 18.6% of all primary pupils and 5.8% of all secondary pupils attend these schools and these percentages in each case are growing.[2]

Following a report[3] by the Dearing Commission in 2001, the General Synod of the Church of England embarked on an ambitious development of 100 additional secondary schools. By October 2004 over 25 had been opened or expanded, with a further 15 due to open within two years and 36 more at various stages of planning. Now, in June 2007, 78 additional secondary schools have been created, many through the Academies initiative, and a further 60 are already beyond the 'Expression of Interest' stage in exploring Academy status. By 2011 the target of 100 additional secondary schools will have been exceeded. All these schools, mostly in areas of sharp social need, are promoted on principles and practices of social inclusion.

The indisputable fact is that faith schools nationally in England have a generally excellent academic record, which, not surprisingly, attracts candidates for admission. The suggestion by some is that there is a sort of vicious circle at work ~ that is, the success of faith schools encourages high levels of applications, and admission policies which offer Church places are, thereby, selective and this allows (it is argued by detractors) for tacit selection on grounds of ability or class, in a way that reinforces existing standards of achievement, and, by default, also reinforces existing social divisions.

If this was true it would, of course, be a serious matter suggesting that faith schools have wholly bought in to the competitive ethos of twenty-first century education in England and are colluding with trends that dig deeper trenches between economic and social groups. However, when one looks beyond anecdote primarily from London and takes account of statistical evidence, the picture is much more encouraging. In fact, the statistical evidence[4] publicly available makes it plain that the proportion of Church of England schools with significantly high numbers of students from disadvantaged backgrounds is much the same as the average within the community sector. The often forgotten fact that church schools are the main educational presences in some of our most deprived communities means that it cannot simply be said that these schools somehow have a policy of segregating. Furthermore, of the church schools recently agreed or opened, over two thirds are in areas of significant social deprivation. Church schools in such contexts are not recruiting agencies for the church. Rather, they are there because of concern for a whole community, which is frequently reflected in both the inclusive admissions policy and in its administration.

The Church of England is in no doubt that it must continue to learn about newly-developed good practice in social inclusion and not rest on past laurels. Equally, we know ourselves to be significant providers of education throughout England. We believe inclusive faith-based education is the best provision that can be made for the growth into wholeness and fullness of life of each person. We believe that provision benefits social cohesion and we are fundamentally committed to offering it, in respectful partnership with others, wherever the opportunity might be.

## 3. COMMUNICATING FAITH IN SCHOOLS: THE TOUCHSTONES AND PRESSURE POINTS

One of the greatest opportunities for offering inclusive faith-based education lies in nurturing the leadership of Church Schools. Communicating faith cannot happen effectively where the Headteacher and other members of the senior leadership team are uncertain or ambivalent about their own faith or about its impact on the ethos of the school and relationships with the Church. The responsibility of assisting Governors in discerning these sensitive aspects of candidates for Headships is usually taken very seriously by Diocesan Directors who attend in person where possible. This builds the Director's collaborative relationship with Governors and also with the successful candidate. All involved need to ask, "What does it mean to be the leader of a Church school?" Headteachers of Anglican schools need to maintain the inclusiveness of their schools in serving each local community but not be afraid to put forward in attractive ways the distinctive Christian beliefs which undergird our common educational values. Collaboration is underway between representatives of the National Association of Diocesan Directors and the National College for School Leadership who, along with the London Leadership Centre, are exploring how the next generation of school leaders can be identified and prepared. The question is, "How do you capture the imagination and motivation of young teachers, and begin nurturing this, as they embark on a career in the profession?" It is clear to most English Diocesan Directors that the Church stake in the maintained sector is so large as to justify the training of all potential heads in understanding what Church schools are about ~ otherwise, candidates are disadvantaged if considering a move into a Church school. In practice, it is good that we are included in these considerations and we build on such opportunities as we can gain.

One such opportunity, which has been seized by the Church of England, was offered in 1994 when the Office for Standards in Education (OFSTED) was created with the expectation that Church schools would be separately inspected to judge their faithfulness to their Foundation, as established in their Trust Deed. Denominational inspections (first Section 13, then section 23, and now section 48 of the Act) took place for over ten years with increasing rigour. Church distinctiveness was enhanced considerably. From September 2005 the OFSTED inspection process has expected that diocesan education officers will help Headteachers to be self-evaluating. Statutory Inspection of Anglican Schools (SIAS) reports have reinforced this focus. We are reaching a point where regular self-evaluation of Church schools in partnership with Local Authority officers will soon be fully integrated into the whole self-evaluation process. English dioceses are aware that a follow-up process is needed for monitoring action plans after Section 48 inspections. This action is the duty of the Governing Body.

Governing Bodies must be given regular training and support particularly in maintaining and developing their school's distinctively Christian ethos and spirituality, as well as in other accountabilities to the DBE (such as VA schools obtaining explicit permission for buildings works). Local Authority initiatives in promoting Values Education are to be welcomed in embedding common educational values but not to be confused with the promotion of the Church school's distinctive Christian beliefs. More focus on this is needed at an earlier stage of ministerial training, to be reinforced throughout the Anglican Church's ministerial formation (in England: Initial Ministerial Education 1 -7), to equip all ministers to take an appropriate lead on these matters with their local schools. Ministerial training should recognise the massive mission opportunity provided by schools and enskill ministers to be confident and competent colleagues in leading collective worship and acting as pastoral Chaplain to staff and pupils. Ministers will be most effective when they involve their local ministerial team in their nearby schools rather than 'going it alone'. Individual vocation needs to be seen in the wider context of how God will have distributed diverse gifts, which can complement each other, throughout each Church community.

 Having said that, there remains a great need, nationally, for Christians to see teaching as a personal vocation and the sharp need in England is for many more professionally-trained R.E. teachers. The project sponsored by the charity The Jerusalem Trust, "Transforming Lives: Christians as teachers in 21st century schools" has the potential to help here. Its Project Director, Trevor Cooling, lists three worthy objectives:

- to recruit more Christians into teaching

- to support and encourage Christian teachers currently in post

- to articulate a compelling vision for the strategic role of Christian teachers in Britain today and to promote that through the Church.

Professional R.E. teachers are needed who are sufficiently confident in their subject to communicate enthusiasm whilst maintaining the Church school's elusive but essential balance between being distinctive and inclusive.

Diocesan Boards of Education can help Governors and Clergy find this balance by working with local universities to embed life-long learning and to further develop Christian distinctiveness several of the new church academies are working in partnership with Liverpool Hope University or with other church foundations in the higher education sector. Much of this will be action research in schools and, from the Diocesan Board's perspective, self-funded through Service Level Agreements (SLAs) with schools.

Many English Diocesan Boards have established Service Level Agreements with their Church schools whereby schools use delegated funding (from the Department for Children, Schools and Families) to buy in services for curriculum, governance and buildings development as well as support with admissions appeals, headship appointments and personnel matters. The funds obtained from these SLAs fund some officer posts and also enable buying in of appropriate consultancy as required. Service Level Agreements are a major strategic opportunity for creating, within the parameters of the limited budgets of Diocesan Boards, the conditions under which faith might be effectively communicated.

All Church schools operate according to their original Trust Deed by which in England and Wales, a Church Educational Trust owns the land and buildings. Thus, in Voluntary Aided (VA) school this Trust owns land and buildings, to whose maintenance a 10% local contribution is made, and the school is Aided by the Local Authority which appoints only a minority of the Governing Body. The Governing Body is the employer of the staff in VA schools with full responsibility, accountable to the Diocesan Board, for buildings maintenance and replacement. These schools (roughly 50% of all the Church of England's Primary Schools are VA) represent a substantial responsibility for Church representatives, both Foundation Governors and Diocesan Education Officers; in disputes there is a right of appeal to the Diocesan Director in VA schools.

By contrast, Voluntary Controlled (VC) schools, whilst also owned by the Church Educational Trust, are 'controlled' by the Local Authority with assistance from the Diocesan Director. Recent English legislation gives VC schools the possibility of retaining their religious Foundation but operating as a 'Foundation' school which could choose to have a Foundation Governor majority and operate much as a VA school would without having to make the 10% contribution to building costs. This is an attractive option.

Guildford DBE operates a system of affiliation which enables Community schools to benefit from central diocesan support and register their close collaboration with their local church but without changing status. This is a useful 'half-way house'. Community schools cannot have a religious character, which is designated under the English Parliament's 1998 Act, without closing and opening again, but all others can. Thus, regulations and affiliations can be flexibly adapted to facilitate the easy communication of faith in appropriate ways within the state provision of education.

The dual system of partnership in England between Church and state in education, put in place by the 1944 Education Act, is beginning to break down. The Church of England and the Roman Catholic Church used to be the main providers with the LEAs of education. The Local Authority is now the Commissioner of education services as well as the main provider and Academies have opened the doors wide to a plethora of other providers who are their sponsors. The demise of School Organisation Committees, which always included diocesan representatives, gives greater independent power to Local Authorities. The critical question is, "Is the Church of England still at the heart of the system of state provision of education or has it become just another provider?" As Local Authorities, faced with national demographic downturn, look to rationalise their distribution of limited funds, it is inevitable that small rural primary schools will find themselves under close scrutiny, on educational and financial grounds, and not all can survive. Maintaining the Church percentage and geographical spread of its provision is fundamentally important to retaining these unique opportunities for faith sharing in education. At the moment the Church, in its educational context, is in a prime position to communicate faith to the children and young people of the nation. That position is not automatic in England and must not be taken for granted.

Indeed, there are some Secularists who maintain that the law should not, as they see it, favour faith schools and they question the rightness of nurturing a Christian educational ethos in English state schools. My sad experience is that some of them will put even their own children's well being at risk at the centre of their attempts to pressurise Church school governors to break the law which requires them to conduct a daily act of collective worship that is in accordance with the religious tradition of the school. It is worth being clear that all other schools in the maintained sector must conduct daily Collective Worship that is, "wholly or mainly of a broadly Christian character" (1988 Education Act.) Secularists can be a noisy minority who try to divert time and energy away from giving children and young people the holistic education, including a spiritual dimension, as is required by law. They disregard the Church's long history of provision of education for 'the poor' of each community. The Church of England in the twenty-first century offers a high quality education, based on Christian principles respected by the law, to those of 'all faiths and none'. It is central to our Anglican comprehensiveness that we want to offer an inclusive service that respects where people are; however, our efforts are thwarted if they are not met with equal respect and co-operation. Sadly, it seems that some secularists attempt to subvert Anglican good intentions and divert attention from the holistic well-being of every child.

Anglican schools in England want to be able to serve every child in their area. Sometimes that is not possible, particularly for Secondary schools, and so over-subscription criteria are adopted by Governors of Voluntary Aided schools which attempt to fairly divide available places between as many applicants as possible. Many church schools, such as the Bishop of Hereford's Bluecoat School, serve their local area first and only 'fill-up' with Church places. In those cases, our Hereford VA schools use admissions over-subscription criteria recommended by the National Society: first, looking to whether the child is baptised, and if so, asking if the child or family is 'known to', 'attached to' or 'at the heart of' their local church. These criteria are far from perfect but they are an attempt to achieve a degree of national common practice. They will, doubtless, be improved with the wisdom of time. Meanwhile, in most rural areas the Church primary school (generally under-subscribed due to falling rolls, nationally) is the only school for some miles and simply serves all the children in its area. Service in caring for the young, seeking after truth and up-building local community is at the heart of the faith that is communicated implicitly and explicitly in Anglican schools.

This service is not limited to schools. Many DBEs promote voluntary work with children and young people and, in this past year, we have responded to requests from every Further Education (FE) College Principal in our Diocese for closer links with our Diocesan Board. They each want something a bit different but most want part-time Chaplaincy and have offered to seed-fund the establishment of a part-time Diocesan F.E. Officer post. This person will work with each institution to help them find the right Chaplain who will be supported and linked to our Board by the F.E. Officer. An exciting recent initiative has been a shared Chaplaincy pilot project, sponsored initially by our DBE, at Ludlow College. This enjoys high quality support from the local Church and has got off to an excellent start. In due course, a report will be produced of the project which will demonstrate how Chaplaincy enriches College life for both students and staff. We are aware, however, as we move forward in these partnerships that each Principal views communicating faith in different ways and there can be no 'one size fits all' approach.

It will have become clear even from this brief summary of touchstones and pressure points that there are huge opportunities facing the Church for communicating faith in education in England, in its formal and informal contexts. These huge opportunities require similarly substantial capacity to meet them. It is a major question as to whether Diocesan Boards will acquire the capacity to rise to this exciting challenge of communicating faith in these many areas. Academies offer just such an exciting challenge and strategic opportunity.

## 4. AN OPPORTUNITY: ACADEMIES

Certainly, Diocesan Boards establishing Academies is a major strategic opportunity for communicating faith. Cathedral Schools can also now sponsor Academies or, themselves, change status to become one, in both cases without the normally expected sponsorship contribution of two million pounds. Time will tell whether there will be wide-spread take-up for these options. However, what it certain is that many dioceses have seized the opportunity for the Church of England to sponsor previously failing local schools for a one and a half million pound sponsorship donation. That has been a major part of our DBE life in Hereford Diocese for the past 18 months.[5] Through the generosity of an anonymous donor, Hereford Diocese has gone down this road in partnership with Wyebridge Sports College, situated in South Wye, an area of Hereford city in need of community regeneration. As Hayward High School, Wyebridge had gone into special measures but had been gradually demonstrating its capacity to improve throughout the last five years. This is important so that the vast investment of time and capital is not wasted.

Academy status, planned for Autumn 2008, will bring a substantial (91%) rebuild with a Department of Children Schools and Families (DCSF) initial allocation of £20.18m, including £1.62m for an Information and Communications Technology (ICT) managed service. Fundamental to the independence, within the maintained sector, of an Academy is its freedom, whilst teaching the core national curriculum, to think innovatively about modes of delivery, pastoral structures, salaries, appropriate architecture and life-long learning links with the local community. It is expected that The Hereford Academy (as Wyebridge will be known) will be designated with a religious character, allowing it to seek a Principal who is a practicing Christian. However, the school will not give priority in its admissions policy to pupils whose families attend church because we want primarily to serve the local area. The Academy will have a paid Chaplain and operate in the light of a vision statement that sees an inclusive and distinctive Christian ethos as fundamental. This change of status is a marvellous opportunity for ensuring that the communication of Christian faith, from an inclusive Anglican perspective, becomes central to the extended educational community of South Wye.

Such a change of status for a community school to become a Church-sponsored Academy is one of the opportunities for Church influence in communicating faith to grow beyond all previous expectations. It is a foolish Diocesan Director who does not seize the moment, but an equally foolhardy one who does not count the cost. The task of setting up Academies is time-consuming and burdensome for a DBE. We can find ourselves driven by a DCSF Academies Division agenda which is volatile and ruthless. We will be left with the long-term consequences when the Academes Division has moved on to its next project and its realigned priorities. The children and young people in a needy area deserve better than a quick fix and that is where we need to create the DBE capacity to be satisfied with nothing less than the best. Any Academy we promote must sustain and enrich local community, taking emotional and social needs as seriously as intellectual stimulus and vocational development, and it must not be shy of promoting a diverse and exciting range of spiritual possibilities for holistic fullness of life. It is, in truth, a hard call ~ but I believe it is strategically well worth it!

## CONCLUSION

The unique perspective of the Diocesan Director of Education on communicating faith is focused on strategy and support. We rejoice that faith is already being shared abundantly in parishes and schools and seeks collaborative ways of promoting, resourcing and supporting those communications. The Diocesan perspective will benefit from comparisons with other dioceses throughout the world and from direct contact with those forming and guiding national initiatives. It also benefits from close working collaboration with Local Authority officers at all levels and with diocesan and parochial colleagues. The impact of these benefits is upon enhancing the effectiveness of projects with many stakeholders. Projects that include communicating faith in any form will be effective if they achieve optimum stakeholder satisfaction.

For a Diocesan Director this requires much listening and consultation, attendance (either in person or *inter alia*) at meetings and talking with individuals about areas of sensitivity. Much vital networking goes on behind the scenes and during coffee time. There is no substitute for key people knowing that they are taken seriously. Key people move on and one has then to establish a new set of working relationships ~ it's like painting the Forth Bridge! ~ and there must be no painting over the cracks in the relationships; that is, difficulties will be faced positively because of a culture of mutual respect. Difficulties often emerge from differences of perspective and diocesan education officers know that faith is communicated most effectively when distinctive differences are respected.

Inclusion will be sought wherever possible. But this is the see-saw, balancing distinctiveness and inclusion, of effective faith communication which Diocesan Directors ride all the time. We see both aspirations as central to our Anglican valuing of difference and we are pragmatists who use all our skills and sensitivities to find what will work in practice in each situation. Our ideal is no compromise with basic faith principles but much pragmatic flexibility. Similarly, we balance direct communication of faith (by youth workers, FE Chaplains, leaders of children's work and in extra-curricular Christian activities) with creating the conditions under which humanity might thrive and faith be seen at its most attractive. These conditions are created by our School Buildings Officers and those who resource Foundation governors and headteachers as well as in many Local

Authority statutory meetings. Our Children's Work Advisers and Youth Officers create these conditions when they train, encourage and support those in parishes and deaneries who communicate their faith at its most attractive to children and young people.

We are well aware that Christian faith is most attractive when it is seen to be rooted in self-giving service which encourages forgiveness, reconciliation and new beginnings; in other words, when it mirrors the graciousness of God as shown in the self-giving of Jesus of Nazareth. Our strategies and support, our many meetings and messages, will all be as dust in the wind if we forget that. At the end of the day, this graciousness, this precious hope, is what it must all be about.

## NOTES

1   Department for Education & Science, C 5860, *Every Child Matters,* (Norwich: HMSO, 2004).

2   These statistics were current on the National Society website *www.natsoc.org. uk* on 17/05/07

3   Church Schools Review Group [Chaired by Lord Dearing]. 2001. *The Way Ahead: Church of England schools in the new millennium* (London: Church House Publishing, 2001).

4   James Arthur and Ray Godfrey, *Statistical Survey of the Attainment and Achievement of Pupils in Church of England Schools,* (Canterbury & London: National Institute for Christian Education Research, & National Society, 2005).

5   At the time of writing, December 2007, the Hereford Academy project was successfully approaching the end of its feasibility study and was about to appoint a Principal-designate in anticipation of the Secretary of State agreeing early in 2008 to its formally entering the implementation stage of Academy formation. It is hoped that, despite a formal opening in September 2008, the buildings, post-16 arrangements, new curriculum and staffing structures, will be ready two years later, in 2010.

# Chapter 10

## Joining Conversations on Christian Higher Education

*John Sullivan*

For many young (and not so young) people, university is a context for leaving behind who they have been and separating themselves off from those to whom they had previously belonged; it is a time for developing a new sense of identity. For some, it is a moment to cut the strings that tie, and among these might be religious affiliation. The corrosive effects of questioning, one's own questions and those of others, the desire to fit in, the urge to try out new experiences, or some other motivation, leads to the dropping of religious practice. The language of faith here is felt to be tired, irrelevant, perhaps an embarrassment. For others, faith is tested and in the light of such testing, becomes renewed, matured and deepened. Not only are students affected. University can also often be an uncomfortable environment for the expression of faith by staff. Most of those who are believers find that their academic and professional socialisation has encouraged them to leave faith and the language associated with it to the private sphere, for home and church, but to be kept under restraint in the context of university. There is a lack of confidence in how one might speak of faith in that arena, without intruding on the beliefs of others, offending the canons of polite society, undermining the critical thinking required in such a place or infringing the rights of non-believers to a faith-free zone. So far has this secularisation of the academy progressed that deliberate and careful steps are needed to reinstate a legitimate place for religious language within the university context.

Christian educators working in the university find themselves simultaneously involved in several overlapping groups to which they have varying degrees of affiliation and loyalty. They belong to the wider family of the church, as Catholics, Presbyterians, Orthodox, Anglicans, Methodists, Baptists, Mennonites, and so forth. Within that part of the Christian family they may have links with a particular group or religious order. They are under contract to a particular institution which aspires to become a community in its own right. In addition to the mission of that institution, they might have a sense of their own intellectual apostolate, fed by sources and practices external to (as well as internal to) their employing university. As educators, they must be attentive to the very specific and diverse nature and needs of the various learning groups for which they have responsibility. They are citizens, taxpayers, members of local communities and voluntary groups. They are members of academic guilds which play a significant part in their sense of identity and in their professional development. As Caroline Simon says, 'it is important to pay one's dues, to keep memberships current, to stay in touch with what is happening in the outside world, …The guild can remind a faculty member of the general trends of the discipline, the latest debates, the key works a faculty member should read.'[1] These different roles played by Christian educators and the diverse circles of belonging in which they find themselves can pull in different directions. However, although this presents them with the challenge of how to reconcile these diverse calls, it also affords them the opportunity to clarify who they are, what they want, where they stand and where they are going. In sorting themselves out on these matters, as walking anthologies they tell a story made up of elements drawn from all of the groups they encounter and all the experiences they undergo, sharpening their self-perception in the face of other possibilities, developing a narrative that is worked out 'in the face of' and with a view to specific other people.

In Part One of this chapter I bring out some of the conflicting expectations experienced by Christian educators in universities in general and in Christian universities in particular, ending by proposing conversation as central to their work. In Part Two three themes emerging from the literature about Christian higher education are explored. These are the notion of living tradition, the role of theology, and how we might understand religion in relation to the secular. In Part Three I propose, very sketchily, a few communicative virtues, qualities that have a capacity, when exercised together, to sustain the conversations needed to enable Christian higher education to flourish.

## 1. COMMUNICATION CHALLENGES

There are many communication challenges and opportunities facing Christian educators in the university sector. The multiple constituencies they address have different perceptions of reality, different needs, deploy different conceptual categories, are motivated by different concerns and are drawn by different priorities. Nor should it be assumed that there is a high degree of commonality among the Christian educators themselves; not only are there differences caused by contrasting denominational traditions and emphases, but there will often be deep differences within a specific denominational tradition as to the relative weight to be given to particular truths, texts, values, practices and authorities. These different constituencies can require contrasting repertoires of behaviour which sit alongside each other with at least a degree of tension.

Students want us to supply goods and services. Getting a university degree is an expensive undertaking and an investment in life chances. In their role as consumers students have certain expectations about what they are paying for and what they are entitled to. They are encouraged to think of themselves as customers, customers who know what they want and have a right to be satisfied in receiving it. The notion that education might help them to see that what they initially want is not worthy of their attention and allegiance and that they need to come to develop other loves in life does not fit into the customer mentality. Although education is one of those contexts in which the customer is not always right, the university is treated as a supply line of educational services from which students might select as they think fit, with students as arbiters of what is to be sought.

Colleagues too expect us to supply goods and services. Providing a university education is an expensive endeavour, one that requires complex forms of human interaction and it depends on many people cooperating in the task by carrying out their roles in dependable and efficient ways. Curriculum design, timetabling, teaching that is often shared between members of a team, assessment of student work, coherent and interlocking procedures for dealing with student difficulties, performance management of faculty, collaboration in marketing activities – all require that we each play our part in the great university machine. If not, it breaks down, frustrations abound among students and staff, we fail to 'deliver' and our place, individually and institutionally, in the 'pecking order' is lost, either temporarily or perhaps even permanently.

In their dealings with students and colleagues Christian educators in the university, as for their counterparts in schools, have to take into account many factors. They must be discerning about what values and practices are at work in their cultural context. They must be well informed about their students (their development, capacities, needs and interests). With regard to their institution and community, they should bear in mind its relationships, rules and ethos. Attention must be paid to the nature and requirements of what they teach. The art of pedagogy (with a concern to become ever more skilled and effective in how to promote learning) must be nurtured. They cannot afford to ignore or become isolated from their colleagues (being mindful of their intentions, methods, gifts, insights and needs) because teaching as a corporate endeavour benefits from certain kinds of 'keeping company' among colleagues.[2] Nor should they forget themselves, for it is incumbent on educators to be aware of how their own personality and character is influencing, positively and negatively, the promotion of learning, and, at the same time, they should remain conscious of the effect that the work is having on them – for if they wish to make a long-term contribution, they will need to pace themselves and live in rhythm with their own energies and sources of satisfaction so as not to suffer burn-out, exhaustion or loss of morale.

There is likely to be a clash, or at least tension and confusion, between the attention given, on the one hand, to standards and status, order and authority – for many academic tasks are tightly prescribed and many activities (of students and staff) have to be carried out in specific ways and according to set patterns if they are to 'count' – and, on the other hand, the nurturing of equality, collegiality, independence of thought and lack of deference as elements in fostering the development of critical questioning capacities. Such tensions might include 'control of course content versus going with the flow; facilitator versus evaluator role; and a focus on the subject versus a focus on learners' needs.'[3] Teachers cannot simply be friends, in the normal sense, with their students, although they can, of course, be friendly. Establishing appropriate boundaries and distance is a necessary professional responsibility, if one's duties are to be carried out equitably and if the quality of the services one is expected to provide is not to be dependent upon the degree to which one feels emotionally connected to particular people (again, students or staff). Receiving a disappointingly low grade for an assignment or in a performance appraisal is made harder to bear when the link between the assessor and the assessed is too close. However, neither is it desirable for the relationship between lecturers and students or between managers and staff to be that of strangers; this would undermine the bonds of collegiality, the well-springs for collaboration, and the associated sensitivities that assist in matching professional conduct to the needs and capacities of those we serve and of those with whom we work.

Another source of tension, for Christian educators, might be the differing expectations of the academy and the church, as to the salience of and the treatment of religion. In the academy there is the expectation that religion is an object of study, to be kept at a distance, subject to question and exposed to scrutiny by criteria coming from traditions and practices external to faith. On the other hand, faith communities look to Christian higher educational institutions for fostering creative fidelity to tradition, as places where the perspective of faith can be a lens through which to examine the world and the various academic disciplines.

The word 'conversation' in the title of this chapter is meant to indicate how central conversation is to the nature and tasks of any higher education, including Christian higher education. One the great philosophers of the twentieth century, Michael Oakeshott, envisaged the whole process of education as being one in which the younger generation were taught how to join the conversations of humanity. In this way they would be initiated into civilization. Of education, he said 'We may regard it as beginning to learn our way about a material, emotional, moral and intellectual inheritance, and as learning to recognise the varieties of human utterance and to participate in the conversation they compose.'[4]

Professor of English, Gerald Graff, also makes conversation central to what it is that academics are inviting their students to join. Pivotal for education is what he calls argument literacy, the ability to listen, summarise, and respond.[5] Drawing on John Stuart Mill, Graff says 'We do not understand our own ideas until we know what can be said against them.'[6] Graff wants students to have access to the points of disagreement within their field of study, pointing out that this presupposes that they at the same time become aware of what is taken for granted and agreed upon.[7] He identifies the rudiments of intellectual life: 'how to make an argument, weigh different kinds of evidence, move between particulars and generalisations, summarise the views of others, and enter a conversation about ideas.'[8] The metaphor of joining conversations as being at the very heart of academic life for students and for staff is deployed throughout his book *Clueless in Academe*. However, he is concerned that, from his observations, too often academics inhibit rather than assist access to the conversations from which they derive their interests and energies. 'Most students experience the curriculum not as a connected conversation but as a disconnected series of courses that convey wildly mixed messages.'[9] He blames this situation on the fact that 'teachers know little about what their colleagues do in their classes.'[10] The reason for this is that they talk too little to each other about what they are teaching, that they work too often in isolation, they fail to keep each other company as pedagogues. I have explored elsewhere the importance for teachers of 'keeping company' and so will not press that point further here.[11] The failure to share intentions and experiences among faculty is, for John Bennett, a sign of the 'insistent individualism' he sees as too prevalent in universities.[12] He comments 'These institutions offer a philosophy of atomism, an ethics of opportunism, and a spirituality of self-preoccupation.'[13] Given that 'The prevailing culture encourages faculty to feel primary obligations to disciplines and disciplinary colleagues – not to students, institutions, or the broader public,'[14] they give insufficient attention to conversations internally, especially with their fellow teachers and with their students. This leads to the mixed messages conveyed through the curriculum experienced by students, a feature lamented by Graff. Yet, as Bennett argues, 'Conversation is the key ingredient in teaching and learning, building community, supporting colleagues, and providing leadership.'[15]

Conversations are vehicles for travel from our starting points to other destinations. They make it possible for us to enter into other ways of perceiving, thinking and valuing. None of us, it should be remembered, begin with a clean slate, unencumbered by prior intellectual 'baggage.' We are all already named and claimed, in the sense that we are already using a particular language, a set of concepts, a range of criteria, a particular narrative and draw from one or other tradition.

> Multiple voices are present already as ideologies that pervade the pedagogical space. Students are constructed variously as units of resource, as consumers, or as potential actors in the labour market, or possibly even as 'deficient' individuals in need of compensatory 'widening participation', or even as only partly formed persons now deserving counselling and therapeutic

interventions. These are, in turn, ideologies of economy, of efficiency, of marketability, of performance, of necessary participation and of therapy.[16]

Before they have entered the university, students have been subject to lengthy socialisation processes that have embedded in them ideological elements. Some of these have been seen as prejudicing young people against the claims of faith. Thus in a book that sharply challenges Christian universities to decide whether they are church-related and liberally-based or, alternatively, they are church-based and liberally-related, Michael Budde claims:

> liberal commitments have become more determinative for Christians than the commitments arising out of baptism. ... By creating the realm of the private, autonomous individual and then placing religion within this realm, liberal theory separates Christianity from the communal base that renders it viable across time. ... The use of compulsory mass education to diminish and dilute the integrity of particularistic communities like the church has been a constant of the modern state for so long that few notice it anymore. Under the rubric of individual freedom, ... personal autonomy, and progress, child and adolescent education has functioned to undercut those religious loyalties, practices, and affections it could not co-opt, transform, or subordinate.[17]

He continues: 'Nearly all children and adolescents in advanced industrialised countries are already the objects of programs aimed to socialise them into a powerful set of political assumptions, affections, and practices.'[18] So much is this so, that Stanley Hauerwas comments 'The habits that now constitute the secular imagination are so imbedded in how Christians understand the world we no longer have the ability to recognise the power they have over us.'[19] Bearing this in mind, I would suggest that, without leaving completely behind us how we have already been so named and claimed (for the prior voices that have influenced us remain part of us), conversations allow us to try out alternative ways to speak, value, judge and act.

## 2. CHRISTIAN HIGHER EDUCATION

What do the conversations about Christian higher education indicate are current issues of concern? I have elsewhere examined works that probe Catholic universities, especially the challenges they face, the factors operating in them that inhibit their fully flourishing and the issues that need special attention, drawing on two key recent studies. [20] Glanzer surveys the history of Christian HE in the UK, brings into light contemporary public rhetoric about their Christian mission and explores the degree to which this public rhetoric is matched by a range of practical markers in their day-to-day running.[21] There have been many other studies on Christian Higher Education in the past decade.[22] Many issues receive treatment in such studies. First, there is the Christian university as situated between the state and the church and the relationships to be developed with each of these partners. Second, there is the desire to provide a holistic and interconnected education: learning in the light of a big picture of reality, humanity and society that provides an alternative account of human flourishing to that prevailing elsewhere, one that is illuminated, underpinned and guided by scriptural reading, sacramental life, spiritual disciplines, prayer and formation as disciples, as well as by the workings of grace. Third, character, not just competence, wisdom not just career-training, is a desired emphasis in teaching. Fourth, distinguishing and relating religious and secular remains a complex task on which much hangs. Fifth, what is the role of theology in the curriculum? Sixth, there is the challenge of ecumenical learning. I cannot explore all of these here. Instead I limit myself to attending to the notion of living tradition (2.1), make brief comments on the role of theology (2.2) and analyse the thorny issue of how the religious relates to the secular (2.3).

## 2.1. LIVING TRADITION

A living tradition, if it is to be critically appreciated and creatively appropriated, requires (at least) five things to happen. First, it must be transmitted and mediated through polices, practices and personal example; without this it would be simply abandoned, at best a historical memory. Second, it should be questioned and critiqued; in the university it is vital to avoid simply reproducing the past or seeking blind submission, for that would be imply that clones and doormats suffice as products of our work. Third, the tradition needs to be articulated, explained and interpreted in the face of people's very different starting points; otherwise we fail to connect and thereby cannot carry people with us. Fourth, it needs to be deepened and transformed; otherwise it remains shallow, without making a real difference. The modifications and adjustments that contribute to such transformation allow members of the tradition to stay alert and responsive to new circumstances. Fifth, it should be applied to the needs we come across, personal and professional, internal and external, local and more widely; without attention to meeting such needs, it remains self-indulgent, isolated, infertile and fails to promote the common good.

This living tradition, carried forward in a Christian university, in its efforts to be distinctive, inclusive and effective, will need to clarify what it holds in common with and where it differs from alternative traditions, religious and secular. 'Christian higher education should be counter-cultural, engage the whole person (feelings, imagination, habits and virtues), and address and learn from opposing points of view.'[23] Conversation will be integral in the tradition's work in conveying distinctiveness, in striving for greater inclusivity and in displaying the capacity to continue learning from other individuals, institutions, groups and faith communities, since all these are gifted by God, even where they differ from our own tradition. With regard to the need to display openness, it needs to be remembered that we are finite and fallen. We experience limitations right from the start and thereafter throughout our lives. There is limitation from our initial endowment: there are always some things we cannot do; they remain beyond our repertoire, however hard we try. There is limitation stemming from our environment and surroundings; some opportunities do not come our way or remain beyond our resources. There is limitation because we have decided one way and not another; choices have consequences; some doors open while others remain closed; a pattern of choices also develops character; however rounded, characters are incomplete. Because of our limitations, whatever their source, we need supplementing and enrichment from others. Thus we should be open to other people, to other perspectives and (in the university context) to disciplines other than our own.

The Christian university also needs to offer comprehensiveness and coherence of viewpoint for fragmentation and disconnectedness fails to do justice to the integrity of the tradition and deprives students of the necessary equipment to engage robustly and perceptively with the surrounding culture that threatens to colonise its members. However, in acknowledging our limitations and the ambiguity built into ourselves and our world, the comprehensiveness and coherence being aimed for should be combined with openness, avoiding over-prescribed modes of thinking.

## 2.2. THEOLOGY

How could theology engage fruitfully with other disciplines in promoting a more coherent educational programme at university level? This should be one that is neither too prescriptive/foreclosed (thus remaining open and leaving room for students to make their own contribution and to realise and take ownership for themselves of what they are learning) nor so open and fragmented and disconnected that it inhibits people achieving a rounded and coherent view of things (shades of Newman here). Perhaps theology could help, in close and humble dialogue with other disciplines, in the task of articulating and developing understandings of well-being or human flourishing in the context of contemporary society that are not dictated by state priorities and which derive from sources not normally made accessible in the public square. The English Chief Rabbi Jonathan Sacks and the eminent Muslim scholar Tariq Ramadan have made such contributions, drawing upon the Jewish and Muslim traditions.[24] Can we do the same from our own Catholic tradition? Such a contribution would need to connect our particular and necessarily limited work with a bigger picture, both about the academic endeavour and about human flourishing in general. I presume that these two have in common the need to order activities in service of goods in ways that present challenges to key features of our ethos in higher education and society: autonomy, unconstrained choice, decisions made as if there were no consequences, pick and mix curricula, disconnection between the questions and requirements of courses and the questions and requirements of life.

I explore in the following chapter the possible way theology might help promote interconnectedness in the university curriculum. But, of course, potentially, at least, theology should be able to play an architectonic role beyond the curriculum, influencing institutional self-definition and helping to frame the mission. A leading analyst of Christian higher education in the USA, Robert Benne, whose book *Quality with Soul* provided a typology of models for this enterprise, has claimed that 'Without a public theological rationale for the ongoing legitimacy of a religious way of life on campus, that way of life tends to diminish over time.'[25] Furthermore, he asserts, 'The president or another cabinet-level official must be [able to] spell out a Christian vision of higher education that can help to organise the curricular and non-curricular offerings of the college and to differentiate that vision from the secular models that now dominate the educational world.'[26] We could expect theology to exercise a key role here.

## 3.3. RELIGION AND THE SECULAR

While I found very valuable Glanzer's analysis of Christian Higher Education in the UK,[27] I think he does not quite adequately pick up something that is crucial for understanding why these institutions have located themselves in the way that they have in relation to the wider culture. I believe that there is operating, beneath the surface, some kind of implicit rationalisation for the way Christian university educators in the UK have accommodated the requirements of liberal secular democracy. I detect the following elements at work. First, among some there is guilt about Christian dominance and abuse of power in the past. Second, there is a desire to be as inclusive as possible. Third, there is a belief that God is at work beyond the church and in the midst of the secular. Fourth, some fear that being too 'in-your-face' will be counter-productive in eliciting a very negative rejection of Christianity. Fifth, false readings of what people of other faiths might want of Christians make some people reticent about proclaiming their mission too explicitly. Sixth, a self-denying and self-emptying, service mode of Christianity is thought appropriate, where the 'cup of water' is offered without need for an explanatory note as to why or where from. Seventh, Christian faith has been effectively marginalised from academic and professional socialisation and development, and thus privatised and removed from institutional language. Eighth, effective lobbying by secularists (for example about exclusiveness and divisiveness on the part of Christian bodies) makes people nervous about steps to preserve their Christian tradition. Ninth, a fatal separation of worship and intellectual endeavour has taken place, a topic that deserves separate treatment.[28] Tenth, Christianity is often reduced by some of its adherents to being nice; here claims to be distinctive on account of being caring insult people of other persuasions by assuming Christians have a monopoly on such caring and they render faith anodyne and without intellectual purchase.

I do not think subservience to the state is the key issue here, but a lack of confidence, a lack of intellectual equipment and a lack of Christian formation. Very few academics are equipped to articulate how Christian faith has a bearing on their work, the life of their institution or on how they relate to society. In parallel with this, very few academics actually build into their lives patterns of Christian practices that sustain and deepen formation in faith that can permeate all their perspectives and activities. For example, until we pray regularly – and at university as well as at home or in church – we will not think Christianly about the intellectual life or our academic pursuits.

Let me dwell further on the question 'can we distinguish a religious activity from a secular one?' because I think confusion about how these two relate can be damaging for effective Christian witness in the university as elsewhere. Secular does not mean anti-religious, simply an activity not requiring a religious description or interpretation. 'Secular' means 'pertaining to this age and belonging to this world'. To say that something is secular does not mean that it is hostile to eternal life or to the spiritual life.[29] Distinguishing a religious activity from a secular one sometimes matters to secular authorities and agencies when they are seeking to ensure that no favouritism or no discrimination is taking place with regard to funding, access to resources, legislation, the implementation of policy, and so forth. I think that making the distinction matters less to religious people because they would see everything as related to God, nothing being hidden from God and everything as dependent on God.

The context in which an activity takes place can make a big difference to whether it is interpreted as religious or as secular. Thus, a gesture or action that occurs within the context of a liturgy or act of worship or sacred scripture study group – where the participants know what is happening and why they are gathered – can be assumed to belong to a religious family of actions and be subject to a religious frame of reference. For example, even a gesture that might be replicated outside this context, such as shaking hands, takes on a meaning beyond simply human greeting; it becomes a reminder of solidarity in the body of believers, of shared status as children of God. Even studying sacred scripture can be a secular activity, in that it can have no religious intentions; it can take place for educational purposes that have no religious 'baggage', or in order to promote mutual harmony or social understanding, again, not necessarily with any religious goals in mind (this despite the fact that for many religious people, education, working for mutual harmony and social understanding are deeply religious activities, carried out in service of God's will and for the sake of God's kingdom).

People can carry out actions that on the surface look identical, for example, in schools and hospitals, in youth clubs and in social welfare, but which have significantly different meanings for the people involved, whether these be on the 'giving' or the 'receiving' end. How they perceive what they are doing and what is happening to them depends not only on the surface nature of the action – being told something, receiving treatment in some way – but the 'story' they tell themselves about it, the narrative into which the action is inserted or finds its location. And, of course, often, though not always, the way an action is received contributes to the way the actor perceives the meaning of her or his action. If someone welcomes my contribution as some kind of blessing, this might reinforce my intention that it should be a blessing; if someone rejects it as such, this may not prevent me from hoping it will be such a blessing but it may press me to question my motives or my methods.

We may say that an action is religious in nature if it is driven by (in terms of the motivation behind the action), drawn by (that is, with the intentionality of, aiming for, having as its goal) and conducted in the light of some religious teaching, person or community. The fact that on the surface the action or set of activities seems identical to an action or set of actions carried out for non-religious motives, in aid of non-religious goals and not illuminated by religious teaching should not prevent religious people from calling such an action or set of actions religious for them. Nor should the fact that they have these motivations, goals or sources of guidance prevent them from being permitted to carry out the actions or receive support for such action, if such acts as carried out by non-religious people are being allowed or supported. In very many human activities it is possible for a great deal of cooperation to occur between people with radically different motivations, goals and interpretative frameworks.

This analysis of the features that make an action or set of actions religious in nature is complicated by the fact that, quite often, we act from a spectrum of motivations, intermingled so inextricably that it would be very difficult to unravel them or set them in any clear order of priority. We can also have in mind a plurality of aims, often overlapping and even sometimes contradictory aims. For example, we may wish to elicit conversion, to show what fidelity to a tradition entails, to promote critical thinking, to increase people's sense of independence and agency, to promote justice, to invite participation in some endeavour, to deepen affiliation to a community, to critique its shortcomings. Some of these will be in tension. Similarly, the guiding principles that steer how we go about an activity (ethical and otherwise) can modify the manner in which we act. While we might be tempted to say that it is what is done that matters, something that can be seen by all, and thus to pay no attention to the invisible working of motivations, intentions or accompanying narratives, we know from our own actions and from our experience of being on the receiving end of other people's actions that what is done cannot be experienced without being connected with how it is done and that how something is done is likely to be strongly influenced by why it is done and what the actor thinks about what she is doing.

There is a different aspect to the question of distinguishing a religious from a secular action. This concerns the degree to which an actor's conduct is carried out in the light of religious teaching. There is a very wide spectrum possible here. Many religious people separate out their religious life from their public, secular life. That is, they allow their faith to become privatised, for home (perhaps) and for church; but not directly impacting on their jobs, politics, pattern of economic activity, leisure and general mode of operation. Yet the features of a religious account of life include that it presents something comprehensive, overriding and unsurpassable.[30] A religious account of life is comprehensive, in that no aspect of life is untouched by it. It is overriding insofar as, when conflicts of priority arise, religious considerations are expected to trump other considerations. Furthermore, despite the developments inevitably brought about through a long history, a religious account of life remains, for its adherents, unsurpassable in the sense that, while critical intelligence and creativity can be applied in reaching new understandings of the tradition, the basic framework or 'ecology,' the body of teaching and its key elements remain. Yet, for many believers, the challenge remains to establish how their ways of perceiving, reflecting, deciding and acting in the diverse circumstances of their lives, and most especially in their work should be illuminated, clarified, guided and directed by the worldview offered by their faith. Where religious faith is a private option and frequently marginalised in the public sphere, it is only too easy for the norms of behaviour that we abide by and for the principal categories through which we think to be permeated by notions that are indifferent to and often hostile to Christian (or other religious) beliefs and values. Thus, while we might maintain a corner of life in which we allow faith perspectives and practices that sustain these to hold sway, for many areas of life we find ourselves colonised by, and operating according to ideas, habits and allegiances that do not fit well with discipleship.

Many commentators support the view that such colonisation has taken place in the public educational sphere. According to Warren Nord, 'Public education unrelentingly and uncritically nurtures a secular mentality.'[31] The philosopher, Jeffrey Stout, believes that we should be careful here to distinguish secular from secularist. He says that the discourse of most democracies is *'secularised* [in the sense that it] is not "framed by a theological perspective" taken for granted by all those who participate in it. But secularisation in this sense is not a reflection of commitment to *secularism*. ... But this just means that the age of theocracy is over, not that the anti-Christ has taken control of the political sphere.'[32] Just as secularists often treat expressions of religious faith as conversation-stoppers, so Christians can treat the secular in a similar way. Yet, as I have argued above, conversation is just what is needed between people of different perspectives, for the enrichment of all. Stout affirms this too: 'Conversation is a good name for what is needed at those points where people employing different final vocabularies reach a momentary impasse.'[33] In using the phrase 'final vocabularies' he is referring to Richard Rorty:

> All human beings carry about a set of words which they employ to justify their actions, their beliefs, and their lives. These are the words in which we formulate praise of our friends and contempt for our enemies, our long-term projects, our deepest self-doubts and our highest hopes. They are the words in which we tell, sometimes prospectively and sometimes retrospectively, the story of our lives. I shall call these words a person's "final vocabulary."[34]

Stout indicates some of the communicative virtues necessary for good conversation when he complains that

> There are people who lack civility, or the ability to listen with an open mind, or the will to pursue justice where it leads, or the temperance to avoid taking and causing offence needlessly or the practical wisdom to discern the subtleties of a discursive situation. There are also people who lack the courage to speak candidly, or the tact to avoid sanctimonious cant, or the poise to respond to unexpected arguments, or the humility to ask forgiveness from those who have been wronged.[35]

### 3. COMMUNICATIVE VIRTUES

Critical and friendly conversations require certain qualities. We are advised 'Always be ready to make your defence to any who demands from you an accounting for the hope that is in you; yet do it with gentleness and reverence.'[36] As we do so, and as we enter into and engage with the mindset of another, we learn new things about the faith and hope that sustains us. Such defence (or apologetics) requires of us a careful balance between and a combination of tact and courage, clarity and charity, humility and conviction. We will also require patience, mutual trust, perseverance, empathic imagination, sustained listening, not seeking control, willingness to admit mistakes and learn from others, acknowledgement and appreciation of the other's gifts, hurts, and insights, and openness to the grace and work of the Holy Spirit.

Perhaps the most famous advocate of communicative virtues is the German philosopher, Jürgen Habermas. He describes the conditions for communication as including a belief that genuine consensus is possible, equality among participants, freedom from constraint, no premature closure, and that all participants have voice, respect and attention.[37] However, valuable as these conditions are, the kind of conversation I have been advocating would require the qualities eloquently advocated by Jon Nixon and John Bennett.[38]

Bennett links hospitality and humility. Both these qualities are about relational power, which means 'allowing the other to make an inner difference, ... receiving as well as sharing.'[39] As Bennett says, 'Without an ethic of hospitality (and the community of inquiry which makes it possible), scholarship borders on parochialism, teaching is reduced to credentialing, and learning comes close to the receipt of information without internal impact.'[40] This kind of hospitality entails positive space-making; it is not intrusive. As Philip Sheldrake puts it, 'Hospitality is not the same as assimilation of what is 'other' into me. ... At the heart of hospitality lies a commitment to listening. For this we need to learn silence, to cultivate attentiveness, so that we become capable of receiving what we are not.'[41] Bennett understands education as conversation. To do so is 'to appreciate the different kinds of liberation learning promotes – from ignorance, parochialism, lack of self-insight, and obsession with power.'[42]

Nixon makes a strong case that the health of a university depends on the mutually reinforcing virtues of truthfulness, respect, authenticity and magnanimity. He links care and autonomy. 'Only an autonomous person can care for the autonomy of others; without autonomy, care is likely to collapse into dependency. Similarly, only a caring person can ensure that autonomy is disposed towards magnanimity; without care, autonomy collapses into self-regard.'[43] What I particularly resonate with, in Nixon's delineation of the virtuous university, is the question he poses as central to its rationale, a question that Christian universities should also ask in relation to their practices, 'why we do what we do.' Nixon rightly says that in enabling this question to be raised about any aspect of their work, universities find themselves opening out to the wider question 'about the ends and purposes of a human life.'[44] It is therefore advisable to monitor 'who speaks to whom, under what circumstances, in what register, and to what ends' if we wish to ensure that no one is excluded from the conversation.[45]

In the conversations about Christian higher education, our tone of voice should be confident, clear, open, humble, respectful, invitational, imaginative, constructive and collaborative. Key qualities for promoting Christian education, in the university as elsewhere, will be a blend of realism and hope, patience and courage, honesty and hospitality, invitation and accompaniment, humility and critical questioning, all underpinned by prayer and attentiveness to God's Spirit.

## NOTES

1 Caroline Simon (et al) *Mentoring for Mission* (Grand Rapids, MI: Eerdmans, 2003), p.62.

2 John Sullivan, 'Keeping Company', *The New Theologian*, vol. 13, no. 2.

3 Elizabeth Tisdell, 'Spirituality, Diversity, and Learner-Centered Teaching' in *The American University in a Postsecular Age,* edited by Douglas and Rhonda Jacobsen (New York: Oxford University Press, 2008), p.152.

4 Michael Oakeshott, quoted by Nicholas Rengger, 'The Idea of Politics in a Christian University' in *The Idea of a Christian University* edited by Jeff Astley, Leslie Francis, John Sullivan and Andrew Walker (Milton Keynes: Paternoster, 2004), p.238.

5 Gerald Graff, *Clueless in Academe* (New Haven: Yale University Press, 2003), p.3.

6 Ibid., pp.12 -13.

7 Ibid., p.28.

8 Ibid., p.217.

9 Ibid., p.27.

10 Ibid., p.30.

11 See note 2.

12 John Bennett, *Academic Life* (Oregon: Wipf & Stock, 2003).

13 Ibid., p.38.

14 Ibid., p.36.

15 Ibid., p.xi.

16 Ronald Barnett, *A Will to Learn* (Maidenhead: Open University Press, 2007), p.98.

17 Michael Budde and John Wright (eds) *Conflicting Allegiances* (Grand Rapids: Eerdmans, 2004), pp.19, 21, 258.

18 Ibid., p.260.

19 Stanley Hauerwas, *The State of the University* (Oxford: Blackwell, 2007), p.173.

20 John Sullivan, 'Catholic Higher Education', *The Heythrop Journal*, vol. 49, No. 5, pp.860-867. James Arthur, *Faith and Secularisation in Religious Colleges and Universities* (London: Routledge); Melanie Morey and John Piderit, *Catholic Higher Education* (Oxford: Oxford University Press, 2006).

21 Perry Glanzer, 'Searching for the Soul of English Universities: An Exploration and Analysis of Christian Higher Education in England', *British Journal of Education Studies*, vol. 56, no. 2, June, pp.163 – 183.

22 Paul Dovre (ed) *The Future of Religious Colleges* (Grand Rapids, MI: Eerdmans, 2002); Stephen Haynes, *Professing in the Postmodern Academy* (Waco, TX: Baylor University Press, 2002); Douglas Henry and Michael Beaty (eds) *Christianity and the Soul of the University* ( Grand Rapids, MI: Baker Academic, 2006); Richard Hughes and William Adrian (eds) *Models for Christian Higher Education* (Grand Rapids, MI: Eerdmans, 1997); Mark Noll and James Turner, *The Future of Christian Learning* (Grand Rapids, MI: Brazos Press, 2008). On Catholic higher education, see two works edited by Anthony Cernera and Oliver Morgan: *Examining the Catholic Intellectual Tradition* and *Examining the Catholic Intellectual Tradition, Volume 2* (both Fairfield, CN: Sacred Heart University Press, 2000; 2002) and another book edited by Anthony Cernera, *Lay Leaders in Catholic Higher Education* (Fairfield, CN: Sacred Heart University Press, 2005). See also John Wilcox and Irene King (eds) *Enhancing Religious Identity* (Washington, DC: Georgetown University Press, 2000).

23 Charles Scriven, 'Schooling for the Tournament of Narratives', *Religious Education* vol.94, 1999, p.40.

24 Jonathan Sacks, *The Home We Build Together* (London: Continuum, 2007); Tariq Ramadan, *Western Muslims and the Future of Islam* (Oxford: Oxford University Press, 2004).

25 Robert Benne, *Quality With Soul* (Grand Rapids, MI: Eerdmans, 2001), p.45.

26 Ibid., p.189.

27 Glanzer, 2008, loc. cit.

28 I hope to address this in a book I am working towards, *Scholarship, Standards & Spirituality*.

29 Robert Markus, *Christianity and the Secular* (Notre Dame, IN: University of Notre Dame Press, 2006).

30 Paul Griffiths, *Religious Reading* (New York: Oxford University Press, 1999).

31 Warren Nord, 'Taking Religion Seriously in Public Universities' in Jacobsen, op. cit., p.171.

32 Jeffrey Stout, *Democracy & Tradition* (Princeton: Princeton University Press, 2004), p.93.

33 Ibid., p.90.

34 Ibid., p.89, quoting Rorty.

35 Ibid., p.85.

36 1 Peter 3: 15 – 16.

37 Nicholas Adams, *Habermas and Theology* (Cambridge: Cambridge University Press, 2006).

38 Jon Nixon, *Towards the Virtuous University* (New York & London: Routledge, 2008); John Bennett, op. cit.

39 Bennett, op. cit., p.41.

40 Ibid., p.59.

41 Philip Sheldrake, 'Becoming Catholic Persons and Learning to Be a Catholic People' in *Receptive Ecumenism and the Call to Catholic Learning,* edited by Paul Murray (Oxford: Oxford University Press, 2008), pp.56 - 57.

42 Bennett, op. cit., p.103.

43 Nixon, op. cit., p.100.

44 Ibid., p.43.

45 Ibid., p.92.

# Chapter 11

## CONNECTION WITHOUT CONTROL:
## THEOLOGY AND THE UNIVERSITY CURRICULUM

### JOHN SULLIVAN

A Christian university should be able to prompt its members to see the connectedness of the many forms of knowing. Faith and learning should be envisaged as allies rather than as opponents. The critical thinking developed across the disciplines, and the diverse perspectives on reality these disciplines offer, should be seen as capable of being harmonised with the kind of commitments that flow from Christian faith. However, any integrated view of human understanding faces complexities and challenges, both in principle and in implementation, not least one that is theocentric. In the university, disciplines become fragmented; scholars become more and more specialised; modularisation of courses encourages a consumerist attitude toward knowledge rather than a cumulative and long-term development by students, inhibiting even a sense of the wholeness of the particular subject they are studying, rendering it a loose collection of bits and pieces. Surely the meaning to be gleaned from any segment of knowledge is dependent on and enriched by a sense of a larger Meaning that the segments draw upon and feed into. A Christian University should be able offer students the opportunity for a holistic education.

How can we provide students with a coherent curriculum? Should coherence be left to students to construct or should faculty seek to build coherence into the curriculum? How can any attempt to offer coherence avoid imposing controls that inhibit freedom of thought, student choice or the autonomy of the disciplines? What is the role of theology in fostering coherence and connectedness in the university in the contemporary context? I take it that any university should aim to develop in students some combination of comprehensiveness of view, coherence between the parts of their thinking, together with open-mindedness, which entails recognition of our limitations, our partial vision, and ambiguity in our experience of self and world, while avoiding over-prescribed modes of thinking that are too tidy and too self-assured. A Christian university should seek to be a place that goes beyond building community, providing care, promoting worship, and serving those in need.[1] It should also draw on the Christian intellectual tradition to facilitate the development of Christian thinking, about all aspects of reality.

In this chapter, three questions are addressed. First, why should theologians promote inter-connectedness in the university? Second, why is this problematical? Third, how might we conceive of this being done, in particular with what kind of tone, style and intention? Why do these questions matter? It is important, if students are to reach any adequate level of understanding and to have the possibility of developing an integrated worldview, that bridges are built, not only within the ecology of concepts and practices at work in any particular discipline, but also between different areas of the curriculum. Some of the obstacles to such integration and to the role of theology in fostering interconnectedness can be attributed to the wider culture, some to the working practices and operating principles of modern universities and some are brought about through the misguided strategies of theologians themselves. Theology cannot dictate or dominate without damaging either the educational process or the cooperative culture and community in the university. Interconnectedness can be neither imposed nor guaranteed. Thus I argue for theology to be a source of connection in the university, but without control. I suggest that a variety of connections should be promoted, without advocating any particular model. It should be noted that seeking connectedness is something much less systematic and developed than attempts at a more full-blown integration. I believe this more modest effort is more likely to be effective in facilitating dialogue in the contemporary context of universities. One outcome we might hope for from such efforts at inter-connectedness is a more integral vision, a greater sense of coherence and a heightened (and better informed) commitment to the common good.[2]

## 1. NEED FOR INTERCONNECTEDNESS

One reason why theologians should press for interconnectedness in the curriculum flows from a belief in the unity of all truth. Ralph Wood reminds us of the Protestant refrain "All truth is from God" and the Catholic equivalent, that we should seek to "find God in all things."[3] This suggests that Christians should expect to find an essential harmony and coherence between the different kinds of truth they encounter, though, of course, this may not be immediately apparent and may require immense work before we can come to appreciate this unity. Theology is about how all things relate to God. Thus, in a sense, a Christian cannot rule out any area of knowledge as irrelevant to our appreciation of God, even though, for practical purposes, she may restrict her attention to a particular area, while always being conscious that such an area is only ever a part of a much larger whole and needs to be related to and incorporated into a bigger picture. In Matthew 22:37, we read "You shall love the Lord your God with all your heart, and with all your soul, and with all your mind." This reminds Christians that they have a duty, as disciples, to deploy all the capacities of their intellectual endowment, alongside their other human capacities and gifts, in service of the gospel. While the intellect is not everything, it is part of who they are, what they have been given, equipment to be appreciated, developed and deployed. In 1 Corinthians 12: 4 – 6 we read "There are varieties of gifts, but the same Spirit. There are varieties of service, but the same Lord. There are many forms of work, but all of them, in all men, are the work of the same God." And in James 1: 17, we are told "Every good thing bestowed and every good gift is from above, coming down from the Father of lights." For the purposes of this paper, these quotations remind us that, though we might need to specialise in our research, scholarship, and teaching, in order to achieve any penetration in our personal learning and so that we can offer something original, reliable and credible to the stock of knowledge, we must always be keenly aware that God is also operating outside our own specialisms, in other people and through other disciplines. Thus, it is fitting that we enter into dialogue with scholars working outside our own niche in the academic market-place, in order to widen our appreciation of God's ways, purposes, nature and call.

Second, there is an essential open-endedness in each of the disciplines and fields of inquiry. They are incomplete, unfinished, on the way, constantly developing, encountering new questions and problems. We can acknowledge this even as we feel committed to their key values, insights, concepts, methods and structure. Without a degree of open-endedness, they would rapidly become fossilised, repetitive, inward-looking, closed, increasingly irrelevant and ultimately moribund. The categories and concepts we deploy can be useful in demarcating part of the world as a focus for our attention, but they can obscure as well as clarify. This happens as they help us to attend to this aspect, while neglecting another aspect, of what we study. One aspect becomes so bathed in light for us that other aspects are hidden in shadow. We can only see so much at a time. But these concepts and categories can be reconfigured when put into another, wider context, when we engage in inter-disciplinary dialogue. Dialogue between the disciplines can help to ensure a balance of continuity and openness. There cannot be any real dialogue if people do not bring to the table something definite that is theirs to share. Nor can there be any real dialogue if people are not prepared to listen and heed what they hear. There is a parallel here with ecumenism. This too depends upon people bringing something definite to the table, but also a willingness to be vulnerable to critique, to have one's position enriched and modified through the reception it receives from others.

Third, central to a Christian's self-understanding is the belief that we are finite and fallen. We are limited through endowment, circumstances and opportunities. We are also limited through choices which make us one kind of person rather than another, choices that have consequences for our future options, closing some down, even as others are opened up. This is one good reason for theologians to wish to go beyond their own discipline and to encourage others to do the same – as part of an effort to transcend our limitations. Other disciplines help us to note the parameters of our finiteness and fallenness. In addition, it may be claimed that theology helps other disciplines by providing an explicit awareness of and vocabulary for these features of our existence, features that can be easily missed or misdescribed. Recognition of our limitations should induce in us greater realism, humility and openness to other perspectives, nudging us to collaborate with others in our explorations.

Fourth, there is our communal nature, as social beings. We need a plausibility structure[4] – that is, we need our beliefs to be reinforced by the consciousness that others share them. The strength of a university rests as much on its quality as a *community* of scholars, fostering and developing a collective wisdom, as on the quality of individual scholars. Inter-disciplinary endeavours can be an important element in countering excessive individualism and also in undermining the tribalism of some forms of intra-disciplinary debates.

Fifth, our belief that all human beings are made in the image and likeness of God is a powerful motive for taking very seriously what other people think and value, how they perceive, evaluate and respond to the world. If there is something of God in them, it behoves us to attend carefully to their investigations, findings and judgments.

In Cady and Brown's book devoted to Theology and Religious Studies in the university there is only one reference in the index to interdisciplinary dialogue, directing us to an essay by Kathryn Tanner.[5] She unpacks some of the reasons for not remaining enclosed within the confines of single disciplinary thinking and the abstractions from the bigger picture this entails.

> Global capitalism, the media reach, an ecological sensibility in biology, systems analysis in the social sciences, the stress in the physical sciences on the complex statistical interplay of multiple forces, interdependent processes, complex configurations of possible events, all suggest an expansive cognitive model attentive to contextual relationality rather than abstract analysis. ... Disciplines that isolate attention on de-contextualised bits of the world of human experience cannot hold off for long consideration of the concrete fullness of that experience, but are forced by the intellectual climate of the times to put their own concerns back into the larger picture.[6]

I take her argument to point towards the incompleteness and inadequacy of working only within disciplinary boundaries, even if for much of the time this is necessary. We must be ready to place our limited inquiries within the wider setting of the work of other disciplines, though there will be multiple ways of so doing, with no particular one way being privileged. Tanner here is stressing the essential complexity that will be missed if we concentrate solely within a single discipline, however sophisticated its methods. Making connections with other disciplines will help to enhance our appreciation of this complexity and inter-relatedness of phenomena. At the moment, as Michael Lawler comments, "there is too little convergence, too little contact among the various faculties, too little mutual challenge and response among them, leaving them all diminished."[7]

Connectedness is also stressed by Kim Phipps. She says: "Scholarship is rooted in connectedness – in mutual assistance, conversation, encouragement, support, and evaluation. Scholarship proceeds by building on what others have done, and it makes sense only in the context of what others are doing."[8] Basically, we need others, not only within our disciplines of inquiry, but also beyond them, in order to appreciate fully the data we come across and to make sense of our world. Scholarly life, even if often carried out in isolation for long periods, is essentially one of interdependence. Such interdependence is stressed by Alasdair MacIntyre in his 1999 book *Dependent Rational Animals.*[9] MacIntyre draws our attention to the goods that come our way through vulnerability and the virtues of acknowledged dependence on others. However, when Phipps emphasises connectedness as essential for scholars, she refers to more than merely a focus on findings and the concepts used in analysing these findings. She also alerts us to the need to pay attention to the personal stories from which the findings emerge, for scholarship is embedded in lives that have other dimensions that impinge upon their academic work. "Scholarship that precludes consideration of the autobiographical perspectives of individual scholars will be severely limited, lacking creative imagination and insights into human nature."[10] Of course in paying attention to the personal stories told by scholars we need to beware unilateral forms of testimony that engage insufficiently with critical questioning and that seek to impose their authority on listeners, seeking surrender, rather than those which invite free responses in a spirit of humility, seeking correction and completion.

Failure to tap into the faith dimension latent in students and subject matter can be countered by attention to curriculum connectedness. Often there is a tendency to ignore what many students bring to the classroom – across the disciplines – in terms of their faith affiliation – or allergies to faith. Yet to advert to the religious implications of what is being learned might be an additional way for teachers to create inclusive and hospitable spaces for learning, by tapping into where students are coming from. I am thinking here as much of student resentments and rejections of religion as of their positive convictions and affiliations. Teachers should acknowledge this aspect of student identity, allow it to enter into the classroom and into educational assignments. Of course, not only is faith (in something) part of the being of the students; it is also integral to some aspects of the realities being investigated in many disciplines. Referring to psychology, sociology, history, anthropology and literature, Jacobsen and Jacobsen say "Since faith is part of the reality that those disciplines seek to study, matters of faith ought not to be banned from the academic dimensions of these subjects."[11] One might add that, even though faith might be less evidently part of some other disciplines, in terms of what they are studying, it will certainly be part of the life of students and scholars in, for example, science, medicine, business, engineering and education, and therefore an element in the operating factors that affect their perception, thinking and evaluating.

I believe that universities should be places where faculty and students raise key questions about the disciplines. What are the philosophical assumptions that underpin them? How is power exercised within them? Who sets the agenda and on what basis? Whose voices are heard, suppressed or ignored? What are the boundaries that separate out one discipline from others? What ethical issues arise out of deploying the key concepts and central methods of that discipline? It is difficult to see how these questions can be adequately addressed without looking 'over the garden fence,' giving at least some consideration to neighbouring disciplines. Theology has always had to do this, for, as Kathryn Tanner says "specifically Christian sources and norms have never been sufficient for theological instruction."[12] There has always been engagement with concepts and cultures external to the faith. "The very *meaning* of even the most fundamental theological claims is determined by what theologians do with the notions and affirmations of other intellectual and cultural areas."[13] One draws upon the intellectual terminology or currency available at the time even if one 'buys' something different with it. Tanner claims that "One cannot be a constructive theologian for the present day without familiarity with the currency of the other intellectual or cultural fields of the day, and it is through the assessment of how other theologians of the past and present have dealt with comparable material of their own times and places that one develops a sense for what needs to be done now."[14]

John E Hull provides two additional reasons for theologians to engage in inter-disciplinary dialogue. First, they cannot be counter-cultural in the university context if they remain within their own field of study and accept the reigning ' rules' of the academic environment. If they "submit to the 'wisdom' of the incumbent paradigm" they "relinquish [the] right to pose the central questions, redefine limits, set priorities, or offer alternative answers to society's questions of ultimate concern."[15] Second, if they abdicate responsibility for engaging others in dialogue about scholarly questions, methods, findings and their practical implications, they run the risk that the Christian perspective will function simply like "bookends – God talk will appear [at the best] at the beginning and end of lessons, units, courses and years, but what lies in between will remain largely unaffected."[16]

## 2. OBSTACLES

There are many different kinds of obstacles to the establishment of connection between the disciplines. Among some Christians there has been a marked anti-intellectualism, as if a faith separated from scholarly and academic concerns was somehow more pure, more trusting, less reliant on human achievement, more open to God's revelation. Faith alone or Scripture alone is required by the disciple. Academic learning clouds the vision, relies too heavily on anti-Christian assumptions, invites pride, and leaves less room for God in one's life. Fideism, however, undermines the credibility of Christian faith in the long run and refuses to use one of God's great gifts, rationality.

Among other Christians who seek connections between theology and other disciplines, sometimes the kind of relationship sought invites suspicion. This might be because the relationship being pursued seems too unilateral, with theology influencing the other discipline but not in turn allowing itself to be influenced, as if theology is already complete while the other partner is deficient. Nicholas Wolterstorff refers to Abraham Kuyper's "one-directional, non-interactionist view of the relation between religion and the practice of scholarship."[17] Or, suspicion might be aroused by fears that the academic agenda of a discipline, and following from this, the distribution of power and opportunities, might be altered by a dominant religious group. This might render as second-class academic citizens those scholars who are not members of the faith or denomination in question. This fear certainly prevails in some Catholic universities.[18]

Jacobsen and Jacobsen bring out two important limitations of earlier integration models.[19] They claim, with some justice, that these models often depend rather closely on a Reformed, Calvinist view of Christian scholarship and fit much less easily with other Christian emphases, among which he mentions Catholic, Wesleyan, Lutheran, Pentecostal, Baptist and Orthodox approaches. Some of these give less emphasis to the intellectual dimension and more to other dimensions of Christian life, for example, the liturgical, sacramental, communal, practical, political and aesthetic. They also point out that typical models of integrating faith and learning fit better areas of study that by their nature are more philosophical or theory-based, for example sociology, rather than chemistry, or literary criticism rather than engineering. Partly because of the cogency of these points, I am advocating in this chapter, not a full-blooded integration, but a much looser and less systematic exercise in establishing connections, without seeking to specify the expected outcomes or nature of these connections.

Such lack of clarity, however, about what is being aimed for in inter-disciplinary dialogue, can itself be an obstacle. This might be related to lack of realism about what can be expected, how open people are prepared to be, how much time they can devote to dialogue beyond their discipline, and how many resources can be allocated for this kind of activity. It might also be linked to an attempt to seek too tidy an approach to inter-disciplinary dialogue and projects, perhaps importing a monistic attitude, envisaging a strategy that is insufficiently pluralistic or flexible. Too systematic an approach can be both threatening and narrowing. Disciplinary affiliations among faculty can lead to connections with their international colleagues in the same field being prioritised over those with their colleagues from other disciplines in their own institution. Then there are defensive mechanisms and territorial sensitivities that operate, for example, in protecting budgets, in preserving a curriculum into which one has invested much time and effort, in the drive towards empire-building, combined with a mixture of both excessive confidence in a discipline and a fear of the unknown. In the collaborative project management of people drawn from different disciplines attention has to be paid to the identity, security and motivation of those involved. Ways have to be found to balance the risk-taking required for inter-disciplinary endeavours with the familiarity and stability provided by the home-base discipline.

Lyon and Beaty succinctly indicate three considerations that can inhibit interconnectedness between theology and other disciplines in a university setting. First, some claim that, with regard to their particular discipline, religious perspectives are either non-existent or simply irrelevant. Second, which version and whose definition of 'Christian' is to be used, since there simply does not exist one unified version which can be labelled 'the' Christian one. Third, some take the view that teaching a Christian perspective presents a biased view that is unfair to other religious (and non-religious) perspectives.[20]

With regard to the first of these points, judgment as to whether theology has anything to offer should be withheld until *after* some inter-disciplinary discussion has taken place. My guess is that it is a combination of three factors that leads to a premature judgment of irrelevance. Many theologians have simply not considered the implications of their work for other disciplines. Similarly, many theologians have failed to listen carefully to what scholars in other disciplines are up to and are thus unaware of how theology and other studies might be linked. Likewise, scholars in other disciplines rarely consider the potential relevance of theology, remaining largely in ignorance of its potential contribution to their work.

As for the second consideration, the sheer multiplicity of Christian voices, I do not think this should be especially problematical, (given the multiplicity of voices often clamouring for attention in other disciplines). When the particularities of the tradition being represented by a theologian are specified, there should be humble acknowledgement of the limited degree of authority these hold for other Christians. Also, the theologian must be willing to learn from Christians of a different persuasion and open to other disciplines.

As for the third possible objection to theology being brought to bear in inter-disciplinary dialogue, that inviting the Christian voice into the academy is unjust to non-religious and non-Christian views, this is specious reasoning. It presupposes that the Christian speaks without respect for others, without knowledge that there are other points of view and that others are not allowed to speak for themselves. None of these conditions need apply when Christian theologians contribute to inter-disciplinary dialogue.

It might be thought counter-intuitive to assume that the academy is ready for theology to make a constructive contribution to cross-disciplinary dialogue. There are intellectual trends that seem to count against such an undertaking. First, there is the hermeneutics of suspicion (all is power-play and the expression of vested interests). Second, there is a strong sense of the situation-specific nature of all claims (relativism). Third, there is resistance to meta-narratives. Fourth, often this is linked to the discrediting of authority, heavy weighting given to individualism and strong emphasis on autonomy (rather than inter-dependence) as a major value. Fifth, there is the privatisation of religion and its relegation to a marginal and merely optional activity. Sixth, there can be a tendency to believe that we can develop the 'software' of skills and competences without the 'hardware' of character. Here the assumption is that what we learn in class is something quite disconnected from (and thus uninfluenced by) the company we keep, what else we are learning, the kind of life we live and the persons we are becoming. Marcia Bunge identifies both a negative and a positive feature in the modern academy. "On the one hand, many students and faculty seem to hold onto the very modern assumption that faith and learning are separate realms and that religion is personal and private and therefore irrelevant to academic life. On the other hand, there appears to be a growing openness to religious perspectives among scholars in several fields that some attribute to the postmodern critique of objectivity and emphasis on pluralism."[21]

Such openness to the religious voice as one among many contending for our attention in the market-place of ideas is very different from the position of religion in a religiously affiliated university. It is plausible to argue that theologians in Christian universities are in some way sponsored by their institution, perhaps considered as spokespersons for it, guardians of orthodoxy, in a privileged position *vis-à-vis* other disciplines. When they speak, they can be heard by faculty from other disciplines as if they are speaking with more than just their own voice, with an institutional mandate. Of course, this is often not the case at all, for many Christian universities in practice give far too little support to the position and healthy functioning of theology, thereby undercutting the capacity of the institution to articulate its identity and to communicate intelligently its *raison d'être*. Secularisation has frequently deeply permeated even religiously affiliated universities, influencing their operating assumptions and practices. Secularisation occurs for many reasons. We want to widen the field and improve the quality of our staff; reducing the focus on religious affiliation and commitment allows us to widen the net in recruiting the best staff. We want to avoid heavy-handedness and compulsion in imposing a religious ethos and so step back from many of the kinds of requirements – in curriculum and in student life – that once might have been normal.

We need to maximize our recruitment of students, of all kinds, including the brightest, in order to compete and to remain viable; thus we minimize the religious character of our institution in our promotion of it, lest this should put them off coming to us. It is not surprising that cumulatively the obstacles indicated in this section lead some colleagues to see the religious and the academic mission of Christian universities as existing in tension. While acknowledging this, I believe the tension can be a creative one.

### 3. PROMPTING CONNECTIONS

Theology should not be considered as a competitor against other disciplines, but their partner. Although there is, in my view, a place both for apologetics - a defence of the faith we hold - and for critique - exposing the false assumptions, misguided priorities and distorted values of some worldviews and ideological contenders in the university - the primary role of theology, in the context of inter-disciplinary inquiry, is as humble contributor to the debates and investigations. All knowledge involves interpretation. And this emerges from our worldview fed by prior inclinations, judgments, commitments and aversions. Neutrality might be often claimed but is rarely displayed in practice in the academy.[22] Theologians should ask their colleagues what view of persons, society, knowledge and learning underlies their current practices and proposals – and be ready to be questioned in turn on these points. They should open up for their colleagues the possibility of seeing all of reality as the theatre of God's work. As Harry Lee Poe puts it, "faith intersects an academic discipline at the point where it asks its fundamental questions, ... appropriates its most fundamental assumptions, ... [and] establishes its core values."[23] Poe provides a useful set of questions that can facilitate interdisciplinary dialogue:

- With what is your discipline concerned?
- What characterises the methodology of your discipline?
- On what other disciplines does your discipline build? To what other disciplines does your discipline contribute?
- What are the values on which your discipline is based? At what point do these values come into conflict with other disciplines?
- Over what values within your discipline do members of your discipline disagree?
- What is the philosophical basis for your discipline's values?[24]

He also provides examples of questions for particular disciplines, from which I select just five as examples:

- For Biology: To what extent, if any, should genetic engineering be used to enhance human beings?
- For English: What are the similarities and differences in interpreting biblical texts and other literature?
- For Political Science: What is the role of forgiveness in international relations?
- For Fine Arts: What are the limits, if any, on the freedom for human creative expression?
- For Economics: What is the relationship the quest for profitability and the Christian call for compassion and justice?[25]

These kinds of questions facilitate the development of a wisdom that transcends mere knowledge.[26]

At the same time theologians must show that they are open to the possibility that faith can be illuminated, engaged, interrogated, and challenged by the findings of other disciplines, so that it is tested, purified, clarified and kept humble. The tone of engagement between the disciplines fostered, facilitated and supported by theologians should be dialogical rather than conflictual. My assumption here is that a Christian university will function more like an umbrella than something more systemic, to use the terminology of Duane Litfin. An umbrella organisation "seeks to house a variety of perspectives without sacrificing its sponsoring perspective; ... to create an environment congenial to Christian thinking, but without expecting it of everyone."[27] Such an idea has implications for the kind of hospitality offered by Christians, the tone of voice they adopt and the quality of listening they exhibit.

There are various ways that theology can contribute to inter-connectedness in the university. Tanner argues that theology can help to focus the university's attention on the most pressing problems and challenges of contemporary life.[28] This view is echoed by Wood, who believes that a Christian university should help faculty and students to discern "how the Gospel impinges upon all humanistic and scientific questions." These questions include: "What constitutes the human person, the quality of the good life, the purpose of social existence, the nature of the physical universe, the structure of political and social order."[29] In this way theology can influence the way other subjects are taught, ensuring that they address the big questions about life and the world. Joseph Komonchak powerfully brings out the potential relevance of theology for the wider curriculum in the following way.

> Whether or not the human person is reducible to the dumb play of material forces, whether or not he has a destiny beyond the grave, whether or not he can attain truth, whether or not there is a God, whether or not this God has a redemptive care for us, surely have consequences for the way in which we conceive not only our private lives but our social lives as well, for the fashion in which we deal with one another, for the criteria by which we measure success or failure, for the means we consider whereby to render human life, not just our own, not just our nation's, but the whole world's life, less unworthy even of the human, never mind the divine."[30]

Attention to their apophatic tradition should make Christians ready to acknowledge the limitations of their language and its 'reach', its match with and adequacy to reality. This should prompt them to take pains to avoid being over-dogmatic in dialogue. However, the openness and flexibility suggested by such awareness of the limitations of language does not imply that Christian theologians should be unprepared to bring to the table something stable and substantial. Being open-minded does not mean being empty-headed. For, as Tanner says, "Theologians on the basis in great part of distinctively Christian sources and norms purport to say something important about the nature of human flourishing."[31]

What will be needed if the kind of interconnectedness I have advocated is to occur? Among a number of recommendations, Gasper includes the following three. There should research groups that deliberately include faculty from different disciplines. At least some professors should serve two departments. Research students should follow a minor subject, in addition to and from a different discipline than their major area of investigation.[32] The encouragement of collegiality can be a strong incentive to greater academic interconnectedness. This implies joint collaboration in service of a cause – for the Christian community, subscribing to the Kingdom of God - that is bigger than any single individual or discipline. Theology – through its clear distinguishing of what is ultimate and what is penultimate - has a role in questioning modes of university management and aspects of academic culture that can slide into forms of totalitarianism and idolatry that colonise our life-world.

Interestingly, Gasper suggests that "Interdisciplinarity will work more readily when people act not as representatives of disciplines but represent themselves, their experiences, values and insights."[33] When his insight is applied to theologians in the Christian university, I would add that they have an opportunity to help colleagues in other disciplines to see that their work could be interpreted as a vocation, a co-operation with God's grace in a particular, positive if limited way, in preparing for the Kingdom. Thus understood, when 'speaking for themselves' they would do so with an enhanced sense of responsibility, not only *for* the subject area they represent, not only *with* their fellow academics, but also with a deep sense of *who* they are (a child of God with a particular calling) and responsive *to* the source and goal of all knowledge, God our Creator, Redeemer and Sustainer. This kind of thinking will require ongoing staff development for mission, gradually building up confidence in the relevance and applicability of Christian language and lifestyle to the academic world.

*** *** ***

The kind of role in promoting connections across the curriculum that I have described for theology avoids the extremes of either abdication or domination, of silence or shouting. It links with the Christian university's *raison d'être*. It accepts theology's role in showing how all things relate to God. It draws upon and displays the relevance for academic inquiry of the Christian intellectual tradition. It questions the fundamental assumptions at work in the academy. It invites others into dialogue and it listens respectfully and humbly to what they have to add and shows itself willing to learn from them. Thus it makes possible connection without control.

## NOTES

1   Ralph Wood, *Contending for the Faith* (Waco, TX: Baylor University Press, 2003), pp.91-93, 107.

2   Terence Nichols, "Theology and the integration of knowledge." In *Enhancing*

*Religious Identity*, edited by J. Wilcox and I King, p.242 (Washington, DC: Georgetown University Press, 2000).

3  Wood, p.89.

4  Peter Berger, *The Heretical Imperative* (London: Collins, 1980).

5  Linell Cady and Delwin Brown, eds. *Religious Studies, Theology, and the University*. (New York: State University of New York Press, 2002). Kathryn Tanner's chapter is "Theology and cultural contest in the university," pp.199-212.

6  Tanner, pp.204-5.

7  Michael Lawler, "Introduction," in *Catholic theology in the university* edited by V. Shaddy, p.1, (Marquette, WI: Marquette University Press, 1998).

8  Kim Phipps, "Campus Climate and Christian Scholarship," in *Scholarship & Christian Faith*, edited by D Jacobsen & R.H. Jacobsen, p.172 (New York: Oxford University Press, 2004).

9  Alasdair MacIntyre, *Dependent rational animals*, (London: Duckworth, 1999).

10  Phipps, *loc. cit.*, p.177.

11  Jacobsen & Jacobsen, p.161.

12  Tanner, p.209.

13  Tanner, p.210.

14  Ibid.

15  John E. Hull, "Aiming for Christian education: settling for Christians educating: the Christian school's replication of a public school paradigm," *Christian Scholars' Review* 13 (2002), pp.203-223, at p.216.

16  Hull, pp.222-3.

17  Hull, quoting Wolterstorff, p.213.

18  John Langan, "Catholic presence in the disciplines." In Shaddy, p.96. See note 7.

19  Jacobsen & Jacobsen, pp.15-31.

20  L. Lyon and M. Beaty "Integration, secularisation, and the two-spheres view at religious colleges," *Christian Scholars' Review* 23, no. 1 (1999), pp.73–112, at p.85.

21  Marcia Bunge, "Religion and the curriculum at church-related colleges and universities," in *Professing in the postmodern academy*, edited by S. Haynes, p.249 (Waco, TX: Baylor University Press, 2002).

22  Roy Clouser, *The myth of religious neutrality* (Notre Dame, IN: University of Notre Dame Press, 1991).

23  Harry Poe, *Christianity in the academy* (Grand Rapids, MI: Baker Academic, 2004), p.138.

24  Poe, pp.138-9.

25 Poe, p.159.

26 Nicholas Maxwell, *From knowledge to wisdom* (Oxford; Blackwell, 1987).

27 Duane Litfin, *Conceiving the Christian College* (Grand Rapids, MI: Eerdmans, 2004), pp.17-18.

28 Tanner, *loc. cit.*, p.206.

29 Wood, *op. cit.*, p.120.

30 Joseph Komonchak, "Redemptive identity and mission of a Catholic university." In Shaddy, p.82. See note 7.

31 Tanner, 207.

32 Des Gasper, *Interdisciplinarity* (The Hague: Institute of Social Studies), 2001), p.17.

33 Ibid, p.15.

# Part Four:
# Expanding horizons

# Chapter 12

## RELIGIOUS SPEECH IN THE PUBLIC SQUARE

### John Sullivan

In the light of their past experience of dreadful internal divisions and mutually destructive murderous behaviour by people with different religious affiliations, many societies in the West have, over a long period of time, worked out ways of reducing conflict and the discrimination and pain associated with such conflict by removing religious speech from the political arena. Religion became an optional element in private identity, free from state interference, except where it jeopardised public safety or offended public morality. Accompanying this freedom from external interference, there was an expectation that religious communities would practice their faith with a degree of restraint. They would not flaunt it in public; they would not impose it on others; they would not seek special favours; they would demonstrate loyalty and commitment to the society which offered them tolerance and freedom from oppression; they would both accept and promote the prevailing values of liberal democracy.

It has often been assumed that the ground-rules which have been established for maintaining this *modus vivendi* operate benignly and impartially, offering a balanced neutrality on the part of the state and civil society in the face of diverse religions, worldviews and moral stances, favouring none and discriminating against none. Policies and debates in the civil zone - by which I mean all those areas of life we share with the general public, comprised of people of diverse worldviews - were expected to be conducted on the basis of principles, values and arguments that could secure a wide measure of agreement. While these principles, values and arguments might in many individual cases be drawn from a more substantial, highly developed and complexly interacting 'thick' set of beliefs, they could be appealed to in the public domain more thinly, in isolation from and without explicit reference to these underlying justificatory matrixes. Thus, in order to keep the peace, to prevent religious conflict and in the interests of social harmony, religious language and argument should be kept away from the public square.

Decision-making was to take place in religion-free zones. This applied to the world of work, the arts and the media, education (with the exception in some countries of religiously affiliated schools, colleges and universities). It also applied to the law, health care, social services and politics.

The assumption here was that the restraint required of religious believers through this arrangement was either minimal, since it still left them with sufficient space to live out their faith in their private lives, or – because of the peace it secured – was a price worth paying. It might well be thought that to concede a greater public role for religion, to allow religious language once again to enter civil society and its various institutions and groupings that often mediate between the individual and the state, would be to threaten a hard-earned social harmony. It might seem to pander to extremists. It could entail turning one's back on rationality. It might include caving in to self-serving clerical elites. Such moves jeopardise freedom of thought and lifestyle and cumulatively undermine democracy. For a while, many religious believers seemed to accept the self-denying ordinance required of them as a necessary price for social harmony. They learned to be bilingual, reserving the language of faith for their private lives while deploying secular language in all their dealings with others in the public domain. The upshot of this bilingual practice for many was a split personality and a dualistic outlook. Yet, religion claims to offer an integrated life, where all aspects of one's life are bound together, co-ordinated into a whole, directed towards a goal that comprehends and includes everything we are and do. If the limits of one's language are the limits of one's world (according to Wittgenstein) then to spend most of one's time not speaking of God is to live most of one's life each day as if God does not exist and does not matter. A strange situation arises for the religious believer in a secular society. God is simultaneously the Supreme Being, of overriding importance. Ultimate obedience is due and anything less than worship is to relate wrongly, to live out of synchronisation with reality. Yet such a belief is to be suppressed for one's own convenience and so as not to upset others.

There is a problem here! On the one hand religious believers feel the need to relate their faith to all aspects of life. So we find that 'Religious traditions wish to be heard in debates about law, medical ethics, international security, the environmental crisis, education and economic development.'[1] On the other hand, any attempt to allow religion back into the public square arouses fear, prompts suspicion and sparks off hostility. In this chapter I have three aims. First, I analyze why allowing religious speech in the public square is perceived as problematical, dangerous and to be avoided. Second, I argue that suppressing religious speech is itself dangerous and wrong and that religious speech *should* be welcomed into the public square. Third, I propose some qualities and virtues required by religious believers if their speech in the public square is not to lead to the problems and dangers identified in part one. Thus, once I have tried to establish in part two that religious believers should be given permission to use religious language in a pluralist and secular context, I shall be concerned in part three to articulate *how* such language ought to be used. When religious beliefs and language are included in public argument, advocacy and commendation, in what style and with what tone should this be done?

## 1. RELIGIOUS SPEECH PERCEIVED AS A PROBLEM

Two days before Christmas 2006, on its front page, in large bold headlines, *The Guardian* - a national newspaper in the UK - claimed, based on an opinion poll, that a majority of people in the UK thought religion is a cause of more harm than good. Let me leave aside here such issues as the size of the sample of people invited to comment, the way the question was posed, and whether or not the views were justified. Let me accept at face value, for a moment, the growing concerns in some quarters that liberal democracy is facing a threat from religious believers who want their religious views to influence the way society is organised, what is permitted and what is prohibited.

English newspapers and television news programmes in the weeks leading up to Christmas 2006 also reported on several issues where religious commitment and its public expression were perceived as unduly vocal, intrusive, divisive or disproportionate. Christian Unions in universities (for example, at Exeter, Birmingham, Edinburgh and Heriot-Watt) were accused of being exclusive in requiring their officers and their members to be committed Christians and as a result were suspended in some places from being recognised as official university bodies.[2] These Christian Unions rejected current acceptance of same-sex relationships and wanted to articulate views contrary to those that hold sway now. In a letter to *The Times Higher Education Supplement,* one commentator on the controversy over Christian Unions in British universities said: 'If you can have a meat eater running a vegetarian society, why can't you have an atheist running the Christian Union? Faith is not required, merely competence and responsibility to its members.'[3] I find this an amazingly misguided response. It seems to bypass any question of credibility of leadership, of match between office and commitment, of concern for the purpose and nature of a group's gatherings.

Another example of religious expression in the news is when a British Airways worker was suspended from work because she insisted on wearing a small cross.[4] Her company has a policy that employees cannot wear visible jewellery and her cross was treated as jewellery. She decided to make a stand in conscience against her suspension, refused to take off the cross and became (briefly) a *cause célèbre*. A classroom assistant in a school failed in her court case to establish a right to wear the Niqab, the veil covering her face, since it was deemed incompatible with the requirements of her job, preventing easy communication with children. A senior government minister, Jack Straw, prompted widespread public debate during the autumn of 2006, questioning the appropriateness of wearing a full veil by Muslim women if they wanted to participate fully in a plural society. The nervous and suspicious response shown in the media to Prime Minister Tony Blair's television interview with Michael Parkinson in March 2006, when he indicated that his decision to go to war with Iraq would be subject to God's judgment, showed how uncomfortable many are that their politicians might be motivated by faith.[5]

In a report for the Christian think-tank *Theos,* Nick Spencer lists several other signs of phobia about religion in public, although often disguised by an ostensible desire to avoid offending faiths other than Christian. These include the renaming of Christmas as 'winterval', the removal of Christian signs from a crematorium, and warning charitable bodies offering various forms of social services, such as drug rehabilitation or shelters for the homeless, that their funding would be cut unless they stopped overt Christian practices.[6] He also reports that 'Edinburgh University was considering banning Bibles from its student halls of residence on the basis that they are "discriminatory" and make students of others faiths feel unwelcome.'[7] Members of minority religious groups, on the whole, do not experience these moves as being inclusive of them by avoiding favouring Christians, but as threatening to their own culture in denying the rightful place of religious faith in life and in seeking to impose an artificial (and damaging) division between the private and public sphere.

Earlier in 2006 there had been large-scale public protest demonstrations by Muslims in many countries about cartoons of Muhammad, originally published in Denmark. Violence had flared up and several deaths can be attributed directly to this particular issue. The UK in 2005 had seen strong protests by some Christians about the show *Jerry Springer – The Opera* and demonstrations about a play in Birmingham that depicted sex and murder in a Sikh temple. The play was called off, after several, increasingly violent, public demonstrations by offended Sikhs. In these early years of the twenty-first century, France has been wracked by similar turmoil about how to maintain the secular principle of *laïcité* in the face of increasingly resentful Muslims who feel rejected by French society. The Centre for Cultural Renewal, Canada, constantly reports cases where militant secularists seek to drive out of the public square the rights of religious believers to influence policy, legislation and mores, for example, with regard to pro-life issues and to same-sex unions.

I do not want to comment on the specific details, merits or demerits of these cases. It may be that the religious believer at the centre of a particular controversy was entirely justified in her or his stance or closer investigation may show that she or he failed to display the kinds of qualities and virtues I advocate in part three below. My point here is simply to note the growing controversial nature of religious language, dress or communication in public. Religion that rears its head in the public square is frequently seen as an 'authoritarian, backward-looking, toxic contribution.'[8] The fear is that 'a sectarian mode of religious participation is more likely, when successful in achieving its political objective, to tear the bonds of political community than to strengthen them.'[9] This danger stems from the overriding authority that religious faith has for many adherents – obligations to family, friends, colleagues, class, race and the state are superseded by the claims of religion. This overriding authority becomes more threatening when the scope of religion is acknowledged. Eberle refers to this scope as 'totalising'; theists 'take the scope of their obligation to obey God to extend to whatever they do, wherever they are, and in whatever institutional setting they find themselves.'[10] The internal divisiveness that is a feature of many religions, with serious conflict about identifying which interpretations of religious authorities are correct, tends to render religious contributions to the public square unpredictable as well as dangerous.[11]

There is real tension in many societies about the role of religious speech in the public square. Despite the obstacles put in their way, religious groups have shown a new-found confidence and desire to contribute to public debate, for example, about law, medical ethics, the environment, education, immigration, how to respond to terrorism and so on. On the one hand, to prevent such interventions in and contributions to public argument from drawing upon religious reasoning seems unduly restrictive to religious believers and to assume false neutrality as the default position in liberal democracies. On the other hand, there still remains a bitter memory of how, in the past, religious voices dominated the public square and suppressed alternative points of view. Fear of resurgent and narrow traditionalism, in various guises, encourages a militant secularism that wishes to keep religion confined to the private domain.

The view still prevails, in many circles, that 'Christianity is mere "superstition," faith a process of "non-thinking," God a virus, religion the "root of all evil," religious people "cloth heads."'[12] It is often believed that, due to the overriding authority and totalising scope of their faith, as described above, religious believers will prove themselves to be inflexible in argument and demonstrate unwillingness to compromise. It is assumed that they will draw upon obscurantist reasoning, rely on inaccessible authorities and texts, privilege past tradition over the needs of the present and promote their own perspective on truth while displaying inadequate concern for the truth-claims made by their neighbours. The sanctions sometimes used to buttress religious argument, such as excommunication, or the implied threat of damnation for rejecting God's will, seem insidiously to undermine the appeal to higher grounds than self-interest.[13] Given the intractable and bitter divisions caused by religion, it is understandable that removing it from the public square can seem an attractive option.

The German philosopher Habermas wonders how communities with different, sometimes contradictory, narratives can meet peacefully in public and engage in debate constructively on moral and other matters. His remedy is to ask particular groupings to suspend their own narratives in order to rely on universally binding procedures that frame public discussions. He is ambivalent about religion. He recognises, on the positive side, that religion for many people is a major provider of visions of the good life and a principal motivator of behaviour in pursuit of such visions. However, he is concerned that, on the negative side, religions seem to encourage uncritical and passive acceptance of authority and unhelpful stances when debating with those who differ from them. He sees religious traditions as being simultaneously powerful in what they inspire and dangerous in what they entail. His particular interest is not religion (or theology) in itself, but its potential contribution, positively and negatively, to communication in the public sphere.

He wants to retain the motivation to live ethically, while stripping religion of its worldview-sustaining role. Modern society, for Habermas, buys an enhanced freedom, one that comes from its ability to question and criticise, at a doubly high price.[14] First, there is distancing from traditions that once provided motivation for living a good life. Second, there is loss of solidarity. These traditions fixed too firmly what the good life consisted in – that was their defect. But, their advantage over current pluralist societies is that they supplied motivations for behaviour and parameters for debate that made debate possible, since disagreements were based on a foundation of basic agreements. Where will the new foundation come from? The conditions for communication proposed by Habermas in several of his works include belief that genuine consensus is possible, equality among participants and freedom from constraint, with all having a voice and receiving respect and attention.[15]

If Habermas has sought, by philosophical analysis, to identify the conditions that optimise the chances of constructive communication between different groups in society, an alternative approach by some Western governments recently has been to draw upon the notion of 'social capital'. It is recognised that religious groups are prime – but not the sole – examples where social relationships and networks can provide support for positive human development, 'contributing to better educational attainment, lower crime rates, improved health, more active citizenship, better functioning labour markets and higher economic growth ... and sustainable neighbourhoods.'[16] One does not have to accept the truth of religious beliefs to be able to see that communities built around responses to these beliefs seem to have the capacity to make a positive difference to the lives of their members and to develop a motivation and support structure that enable them to reach out to others, to non-members who are in various kinds of need. In Britain and in the USA, governments have acknowledged the potential of religious groups to address social problems that have been stubbornly resistant to secular social welfare attempts to resolve them.[17] However, Furbey emphasises that reaching out from religious communities is by no means automatic, guaranteed or smooth.[18] Getting outside its own walls is not easy for many faith communities. Furthermore, when attempts are made to do so by social activists within a faith tradition, this can weaken links with those left behind. 'Social capital,' for all the positive achievements of shared norms, mutual trust, frequent contact, cumulatively enabling people to achieve more together than as isolated individuals, also has a shadow side. It can be 'exclusive of others, a perpetuation of stereotypes of "outsiders," tribalist and oppressive to members, punitive to deviants, an inhibitor of new knowledge, a source of stagnation and isolation, and a source of inequality.'[19]

## 2. WRONGFUL SUPPRESSION OF RELIGIOUS SPEECH

There clearly is a shadow side presented by religious communities. Could we not say the same about families: that instead of being places of warmth, acceptance, blessing, encouragement and growth, they can slip into being cold, even cruel cages, rejecting, crippling, alienating and distorting? However, this does not lead us to dismantle the family, for we remain confident that, on balance, despite the frequent falling short in family life, families constitute for most people havens of (often unconditional) care, support and acceptance. Similarly, despite the damage sometimes done in the name of religion by zealous adherents, those with ill-judged, excessive, unbalanced and narrow convictions, we should beware over-reacting by banning religious speech from the public square in an attempt to avoid conflict. For 'at its best, religious discourse in public culture is not less dialogic – not less open-minded, not less deliberative – than is, at its best, secular discourse in public culture.'[20] It is not appropriate to relegate religion to the private realm, as if it has no place in public affairs, for 'there is no fundamental incompatibility between public religious arguments and the essential conditions of publicity in a pluralistic democracy.'[21] In fact, there is a new realisation of the potential importance of faith groups for creating the conditions for the health of the wider community and for fostering the common good. In the face of the breakdown of a high percentage of marriages, and dissolution of many other social bonds, and all the associated costs - which include not only personal finance and the national economy, but also a negative impact on health, sense of well-being, security, educational achievement - the social capital that can be drawn from faith communities that I referred to in the last paragraph becomes more important than ever. Thus it has been argued that 'local authorities, primary care trusts, police authorities and other such agencies have to develop a much more sophisticated understanding of faith communities with much closer relationships if latent social capital is to be used effectively.'[22]

Arguments in favour of allowing religious speech in the public square fall into several categories. I highlight four types of argument here. One has its focus on personal identity and the potential damage done to this if religion is privatised. Another is directed to the potential moral deficit for society if religious arguments are sidelined. The third argument referred to here attacks the assumption that default secularism is neutral. A fourth emphasises the benefit to religious believers by engaging in the public domain with the discipline of critical dialogue with those who differ from them.

First, banning religious speech in public can lead to the suppression of important aspects of the self, creating internal division instead of fostering the unity of a life. In their stress on freedom of choice, personal autonomy and freedom from tradition, many liberals undervalue the place played by over-arching narratives in people's lives and the way such narratives assist in the process of developing a sense of the unity of life. In a unified life we value a high degree of consistency and coherence between our beliefs and our behaviour, and between one decision and another (at least on major matters). It is confusing (for ourselves and for others) and self-defeating to be at the mercy of conflicting desires and to engage in behaviour that contradicts values we have espoused as central to and directive of who we understand ourselves to be. Of course, consistency and coherence must be tempered by an awareness of complexity and the different roles we play (and the associated different expectations we have of ourselves and that others have of us). But they still exercise crucial functions in unifying our life's projects.

Embracing a religion as a convert, or accepting a religion one has been inducted into, offers a way to bind oneself to a set of ideals. It offers a way to bond with other, like-minded people. It is a basic stance in the face of what one takes to be ultimate reality and a personal response to the source of our being. It brings together our understanding of and relationship with ourselves, society, nature and the whole of what we encounter and believe to exist. It requires of us that we live in the truth, as we see it and this truth, although it must acknowledge the multiple dimensions of life, and the different rules of engagement for these dimensions, cannot be a random set of conflicting beliefs. In order to make sense of our lives our notion of truth will function for us in a way that allows us to decide priorities, and to structure and co-ordinate our values when they appear to conflict. Thus, to act like a father to one's children is not the same as to act like a teacher to one's students. The way we relate to friends would not necessarily be appropriate for the way we relate to strangers. What we offer to clients if we are in a professional relationship with them differs from what we are obliged to offer to others. However, the multiple relationships we find ourselves in – and the diverse responses they require of us – do not mean a fractured self. It is the one self who responds – even if with varying degrees of assurance and adequacy – to these different demands and contexts.

If we are expected to silence, censor and suppress key aspects of our identity, this is bound to have a cumulatively negative impact. We find that such a self experiences exclusion, repression, diminishment; it feels disempowered and treated with disdain. Privatisation encourages forms of bilingualism that slip into double-talking. This is not simply the adjustment of language we use when we switch from speaking to six year olds to speaking with sixteen or sixty year olds, or modifying our speech when we address a group of parents in a school hall as opposed to an academic gathering in a specialist scholarly conference. Being forced to avoid reference to those things that are of ultimate importance to us in all public contexts seems bound to have a damaging effect, both on us as speakers and on those who hear us.

The language we use helps to construct (as well as describe) the world around us; it discloses who we are at the same time as it seeks to do justice to the reality we encounter. It creates expectations in others – expectations of us and of the world we inhabit. If I know that much of what most matters to you is being kept back, I might well wonder about the value of what you are telling me; I might also wonder about how reliable and trustworthy you are for me to listen to. This cannot be good for community relations. If I find myself ignoring, downplaying and translating into another language what I most hold dear, eventually I am not clear about what I really do believe and the purchase this has on my life. This cannot be good for my own self-confidence and sense of identity.

In a recent article in *The Tablet,* Clifford Longley laments the failure in many debates about religion to recognise that 'religious identity is concerned with the basic orientation of the whole person.' Let me quote him more fully.

> In the recent argument about faith schools, any recognition of what makes a Church school's ethos so different was missing. The argument was fought on pragmatic and secular grounds – that such schools were successful, popular and good at inculcating tolerance and respect for other faiths. Nobody asked why. And this is now true of most Church contributions to public debate. Their spokesmen enter the arena as pseudo-secularists themselves, as if these were the only terms on which they are likely to be given a hearing. ... Any body who refers to belief in God as the basis for their actions can expect to be ignored, ridiculed or regarded as dangerous.[23]

I believe it is healthier for society and for the individuals who comprise it if people are encouraged to speak from their sense of identity and allowed to use language that truly represents what their real reasons and motivations are.

A second line of argument, in favour of allowing religious speech in the public square, suggests that to fail to do so would be to deprive a society of key moral forces, arguments and prompts, thereby diminishing the quality of that society. Eberle asserts that enforced privatisation of religion in his country 'denudes the United States of one of its most powerful forces for moral good,'[24] citing slavery, polygamy and civil rights as examples where religious speech contributed positively to social change. A key dimension for Eberle is that faith groups can provide important counter-weights to state power. Acknowledging the increase in state power over the lives of its citizens (through the massive increase in resources available to it), Eberle comments: 'Given that increase, we need to foster communities that can serve as counterweights to state power: any community that equips its members with a moral identity that enables them critically to analyze the state's activities, ... able to reject its pressures as well as its controls and even its gifts' would be an asset to a healthy polity.[25] He admits that religion does not always provide such a counterweight to state power; in fact, only too often in the past it has offered a significant source of legitimacy for the powers that be.[26] However, it is also true that 'the history of religion is replete with religiously inspired movements that challenge a social-political order, whether the state, or some dominant ideology or a widely accepted practice. Religion isn't just an opiate, it's also and "amphetamine."'[27] Those in power have encountered religious groups as catalysts for change as well as defenders of the status quo. Neither role should be underestimated in its effect. Each kind of contribution should always be carefully and critically judged for both its benign and malign outcomes.

One aspect of this argument leans on the opportunity for society to hear arguments contrary to those presented by the powerful agents of the state, when the views of faith communities are allowed to enter the public sphere. Another aspect has as its focus not so much the counterweight effect of religious communities, but rather the different type of arguments they present and, more importantly, the values to which they give witness, values that might otherwise be unfamiliar and unappreciated. Brian Stiltner suggests that intellectual resources drawn from faith communities, and the attention they give to certain personal and community goods, can enrich public debate.[28] Religious perspectives might contribute to social attitudes and policies towards to the disabled, the sick and suffering, the unborn foetus, the elderly, criminals, the poor, immigrants and refugees. Lives that might otherwise seem unproductive and pointless, beyond redemption, unacceptable or undesirable can be perceived in a new light when religious perspectives are brought to bear. One might claim that an airing of religious speech in the public square can provide a valuable alternative to narrow loyalties, to tribalistic commitments and to self-seeking individualism and materialism.

A third reason for advocating the allowance of religious speech in the public square is on the grounds of justice, based on the claim that secularism is itself a worldview, operating much like a religion. Banning religious speech on the assumption that relegation of the expression of comprehensive worldviews to the private zone is equally fair to all viewpoints and favouring none can be shown to be a false move. The so-called neutrality being maintained is bogus, with the referee functioning much like a player in disguise. I draw heavily on a recent book by philosopher Brendan Sweetman as one major exponent of the position to be defended here, although there is a groundswell of literature along the same lines, arguing for a legitimate role for religious speech in the public square.[29]

Sweetman says that 'we have been slow to acknowledge that secularism is a worldview in itself.'[30] His thesis is that it has become so much the default position that its commitments and assumptions have become almost invisible and its universal presence is treated as benignly neutral to all other positions; it is the space within which we operate, the norm whose air we breathe without realising it. 'There are no secularists calling for the restriction of secularism in public life.'[31] Sweetman traces seven steps in the move towards this position of hegemony by secularists.[32] Although he is referring to the United States in particular, the pattern he depicts is recognisable elsewhere. In the relationship between religion and science, science became promoted as the way of enlightenment, knowledge and progress. The sphere of higher education was transformed from religious to secular institutions. Mass primary and secondary education moved from having a curriculum that was principally religiously informed to one that was non-sectarian, and secular. In public culture and philosophy, mainly Protestant custodianship was supplanted with liberal political theory, with an emphasis on pluralism, relativism and procedural justice. In matters of the law, the view became prevalent that religion had no place in public and social policy decisions promoted in the courts and elsewhere. The religious view of the self as a spiritual being and where care of the soul is a primary concern, in which the churches would play a major role, was replaced by a psychological model of personhood, over which therapists and psychologists are the authorities. In the domain of print and the media religion became marginalised, with an apparently neutral approach to news and opinion becoming predominant.

Sweetman's analysis of the steps towards secularism is complemented by Stiltner's summary of the factors that have contributed to the decline of religion's role in a liberal polity. Stiltner refers to five such factors.[33] These relate to pluralism, modes of communication, welfare provision by the state, the effect of the capitalist economy, and the influence of science. The first of these is pluralism – ethnic, religious and cultural; reduced social homogeneity displaces established hegemonies. Second, Sweetman suggests that modern communication technologies have supplanted the cultural unity once maintained, at least in part, by the churches. Third, many of the agencies providing social welfare and care, once the domain of religion, are now resourced by the state. Fourth, the market and materialism intrude so much into our lives that they have changed our preferences and outlook in such a way as to render a religious perspective alien or at least odd. Finally, advancements in science have offered alternative explanations and solutions for life's experiences, challenges and needs.

The upshot of these developments, as described by Sweetman and Stiltner, is that the public square has become a hostile arena for the religiously committed and secularism prevails as the legitimating norm. While assuming the badge of neutrality, however, secularism shows all the signs of a typical worldview, according to Sweetman, and should thus be treated accordingly, with the same rights and the same constraints as upholders of other worldviews. In Sweetman's analysis, secularists display all the formal features of a worldview.[34] They have a philosophy of life, one that embraces the nature of reality, the nature of human beings and the nature of moral and political beliefs. They have beliefs that are life-regulating. Since not all their beliefs can be proven, some are based on faith. They engage in certain rituals, practices and behaviour that reinforce their beliefs. A morality flows from their beliefs, in that some kinds of behaviour are promoted and others discouraged or prohibited by them. They have organs, outlets and authorities to promote their worldview, relying upon spokespersons, advocates, publications and organisations. They engage in "missionary" work in explaining and defending their views and attacking those of their opponents.

Sweetman claims that 'secularists in the United States, as well as trying to establish control of much of the establishment (the universities, the courts, the media, the law schools, TV and Hollywood) are also gaining political clout as a voting block in their own right.'[35] In cogent argument and cumulative detail Sweetman shows that secularists are as likely to draw upon a text, a tradition, an experience and on unproven faith as religious believers; it is the content of their beliefs that differs, rather than the process by which it has been arrived at.[36] 'Secularist believers might appeal to Sigmund Freud or Richard Dawkins or Charles Darwin in the same way that an ordinary religious believer might appeal to St Thomas Aquinas or Billy Graham or Martin Buber.'[37] Sweetman's point here is not to attack secularist views for being wrong but to avoid privileging them over against religious views. 'When you debate an issue *as if* God does not exist you are essentially debating as if secularism is presumptive, as if religion is inferior, as if secularism is true.'[38] 'A school that is in effect a religion-free zone sends the message that traditional religion can be relegated to a private realm and that secularism should be the presumptive view. ... (T)o create an environment in which religious arguments can play no role ... is to advance the secularist worldview.'[39] This is what Sweetman wants to avoid; he wishes to take seriously *both* secularism and religion, not one at the expense of, or to the neglect of, the other.

A fourth argument for inviting religious voices into public debate is that, in doing so, these voices, and the beliefs and values they express, are forced to be subjected to interrogation, to reckon with critique, to face counter-claims, to engage with objections. In doing so, the capacities of religious believers will be expanded, their blind spots will be exposed, their exaggerations tempered, their excesses modified, and greater attention will be paid to rationality. We all need to achieve at least a temporary distance from our beliefs, if we are to see them properly. Engaging with those who differ from us, sometimes radically, will allow us to gain an external perspective on our familiar assumptions, to see them from another angle. If we do not listen to voices outside ourselves, we become constitutionally incapable of hearing the diversity of voices within us. This internal diversity arises from the diversity of roles we play, as worker, citizen, disciple, friend, parent, helper, patient, and so forth, each of which require different performances, responses and qualities from us. Our disciplined encounter with the diversity external to us should assist us in coming to terms with, appreciating and reconciling the internal diversity that life reveals.

To commend a position is not to coerce this on others. To articulate a point of view is not to impose it. To defend a belief is not to denigrate another person's argument. Courtesy and civility do not rule criticism. This works both ways. In showing courtesy and civility in public debate, religious believers should not feel prevented from offering criticism of their opponents. At the same time, when religious believers enter the public domain, while they should not be subject to intimidation or expect to play by rules that are weighted against them, neither can they expect special favours. They are not damaged by having to listen to views contrary to their own. It is a sign that one's views are taken seriously if they are subjected to scrutiny and testing.

Religious believers should demonstrate rationality in the way they offer and respond to arguments. 'A disposition to decide matters on the basis of evidence, a disposition to subject convictions to criticism when called for, a willingness to change even dearly held convictions in light of critique – these are the sorts of virtues required for, and partly constitutive of, rationality.'[40] If believers do not display rationality, they do not deserve to be taken seriously, for such rationality offers a bridge across which people with different starting points can meet and be enriched by their encounter.

Sweetman describes the features of rationality thus.

> Reason is understood as thinking in a logical way, trying to be objective, seeking good arguments, willing to consider evidence. ... To be reasonable means that one must offer arguments for one's conclusions in an attempt to persuade others of their truth or reasonability. One should be willing to test one's views in discussion and debate, to consider objections to one's views and to consider all the available evidence relevant to the subject matter.[41]

Religious believers might gain (from engaging in the public square) greater self-understanding if they deploy in a disciplined and sophisticated way these intellectual virtues. In the face of public scrutiny and correction, they should better appreciate the gifts and insights of others and thereby perceive reality more accurately. Religion should never be in the business of providing its members a safe place where they can hide from reality.

## 3. VIRTUOUS RELIGIOUS SPEECH

I believe that is possible for religious speech in the public square to be respectful, reasonable, reflective, robust, resilient, restrained, revisable, receptive and responsive. That is, it can aim to be simultaneously true to its own faith commitments and committed to the effective and harmonious functioning of a liberal democracy. If religious believers do not bring religious views into the public domain, this is a silent sign that indicates either suppression, where the blame lies outside the religious community, or abdication of responsibility, where the blame rests within the religious community.

The five essential qualities required to ensure religious speech in public is appropriate, by which I mean combining commitment to the requirements of the faith tradition with commitment to the common good, include conviction, clarity, courage, humility and compassion. The first three of these can be stated very briefly. First, conviction: religious believers must speak the truth as they see it, with integrity, meaning what they say, so that it resonates from them as reflecting genuine commitment. Second, clarity: they must make every effort to communicate effectively, in ways that make their message accessible to outsiders, wherever possible. Third, courage: they must be willing to be vulnerable to criticism, unpopularity and resentment in conveying their views. Commitment will often be costly. Being willing to pay the price is a sign of seriousness and a constitutive part of the witness to the truth as they perceive it.

Fourth, humility: they must be willing to acknowledge that they might be wrong; they must be ready to recognise the sincerity of their opponents; they must be aware that we all fall short of our ideals. The tone adopted must be respectful of others and not presume that our side has a monopoly on integrity, concern for truth or morality. Humility also entails that we be willing to learn from and to be corrected by others. Part of this humility will be shown in the way that there is no attempt to secure protection, privilege or rely on special pleading in defence of one's cause.

Fifth, compassion: religious believers must be sensitive to the burdens that might be imposed on others if their views were to prevail; they should accord due weight to the interests and concerns of others; they should willingly give others space to change their minds and time to appreciate religious arguments, showing patience and restraint. They should avoid any sign of triumphalism or of taking pleasure in the setbacks and defeats of those they disagree with. They should endeavour to include outsiders from their tradition in processes of decision-making that affects others, wherever possible maximizing participation in the goods that are being pursued.

This fivefold combination of qualities - conviction, clarity, courage, humility and compassion - should ensure that religious believers, when drawing upon their faith in public, do so in ways that show a willingness to listen to the experience and insights of others. They should also exhibit an earnest desire to engage in dialogue, an informed, self-aware and critical rationality, respect for their conversation partners as well as for truth, together with commitment both to their own particular community and to the common good in a democracy.

Another way of putting this is to say that religious speech in the public square should demonstrably address the needs of citizenship as well as express what is learned from discipleship. There should be some harmony between these twin demands on us, even though sometimes there will also be tension. Citizenship requires (at least) the following eight features. First, we need an informed awareness of public affairs, a degree of political literacy, if we are to contribute intelligently to the public domain. Second we need a moral compass. Its function should be to guide us through complex issues, where the right thing to do is not apparent, where views differ, where there are many temptations to do the wrong thing. It helps us to find a way to pierce false arguments that invite an apparently easy solution to problems without taking into account the long-term effect of such solutions. A third key feature for a good citizen is the active possession of a critical capacity. Without this she or he would be at the mercy of diverse hidden persuaders and spurious arguments. Fourth, there must be a commitment to community and the common good, a willingness to accept the burdens as well as the opportunities, the responsibilities as well as the rights that accrue to membership of a community.

Fifth, we must want to make a positive difference in the lives of others. Effective citizenship cannot flourish if we are passive onlookers and only beneficiaries. We have to be constantly replenishing and safeguarding the treasury of goods available to all, from which we all draw, such as a clean, healthy, secure environment. Sixth, there must be confidence not only in oneself, believing that one does have something to offer, but also confidence in the public sphere itself, trusting in the fairness of its functioning, even when judgments are made that we find it hard to accept. Seventh, citizens require an ability to participate, collaborate and be part of a team: many worthwhile endeavours depend on us mixing our labour and insights with others. In contrast, excessive individualism erodes the protecting walls of community. Finally, we need the ability to respond positively to difference wherever we encounter it. Without such a capacity we run the risks of either monopoly or of jungle. Inadequate response to difference might lead to others imposing a monopoly or unilateral control on us. Excessively strong response to difference might cause us to impose such control on others, one that favours our position unfairly. Inappropriate communal structures and strategies for dealing with differences leads to a jungle, where each person is in constant conflict with others, aiming only for survival against them rather than seeking ways to co-operate.

\*\*\* \*\*\* \*\*\* \*\*\* \*\*\* \*\*\*

In part one I acknowledged that there are good reasons for religious speech in the public square to be treated with caution and as at least potentially disruptive. In part two I argued that removing religious speech from the public square is an over-reaction and is a strategy with its own problems and dangers. In part three I have indicated some of the qualities and virtues that I believe should accompany religious speech if it is to be allowed back into the public square. Without the safeguards afforded by restraint on the part of faith adherents religious argumentation threatens to undermine the conditions of dialogue in the public square. It becomes inhospitable, intimidating and off-putting. It is only too easy (in any setting) to mistake enforced compliance for genuine commitment. Commitment, unlike compliance, cannot be rushed, depends on freedom, and builds up those who offer it rather than constrains or diminishes them.

A degree of plasticity, or willingness to take properly into account the nature of one's audience, if one is to reach them convincingly, need not entail betrayal of one's own principles, for 'what is clearly unethical is to repudiate your main points or deepest beliefs solely for the purpose of winning an audience.'[42] It does, however, probably entail at least a temporary psychological distancing from one's starting point, in order to find a point in entry into the perspective of others. Such distancing, in aid of better communication with those outside one's own immediate primary reference points, ensures that we are not entirely defined by our constitutive communities; and our entry into the public realm assists others in freeing themselves from being fully limited by their own constitutive communities.

The language of faith should not be banned from our public spaces and the political arena. But it should be deployed carefully, with respect for those who do not share such faith, even at the same time as faith emboldens people to speak out against what is believed to be wrong and in favour of what is held to be true and good. In an atmosphere of mutual exchange – and despite understandable fears about the risks of allowing religious speech in the public square - it may well turn out that 'Taking religious discourses seriously ... may be a condition for good-quality argument in the public sphere, not an obstacle to it.'[43] I believe that we have good reason to hope so, if the qualities and virtues I have recommended as necessary accompaniments of religious speech – conviction, clarity, courage, humility and compassion - are evidently exemplified by its representatives.

## NOTES

1  Nicholas Adams, *Habermas and Theology* (Cambridge: Cambridge University Press, 2006), p.201.

2  Isabel de Bertodano, "Christian Unions 'should be more inclusive,'" *The Tablet*, 2nd December 2006.

3  D. L. Clements, letter to *Times Higher Education Supplement*, 15th December 2006, p.15.

4  Stuart Reid, "Crosses and clichés." *The Tablet*, 2nd December 2006.

5  Nick Spencer, *Doing God. A Future for Faith in the Public Square*, (London: Theos, 2006), pp.13 – 14.

6  Spencer, p.14.

7  Spencer, pp.14 – 15.

8  Spencer, p.59.

9  Michael Perry, *Under God? Religious Faith and Liberal Democracy* (Cambridge: Cambridge University Press, 2003), p.129.

10 Christopher Eberle, *Religious Conviction in Liberal Politics* (Cambridge: Cambridge University Press, 2002), p.145.

11 Brendan Sweetman, *Why Politics Needs Religion* (Downers Grove: Intervarsity Press, 2006), p.117.

12 Spencer, p.22.

13 Eugene Garver, "How Can a Liberal Listen to a Religious Argument?" in *How Should We Talk About Religion?* Edited by J. B White, pp.164 – 193, at p.183 (Notre Dame: University of Notre Dame Press, 2006).

14 Adams, *op.cit.*

15 Habermas, as summarised by R. Gaillardetz, "The Reception of Doctrine: New Perspectives," in *Authority in the Roman Catholic Church*, edited by B. Hoose, pp.95 – 114, at p.106 (Aldershot: Ashgate, 2002).

16 Robert Furbey, *Faith as social capital: Connecting or Dividing?* (York: Joseph Rowntree Foundation & Bristol: The Policy Press, 2006), p.1.

17 See, for example, Charles Glenn, *The Ambiguous Embrace: Government and Faith-Based Schools and Social Agencies* (Princeton: Princeton University Press, 2000); Robert Wuthnow, *Saving America? Faith-Based Services and the Future of Civil Society* (Princeton: Princeton University Press, 2004); (UK) Home Office, *Working Together: cooperation between government & faith communities* (London: Home Office, 2004).

18 Furbey, pp.38, 54.

19 Furbey, p.7 is here quoting from A. Gilchrist, *The well-connected community: A Networking approach to community development* (Bristol: The Policy Press, 2004, p.9.

20 Perry, *op. cit.*, p.42.

21 Stephen Post, (quoting Ronald Thiemann) in *Human Nature and the Freedom of Public Religious Expression* (Notre Dame: University of Notre Dame Press, 2003), p.142.

22 Spencer, *op. cit.*, 47 (quoting Furbey 2006).

23 Clifford Longley, "Religious identity," *The Tablet*, 25th November 2006, p.5.

24 Eberle, *op. cit.*, p.175.

25 Ibid., p.177.

26 Ibid., p.178.

27 Ibid., p.179.

28 Brian Stiltner, *Religion and the Common Good* (Lanham: Rowman & Littlefield, 1999), pp.11, 25, 26, 62.

29 For example, Terence Cuneo, ed *Religion in the Liberal Polity* (Notre Dame: University of Notre Dame, 2005); Patrick Deneen, *Democratic Faith* (Princeton: Princeton University Press, 2005); J. Judd Owen, *Religion & the Demise of Liberal Rationalism* (Chicago: University of Chicago Press, 2001); Jeffrey Stout, *Democracy & Tradition* (Princeton; Princeton University Press, 2004).

30 Sweetman, *op. cit.*, p.18.

31 Ibid., p.75.

32 Ibid., pp.67-68.

33 Stiltner, pp.46 – 47.

34 Sweetman, *op. cit.*, 35 – 36, 56.

35 Ibid., p.72.

36 Ibid., pp.95, 98, 116.
37 Ibid., p.118.
38 Ibid., p.129.
39 Ibid., pp.226-7.
40 Eberle, *op. cit.,* p.61.
41 Sweetman, *op. cit.,* p.42.
42 Wayne Booth, *The Rhetoric of Rhetoric* (Oxford: Blackwell, 2004), p.52.
43 Adams, *op. cit.,* p.238.

# *Chapter 13*

## LITERATURE AND RELIGIOUS COMMUNICATION

### TERRY PHILLIPS

When people ask me to make a literary contribution in a religious context, they usually say, 'You could do something on T.S. Eliot'. I ask myself why this is, more than forty years after the death of Eliot and more than seventy years after the first performance of *Murder in the Cathedral*. I suspect the answer is that some of Eliot's writing provides a very rare example of comparatively recent literature which seeks to impart a spiritual subject to its audience. To put it another way, Eliot is out of tune with his age. Neither our own century nor the one which has just finished are very comfortable with the communication of a message and didacticism has become a derogatory term.

This was not always the case. In this chapter I intend to demonstrate the way in which changes in theories about the nature and function of literature from the sixteenth century through to the present time have influenced the way in which writers communicate religious ideas. These changes have been influential in the broad context of western literature and in the particular case of the shared literary traditions in English of both Britain and North America. The move away from the more didactic traditions of sixteenth and seventeenth-century literature which form the cultural inheritance of the United States and Britain has developed in parallel in both countries. While I use examples from British literature, the examples I use have a wide readership in both countries. I conclude my account of changes in the writing and reception of literature with a more detailed reading of a particular text, David Jones's *In Parenthesis*, to demonstrate the way in which, while not being in any sense didactic, it employs religious beliefs in the exploration of his experience as a soldier in the First World War and in so doing contributes to the communication of religious ideas.

## SIXTEENTH- AND SEVENTEENTH-CENTURY LITERATURE: LITERATURE WITH A PURPOSE

The Roman poet Lucretius in his *De Rerum Natura* used poetry to communicate scientific fact and if we turn to the sixteenth-century poet Philip Sidney's treatise on poetry we learn that poetry is 'an art of imitation...that is to say, a representing, counterfeiting , or figuring forth- to speak metaphorically, a speaking picture- with this end, to teach and delight'.[1] He then proceeds to divide such instruction into three categories, 'The chief, both in antiquity and excellency, were they that did imitate the unconceivable excellencies of God'. Interestingly he includes not only scriptural writers such as David and Solomon but Orpheus, Amphion and Homer 'though in a full wrong divinity'.[2] Such an unequivocal and unapologetic assertion is of course alien to our own time as is such a strong belief in poetry with a purpose. This literary context led to some very fine religious poetry. In our own day the metaphysical poet John Donne has come to be associated with some sensual and audacious love poetry; less well known are his Holy Sonnets, written after the death of his beloved wife, Anne, and expressing orthodox Christian beliefs about sin, temptation, suffering, death and judgment. Those familiar with Donne's better known poetry will recognise the unorthodox style:

> Batter my heart, three-person'd God ; for you
> As yet but knock ; breathe, shine, and seek to mend ;
> That I may rise, and stand, o'erthrow me, and bend
> Your force, to break, blow, burn, and make me new.[3]

The theology, in its reference to the Trinity and to the necessity of suffering for spiritual growth, is clearly orthodox while the poem itself with its violent language and forceful rhythms serves to illustrate Sidney's argument that thoughts clothed in poetry, in this case the spiritual message, become more powerful. In short, it meets the expectations of those who enquire about 'religious literature'.

Donne's contemporary George Herbert, the Rector of Bemerton who gave up his ambitions for the service of God and his flock, is better known as a religious poet and in Jordan (1) specifically addresses the question of religious poetry:

Who sayes that fictions onely and false hair
Become a verse? Is there in truth no beautie?
Is all good structure in a winding stair?
May no lines passe, except they do their dutie
Not to a true, but painted chair?[4]

Herbert's poem is entitled 'Jordan' in order to suggest a Christian muse baptised in the waters of Jordan rather than the traditional Muses associated with the springs of Helicon. His plea for religious subject matter is to be seen in the context of the post-mediaeval world in which the range and quantity of secular subjects addressed in poetry had multiplied. While Sidney, for example, places religious poetry first and foremost he certainly does not confine the function of poetry to religious issues, as is well-attested by his own writing.

Herbert was writing within a context which, with the renaissance, had seen a shift from the strongly Christian concerns of mediaeval literature to a much more broadly based range of interests, although both Sidney and Herbert in the passages quoted recognise the continuing pre-eminence of conveying the insights of Christian revelation. The enlightenment, with its emphasis on empiricism sees a significant shift in literary concerns and, with the emergence of the novel in the eighteenth century, literature becomes much less overtly didactic. Nevertheless, it is important to remember that all literature, indeed all writing, is grounded in ideology. As Catherine Belsey reminds us, 'A discourse involves certain shared assumptions which appear in the formulations that characterise it...Ideology is *inscribed in* discourse in the sense that it is literally written or spoken *in it*'.[5] In religious terms, the difference between much, though not all eighteenth- and nineteenth-century literature, and that of our own age is the presence of shared assumptions about Christianity and the values associated with it, even by agnostic writers such as George Eliot.

## EIGHTEENTH- AND NINETEENTH-CENTURY LITERATURE: IMPLICIT ASSUMPTIONS

While no-one would describe the nineteenth century as a Christian century in the sense that the fifteenth, sixteenth and even seventeenth centuries were, the values of liberal humanism, which characterise the age, are in many respects derived from Christianity. Thus the novels of Jane Austen, for example stress a code of conduct which is based on certain Christian values but which emphasises those aspects of Christian values which contribute to the good order of society, particularly in relation to the middle- and upper-class women about whom she writes, and whose sexual conduct is fundamental to the system of inherited wealth and position which governs the social order (although it must be said that despite her conventionality she does assert the right of women to a marriage which accords with feeling). In this sense much eighteenth- and nineteenth-century literature may be seen as imparting religious values in an indirect way, a way to some extent dependent on the reader, who is free to dismiss the message as part of an outdated cultural context.

An interesting insight into the possibilities and limits of liberal humanist texts as a vehicle for Christian ideas is provided in Charlotte Brontë's well-known novel, *Jane Eyre*. At the point in the novel when the penniless Jane discovers that her intended husband, Edward Rochester is in fact already married to the madwoman who inhabits the third storey of his mansion, and hears his justification of his conduct and his offer of a luxurious life as his mistress, few modern readers would even recognise that she faces a dilemma. Nineteenth-century readers did and some even found the novel shocking. Winifred Gérin quotes a review by the future Lady Eastlake in the Quarterly Review of December 1847 which commented that if the book had been written by a woman it must be one 'who had forfeited the society of her sex'. [6] The comment reveals an ethic, which though it may have its foundation in Christian teaching, is primarily focused on the maintenance of the social order.

Nevertheless, a perusal of the novel reveals an unusually overt appeal to Christian values. In the first flush of her grief, 'One idea only still throbbed life-like within me – a remembrance of God: it begot an unuttered prayer...'.[7] After hearing Rochester's powerful justification she almost yields, knowing she is friendless and destitute but finally resolves, 'I care for myself. The more solitary, the more friendless, the more unsustained I am, the more I will respect myself. I will keep the law given by God; sanctioned by man'.[8] She goes on to state, 'Laws and principles are not for the times when there is no temptation: they are for such moments as this, when body and soul rise in mutiny against their rigor; stringent are they;

inviolate they shall be'. It is a powerful appeal against moral relativism, an appeal to what she sees as a divinely sanctioned rule, but also strongly embedded in a rationalist and indeed feminist assertion of the necessity for self-sufficiency. Arguably the novel's liberal humanism is more important than its Christianity. This is demonstrated by the novelist's ambivalence towards the supernatural, although this ambivalence may in part be due to Brontë's aversion to Roman Catholicism, expressed strongly in *Villette* (whose title refers to a fictional Brussels). At the end of the novel, tempted to go abroad as a missionary and the wife of another, Jane hears from many miles away, the voice of Rochester now, unknown to her, a widower. She reacts as a rationalist should, 'Down superstition!...it is the work of nature. She was roused, and did- no miracle – but her best.' Later when Rochester tells her that he uttered the cry and heard her response, after a prayer of repentance, she finds the revelation, 'too awful and inexplicable'. She does not share her knowledge with Rochester as she considers him someone who 'too prone to gloom, needed not the deeper shade of the supernatural'. Biblically she comments, 'I kept these things then, and pondered them in my heart'.[9]

*Jane Eyre* provides a good example of a text whose primary purpose is not to convey Christian beliefs in the manner of Donne or Herbert, but which is yet strongly underpinned by Christian values, within a broadly rationalist liberal humanist context. *Jane Eyre* has been read in a number of ways: as a Cinderella tale of wish-fulfillment written by a lonely spinster (as Brontë was at the time of writing); as a feminist novel; and as a Gothic novel. It has not, to my knowledge, been read as a Christian novel. This illustrates the difference between an overtly religious text such as certain works of Eliot, Donne and Herbert, and a text based on implicit assumptions. The reader is free to ignore such assumptions or relegate them to the sphere of the irrelevant, as modern readers usually do.

## POSTMODERN LITERATURE: THE PROBLEM OF 'TRUTH'

Modern readers read in a very different cultural context. In the lines from Jordan (1) quoted above, Herbert is able to make confident assertions about 'truth' as opposed to what is 'false' in the manner of Sidney's dismissal of ancient beliefs as 'wrong', And here is the difficulty for our own time: the inability to proclaim truth. Contemporary literary critics, particularly those influenced by the ideas of Jacques Derrida, challenge the very notion of truth itself, hence the aversion to didacticism. The denial of the 'transcendental signifier' is based on the recognition that all human concepts are constructed by and through language and therefore subject to the play of language which is, according to Ferdinand de Saussure, a sign system based on difference, that is the difference of one sign from another sign in which no sign has intrinsic meaning outside the sign system. Derrida famously plays on difference and the French word 'différance'- deferral in the sense of deferral of meaning, claiming that différance 'cannot be elevated into a master-word or a master concept, since it blocks every relationship to theology'.[10] Deconstruction, as Derrida's project has come to be labelled, has become something of an intellectual commonplace of which the nuances are not always clearly understood. Some of those who employ the term employ it precisely as Derrida would refuse it, i.e. as 'a master concept'. It is a process not a provable essence. As Luke Ferretter observes, 'Christians share with modern literary theorists an understanding of reality whose most fundamental axioms are neither proved nor provable, but in the end simply believed'.[11] What post-enlightenment philosophy tells us is that every philosophical, religious or ideological position held is in fact a leap of faith. Ferretter points out that Derrida's deconstruction of metaphysical theology is just that and does not include all theology:

> Deconstruction repeats for theology a fundamental caveat of which, in its depths, it has always been aware, namely that it exists in a double bind. On the one hand, it does and must use our language to speak of God. On the other hand, our language is as such inadequate to the task. [12]

Some of Derrida's later writing acknowledges this and, particularly his interest in negative theology (the acknowledgement of the limitations of theological language referred to above) has been characterised as a turn to theology.

A Derridean refusal of ontological language and of master narratives characterises the postmodern novel. One of the earliest and best-known postmodern novels is John Fowles's *The French Lieutenant's Woman* which succeeds in being both theoretically informed and eminently readable and was made into a film starring Meryl Streep and Jeremy Irons in 1981. However in the famous chapter thirteen, 'I do not know. This story I am telling is all imagination. These characters I create never existed outside my own mind...' [13] in which he goes on to propound his view of what a novel in the postmodern age should be, Fowles in fact is being nothing if not didactic, thereby illustrating the double-bind, and indeed inner contradiction of postmodernism, or at least of those postmodernists who assert the non-existence of truth. Other postmodern writers, without being overtly didactic use the vehicle of the postmodern novel to propound a particular world view, employing the mechanism of challenging other discourses. This may be clearly seen in the work of feminist writers such as Angela Carter and Jeanette Winterson, and is indeed perfectly in keeping with a Derridean approach to language, since their method is to expose the cracks and fissures in other discourses.

In the largely secular western world a writer employing an overtly didactic approach to convey spiritual insights would be unlikely to find favour, and indeed as I have stated earlier, overt didacticism is out of fashion. I want now to take the example of a postmodern religious writer, Muriel Spark who converted to Catholicism in 1954 and a number of whose novels reflect her religious interests. *The Only Problem* provides a good example of a deceptively profound postmodern approach to a religious issue, that of suffering, 'the only problem' of the title.[14] The very title signals that this is a text which belongs to the field of apologetics rather than that of spiritual enrichment. The novel's central character, Henry Gotham, a Christian disturbed by the problem of suffering, retires to a primitive cottage in the French countryside to write a monograph on the Biblical text, *Job*. The novel provides a feast of possible interpretations. Henry himself is easily identified with Job, his comforters with his sister-in-law, his lawyer and an uninvited guest.

The novel foregrounds the unreliability of interpretation and an understanding of the Bible as narrative. *Job* itself is of course a text about interpretation; Job interprets his suffering as caused by God for no reason; his comforters interpret it as caused by his own sins. Henry's insistence that God comes out badly *in the narrative* [my emphasis], is based precisely on the understanding that *Job* is a fictional representation of a religious insight, but is misinterpreted both by the media, and by his aunt Pet, a fundamentalist Christian as an attack on God. The interpretation of visual as well as textual evidence is problematised, in accordance with the anti-enlightenment perspective of the novelist. Henry remains convinced that the painting of Job's wife in the local Art Gallery (which itself offers an unusual interpretation of the Job text, presenting his wife as tender and kind, rather than the foolish woman of the scriptural account) bears a strong resemblance to his ex-wife Effie. Photographic evidence of Effie taking part in a robbery is questioned and a featuring of her in a TV report of a hippie commune in California proves false. More significantly, the novel itself works within three completely different paradigms. For Henry the narrative is primarily about coming to a Christian interpretation of *Job*. For the local police it is about Effie's involvement in terrorism culminating in the shooting of a policeman in Paris, which constitutes a secondary though not unimportant consideration for Henry. For his Canadian aunt it is about what she sees as traditional Christian values. This disconnection of paradigms is most clearly seen when Aunt Pet arrives from Canada to inform her nephew of what she cannot tell him by letter or telephone that 'Your wife, Effie is consorting with a young man in a commune'. For Aunt Pet this is a serious stain on the family honour, for Henry it is a vital piece of evidence to enable him to call off the police search for her. The fact that it is a misidentification does not invalidate the point.

The reader does not learn the nature of Henry's conclusions about *Job*, only that his monograph is completed. The nearest we come to an understanding of this extraordinary Biblical text is Henry's statement, when asked whether the dead policeman's wife deserved what happened, 'We do not get what we merit. The one thing has nothing to do with the other'. The final message of the novel seems to me to be the message of the text of *Job*, that suffering is not caused by merit, that its purpose or explanation is hidden from us (the wager with Satan being as obviously fictional as Henry's earlier desperate idea that perhaps the human soul makes some kind of pact with God before birth). Its message for our age is that suffering exists and that rational investigation is inadequate in understanding it; and that texts, even Biblical texts, are just that: words which defer meaning, which open up possibilities but can never be owned or possessed.

*The Only Problem* raises important issues for thinking Christians concerned with the problem of suffering and the issue of Biblical authority, and is, I would argue, profoundly religious in spite of appearances. However, I want to conclude by going back some seventy years to a more overtly religious text, also ultimately concerned with suffering, which for me exemplifies some of the best qualities that such a text might offer.

### IN PARENTHESIS: A MODERN RELIGIOUS TEXT

David Jones's *In Parenthesis*, first published in 1937, comes directly from the cultural context of the First World War and its aftermath. Before I consider Jones's text, I would like to say something about the cultural impact of the Great War, which arguably more than any other single event influenced the twentieth century in the western world. It contributed to a destruction of faith, not just of religious faith, but of faith in progress, in politicians and in the media, creating a context in which, as Paul Fussell has argued, 'there seems to be one dominating form of modern understanding; that it is essentially ironic; and that it originates largely in the application of mind and memory to the Great War'.[15] Fussell appears in no doubt that the war renders religious belief impossible. Citing the supreme moment of disillusion as the first day of the Somme offensive on 1st July 1916, he asks, 'What could remain of confidence in Divine assistance once it was known that Haig wrote his wife just before the attack: "I feel that every step in my plan has been taken with the Divine help" '.[16] Fussell's comment of course begs a whole number of theological questions, while nevertheless representing a common enough view. Scepticism is one obvious response to the Great War in a religious context and examples of such scepticism in the work of many, though not all of the war poets, for example, abound. Robert Graves in his autobiography writes, 'That Good Friday was the last occasion on which I ever attended a church service, apart from subsequent weddings, church parades, and so on...If they [his parents] believed that God stood squarely behind the British Expeditionary Force, it would be unkind to dissent.'[17]

Scepticism was one response. Others turned to a number of sources to combat a growing sense of meaninglessness. Much has been written about the superstitions which prevailed in the trenches and at the home front. Vera Brittain, for example reports that she broke her habit of never seeing her brother off at the station, on what proved to be his last journey, but 'compromised with superstition' by leaving the platform before the train left.[18] Fussell comments caustically, 'One would have to be mad, or close to it, to credit talismans, in the first quarter of the twentieth century, with the power to deflect bullets and shell fragments. And yet no front-line soldier was without his amulet, and every tunic pocket became a reliquary'.[19] Yet these men were not mad. In their desperate search for meaning they simply refused to accept the arbitrariness of death; like Job they thought suffering must have an explanation.

There were other more rational ways in which religion was used as a counter to apparent meaninglessness. One of the most common was in the comparison of the soldier to Christ, a comparison which occurs in countless poems and other writing. The figure of Christ provided a useful symbol for those who believed that the war was in some sense a 'holy' war and, as the war progressed, provided at least some kind of rationalisation for large scale slaughter in a just cause. Such a use of the Christ figure allowed some people to make sense of the carnage by privileging his saving role in the Christian view of history, drawing in part on the doctrine of the atonement. Such a view sees the soldier as fighting for king and country in the war to end wars. Alice Meynell for example, at the end of 'Summer in England, 1914', a poem which looks back to the summer before war and speaks with sorrow of the war itself concludes:

> Who said 'No man hath greater love than this,
>     To die to serve his friend'?
> So these have love us all unto the end.
>     Chide thou no more, O thou unsacrificed!
> The soldier dying dies upon a kiss,
>     The very kiss of Christ.[20]

Such approaches, by an unexamined appropriation of Christology, legitimise warfare, an activity which many people see as profoundly anti-human, let alone an affront to God. However a strikingly different and religiously informed example of the use of the Christ figure is provided by *In Parenthesis*, a text which is somewhere between a poetic novel and a prose poem, which emphasises the human dimension in Christ and his role as a sharer in human suffering, an idea present in Christian meditation and reflection throughout the centuries but sometimes lost in a consideration of Christ's divinity. Its author David Jones, better known as an artist than a writer, was born in Kent of Anglo-Welsh parentage and at the beginning of 1914, enlisted in the Royal Welch Fusiliers and served on the Western Front from December 1915 to March 1918. He became a Catholic in 1921. *In Parenthesis* provides an example of a text, the purpose of which is not to communicate an aspect of Christian doctrine, nor to invoke Christian ideas almost incidentally, but which succeeds in providing a deeply religious response to a moment of great crisis in human affairs.

*In Parenthesis*[21] makes a complex use of the figure of the crucified Christ. It draws on a whole range of allusions, including *Henry V,* Morte d'Arthur, *The Song of Roland,* and the early Welsh epic poem *Y Gododdin,* as well as the Old and New Testaments and Roman Catholic liturgy. Bernard Bergonzi argues persuasively that *In Parenthesis* 'remythologises' the war by giving it a frame of reference which takes it out of the realm of the purely personal[22], and allusions to the passion and death of Christ form part of the framework. The religious allusions cannot be read in any consistently allegorical way. As David Blamires points out 'their function is rather to underline the fact that the religious moment breaks into the whole of a man's experience, penetrating it at every point'.[23] In this sense it is profoundly spiritual.

The text is partly focalised through and partly an account of one private in the Royal Welch Fusiliers, Private John Ball who comes to stand as a kind of Everyman figure and who is wounded at the end of the text, in the attack on Mametz Wood which kills several of his friends.[24] The narrative is imbued with references to scripture and to the liturgy of Good Friday. This haunting presence of Good Friday throughout the text makes clear the relationship between the soldiers, and particularly John Ball, their representative figure, and the crucified Christ. It is an experience of shared suffering. In the third section, when the troops are moved from their French quarters to take up their positions in the front line, the text quotes from the Roman Rubric 'Proceed...without lights...prostrate before it...he begins without title, silently, immediately...in a low voice, omitting all that is usually said. No blessing is asked, neither is the kiss of peace given...he sings alone'.[25] The rubric's focus on the singularity and solemnity of this one day in the year, of all that is not said and done, provides a fittingly solemn comment on the awesomeness of this occasion for the motley crew of Welshmen and Cockneys about to take up their positions in the front line.

Echoes of the Good Friday liturgy are taken up again in Part 7, which recounts the first day of the Welch Fusiliers' part in the Somme Offensive, and the ultimate death of John Ball, and opens with a quote from Psalm 131 and the Tenebrae of Good Friday. The title of Part 7 is 'The Five Unmistakeable Marks' which Jones's note refers to Lewis Carroll's 'Hunting of the Snark', but it is difficult to suppose that the five wounds of Christ were far from his mind.[26] The opening page continues to include phrases from liturgical prayer which Jones's note refers to psalms 119 and 123. Interestingly Psalm 119 ends with the evocation:

> Long banished here
> among the enemies of peace,
> for peace I plead,
> and their cry is still for battle.[27]

How then is the reader to interpret the link between Good Friday and the suffering of John Ball and his comrades on the Somme? I do not think that Jones sees the soldiers' sacrifice as a saving act which redeems their fellow creatures.[28] I argue this, partly because of the general anti-war tenor I detect in much of *In Parenthesis*, but for other reasons too. One of these is the emphasis given to Christ as the suffering human being. For the scene in the scriptural representation of the passion and death of Christ, most clearly influential on Part 7 of *In Parenthesis* is the Agony in the Garden, Christ at his most human in his lonely meditation in the Garden of Gethsemane in which he prays not to have to undergo the trial that lies ahead of him. One passage is worth quoting in full for it demonstrates Jones's gift for linking the language and concerns of very ordinary men with the elevated language of epic poetry or in this case scripture:

> Perhaps they'll cancel it.
> O blow fall out the officers cantcher, like a wet afternoon or
> the King's birthday.
> Or you read it again many times to see if it will come
> different:
> you can't believe the Cup wont pass from
> or they wont make a better show
> in the garden.
> Won't someone forbid the banns
> or God himself will stay their hands.
> It can't just happen in our family
> even though a thousand
> and ten thousand at thy right hand.[29]

Jones's treatment of the crucifixion clearly focuses on the figure of the suffering Christ who takes upon himself a share in human suffering.

However, an interesting, and I think important passage clearly demonstrates the difference between the deaths on the Somme and the crucifixion:

> Nor time for halsing
> nor to clip green wounds
> nor weeping Maries bringing anointments
> neither any word spoken
> nor no decent nor appropriate sowing of this seed
> nor remembrance of the harvesting
> of the renascent cycle[30]

This passage conveys a variety of important resonances. It echoes the well-known passage in *Ecclesiastes* which begins:

> There is a season for everything, a time for every occupation
> under heaven:
> a time for giving birth,
> a time for dying;
> a time for planting,
> a time for uprooting what has been planted.[31]

The whole passage from *Ecclesiastes* suggests that there is a right order of things, in which the harshness and suffering of life has its place. However the passage in *In Parenthesis* clearly reverses that language 'there is no time for...' In particular, the reference to the lack of time for the decent or appropriate sowing of seed links with the many references in *In Parenthesis* to the despoiling of nature and the unnaturalness of the effects of warfare. Finally the absence of 'weeping Maries bringing anointments' referring to the women who brought ointments to anoint the body of Christ, and thereby discovered his resurrection, marks a distinct difference between these deaths and the death of Christ. The ritual anointing suggests some element of order and purpose in the death of Christ, to which Jones would have given assent, but which is wholly absent from these deaths. Jones's text, while it allows shared suffering, suggests that the passive suffering of Christ has purpose, which the suffering of the soldiers lacks.

Jones's concern is with suffering human beings, not with any interpretation of their suffering as meaningful in the sense of constituting a purposeful saving sacrifice. This is rather nicely illustrated by a passage at the beginning of Part 2 where the soldiers, newly arrived in France are benefiting from a variety of lectures. The medical officer is described as a man 'whose heroism and humanity reached toward sanctity' while the Bombing Officer, demonstrated new inventions of destruction is 'like a departing commercial traveller'.[32] There is of course an underlying theological reason for valuing human life, which is foregrounded with some irony in a particularly unpleasant passage which describes the removal of long dead corpses from the newly occupied trenches: 'From this muck-raking are singular stenches, long decay leavened; compounding this clay, with that more precious, patient of baptism; chemical-corrupted-once-bodies[...] each day unfathoms yesterday unkindness; dung-making Holy Ghost temples'.[33] The contrast between the theological view of the sacredness of the human being, defined as the temple of the Holy Ghost, and the corpses left to rot without proper burial could not be more explicit, and is a powerful Christian statement against war.

Jones's poetic novel brings liturgical and scriptural language into play with the language of everyday and brings profound religious insights to bear on some of the darkest moments in twentieth-century history. The subject of *In Parenthesis* is the suffering endured in war. Like *Job* it offers no meaning for such suffering. The religious consolation it offers, and profoundly expresses through its use of scripture and liturgy, is that Christ too suffered. Its assertion of the sacredness of the human renders it ultimately positive. This is why for me Jones's somewhat neglected text provides a particularly good example of what we might in a broad sense term religious literature. There is no one definition of such literature. Spark's postmodern game playing is as valid an example of religious literature as one of Donne's Holy Sonnets, and I have demonstrated the way in which even a particular romantic novel may be read as a religious text. One might ask why it is important for religious ideas to be expressed in literature. One answer is that religious experience is a valid part of human experience which we would not expect to find excluded. The present volume examines a huge diversity of ways in which faith is communicated, some directly related to what might be termed an educational or a formational context; others such as literature and the arts derived from a wider sphere of human activity. One reason why literature is a particularly valuable medium in faith communication is the power of narrative or story to move the reader or hearer in ways no straight transmission of facts can do, a fact well illustrated by Biblical parables. Still another is the very particular relationship of literature to language, often making language its own subject. As Terence Wright comments, 'Metaphors...provide perhaps the most important means by which language is stretched beyond the literal in order to talk of God'.[34] The play of language with its constant deferral of meaning, as Derrida points out, makes for a journey with no conclusion which for Christians is a journey of faith.

## NOTES

1   Sir Philip Sidney, 'The Defence of Poesy' in *Sir Philip Sidney Selected Prose and Poetry*, edited by Robert Kimbrough, pp.102-158, at pp.109-110 (San Francisco: Rinehart Press, 1969).

2   Ibid., p.110.

3   John Donne, *Holy Sonnets* in *The Metaphysical Poets*, edited by, Helen Gardner, pp.83-86. (Harmondsworth: Penguin, 1957), p.85.

4   George Herbert, Jordan (1) in *The Metaphysical Poets*, p.125.

5   Catherine Belsey, *Critical Practice* (London and New York: Routledge, 1980), p.5.

6   Winifred Gérin, *Charlotte Brontë* (Oxford and New York: Oxford University Press, 1967), p.345.

7   Charlotte Brontë, *Jane Eyre* (London: Pan, 1967, first published 1847), 321.

8   Ibid., p.342.

9   Ibid., pp.476-7.

10  Jacques Derrida, *Positions*, translated by Alan Bass (London: Athlone Press, 1987), p.40.

11  Luke Ferretter, *Towards A Christian Literary Theory* (Basingstoke: Palgrave, 2003), p.2.

12  Ibid., p.15.

13  John Fowles, *The French Lieutenant's Woman* (London: Triad Granada, 1977), p.85.

14  Muriel Spark, *The Only Problem* (London: Triad Grafton), 1985.

15  Paul Fussell, *The Great War and Modern Memory* (London, Oxford and New York: Oxford University Press, 1975), p.35.

16  Ibid., p.29.

17 Robert Graves, *Goodbye to All That* (Harmondsworth: Penguin, 1957, first published, 1929), p.165.

18 Vera Brittain, *Testament of Youth* (London: Virago, 1978, first published 1933), p.403.

19 Fussell, p.124.

20 Alice Meynell, 'Summer in England, 1914' in Catherine Reilly, *Scars Upon My Heart* (London: Virago, 1981), p.73.

21 David Jones, *In Parenthesis* (London: Faber and Faber, 1963, first published 1937).

22 Bernard Bergonzi, *Heroes' Twilight* (Manchester: Carcanet Press, 1996, first published 1965), p.194.

23 David Blamires, David Jones Artist and Writer (Manchester: Manchester University Press, 1971), p.106.

24 Several commentators have noted that John Ball has same name as the wandering priest executed in 1381 for his part in the Peasants' Revolt.

25 Jones, p.27.

26 Ibid., p.153 and note on p.220.

27 Psalm cxix, vv 6-7, in Ronald Knox, *The Psalms in Latin and English* edited by Hubert Richards (London: Burns & Oates, 1964), p.309.

28 In this respect, Paul Fussell's argument that the text is a conservative text because its use of Arthurian and other historical material ennobles the conflict on the Somme (Fussell, p.147) has been countered by several critics, for example Jonathan Miles in *Backgrounds to David Jones* (Cardiff: University of Wales Press, 1990).

29 Jones, p.158.

30 Ibid., p.174.

31 Ecclesiastes, 3.1-2, *The Jerusalem Bible* (London: Darton, Longman and Todd, 1966), p.982.

32 Jones, p.13.

33 Ibid., p.43.

34 T. R. Wright, *Theology and Literature* (Oxford: Blackwell, 1988), p.129.

# Chapter 14

## THE GOSPEL BRINGS HOPE TO EUROPE.
## THE CONTRIBUTION OF ECCLESIA IN EUROPA

### DAVID EVANS

### INTRODUCTION

*Ecclesia in Europa* has the subtitle: *On Jesus Christ alive in his Church the Source of Hope for Europe.*[1] It was written by Pope John Paul II in the wake of the 1999 Synod of European Roman Catholic Bishops. It is described as a Post Synodal Exhortation on the Church in Europe. The Synod was held in preparation for the celebration of the beginning of the third Christian millennium. The description indicates the style in which the document is written, while its subtitle declares its theme. The author shapes and presents the Bishops' discussion through reflection on passages from the book of Revelation, affirming the perennial structures of the Church and encouraging all members of the Church to proclaim the gospel through the holiness of their lives and their commitment to the gospel proclaimed by Jesus Christ.

The pope's thought is a dialogue between the gospel and contemporary Europe. This makes Pope John Paul both the spokesperson for Christ and the voice of Europe. However there is a stark difference between the two voices. The gospel calls for the joy of a living encounter with Christ (1) but Europe is characterised as having lost its Christian memory and heritage. The continent displays practical agnosticism and religious indifference (7).

This essay takes the form of a personal reflection rather than a critical appraisal of the document, though it points to shortcomings on the document's part. It explores *Ecclesia in Europa* by giving a summary of Pope John Paul's account of the gospel and of the gospel's place in Europe's life and history. This account presents Jesus as at the heart of the Church's proclamation. He reveals the persons of the Trinity and calls humanity to share the life of God by living the commandment of love (4). This is the gospel of hope. The essay also identifies the features of European culture that gave the pope most cause for concern. Finally, after identifying humanity and transcendence as key themes in the pope's thought, it will appraise the relationship between the two voices within a brief discussion of how the pope's project for Europe might be carried further.

Though the document and this chapter concentrate on the Church in Europe and European culture, they have relevance for people from other parts of the world. In the first instance *Ecclesia in Europa* is an example of the dialogue between faith and culture that has become a regular part of the Church's reflection worldwide. Secondly, a large part of the pope's document is an outline of the gospel and the faith it proposes in John Paul II's distinctive style. It will strike a chord with people who already believe what the gospel expresses and provide an introduction to those who are seeking a readily accessible account of Roman Catholic life and belief. The pope's thinking is also of interest to those who want to find a way into the contemporary European political enterprise. By approaching this with approval and also in a critical spirit, the author of *Ecclesia in Europa* demonstrates how the gospel comes to the assistance of a democratic project based on liberty and Christian foundations in any part of the world.

## PART I THE JOY OF A LIVING ENCOUNTER WITH CHRIST

The majority of *Ecclesia in Europa* is devoted to reaffirming the structures and institutions of the Church and to encouraging her members to live the gospel to the full. In the course of this Exhortation Pope John Paul II offers a distinctive perspective on the gospel. Jesus is at its centre as the one who proclaims the gospel and as humanity's saviour. There is nothing out of the ordinary about that, any more than there is in seeing him as the one who reveals the life of the Trinity and who models the true nature of humanity. Hope is central to the gospel the pope is preaching in the light of the Synod. It is a gospel of transcendence in which who God is colours the whole of reality and makes the world as well as the Church the threshold of eternal life.

The gospel has bequeathed Europe 'the joy of a living encounter with Christ' (1). This declaration sets the scene for the pope's exposition of the gospel. Within the pope's perspective Jesus is the source of the gospel. Jesus is risen and he communicates to the present generation the vision of new life that he proposed to the crowds in Galilee and Jerusalem. The state of

Europe at the beginning of the new millennium makes a new proclamation of the gospel necessary (2). This is the task of today's European Church. It is for the Church to communicate faith. The basic structure for communicating faith is presented at the beginning of Chapter III in the course of its opening reflection on Rev 10:8, 9. "Go, take the scroll which is open … take it and eat." Jesus has knowledge which is available to no one outside the Godhead. Because of this, only he can illuminate reality and show humanity the path it should take. The hidden knowledge of the Son of God is inscribed on the scroll given to John and through him to the whole Church (44). The path humanity should take is both personal and political. The goal of each journey is the same: a society based on love and on the dignity of humanity that anticipates the fullness of life which is God's gift to his people when God's work on earth is done.

The significant thing about this scenario is that it is Christ who communicates faith, in the sense of revealing to humanity through the Church truths that people cannot reach by means of their own resources. Earlier in the text, Jesus is identified as revealing the mystery of the Trinity (19) and is claimed to be the future of man (20) as well as granting eternal life (21) thereby giving true meaning to life (21). It is because Jesus reveals the mystery of the Trinity that he is humanity's hope. The pope explains this in a partly political way, seeing faith in the Trinity as reviving the values that are capable of promoting the welfare of all Europe's inhabitants (19). He speaks more explicitly still, comparing the contribution Christian values have made to the continent's past with the values needed to promote the united Europe that is the present enterprise. It does no one any favours to forget Europe's Christian heritage (19). Throughout his Exhortation the pope is aware of the varied landscape of contemporary Europe, east and west. His words are for the whole continent, though he addresses the European Union alone at times.

It becomes clear, then, that *Ecclesia in Europa* has more than a personal significance for its readers. It presents the gospel as a life force active in Europe's past and available now to bring to fulfillment the vision of Europe that its post-Second World War and post-communist leaders are attempting to enact. The gospel retains its personal significance since its initial effect is the holiness of believers. This effect is prevalent in the present era, not just confined to the past. It is visible in people's daily lives and is testimony to their faith

(14). Without holiness there can be no authentic evangelisation. Nor can there be true hope (49). Hope is the primary contribution that the person of Jesus and the gospel make since hope opens up the future and indicates the goal towards which all the human endeavours of Europe are directed.

The goal is Jesus himself. In spite of encouraging Europe's political enterprises a theological point of view is never far from the pope's mind. Christians bear witness to Christ as the future of humanity. Evangelisation is the Church making clear the truth about Jesus that Jesus has entrusted to the Church. Where the gospel is preached Jesus himself is present in his full reality, as the God made man of the gospel days and as the risen saviour shaping human nature for its ultimate reality, reworked into the likeness of God. This is summed up in the figure of Jesus the hope of every person because he grants eternal life. Jesus is the word of life, who shows the true meaning of human existence. This is not confined to this world but is open to eternity (21). Pope John Paul II provides Europe with a rich vision of a transcendent Godhead. The world is imbued with God's presence in a way that makes the transition from this world to the next that of transforming the quality of life here and now into as close a likeness to the life of God as the limitations of finitude allow.

The pope is in no doubt that however politically successful an integrated Europe may be it will lack an essential dimension if it fails to recover its Christian heritage. Yet *Ecclesia in Europa* is not nostalgic in tone nor is the pope intent on the wishful thinking that begets utopia (106). The pope speaks robustly of an eschatological reality and does not call for a return to the past. In fact, he explicitly rejects one element of such a reversal. He asserts that the Church is not calling for a return to the confessional state (117). Nevertheless, he also declares that Europe drew the inspiration for the best of its culture from the biblical understanding of humanity. This applies in the artistic and intellectual spheres as it does in the realm of law and morality (25). The document conveys a strong sense of the lasting value of Europe's high culture. In a way, one might claim that that culture stands alongside and within the Church as a means of transmitting the gospel.

Something vital will be lost if Europe is merely conceived as a physical and monetary reality. For all his appreciation of the efforts that are being made to establish Europe as region of prosperity and peace, the pope's address implies that these efforts will miss the mark unless as much attention is paid to religion as is given to geography and economics (110). Europeans need to open their eyes. The values and institutions they are seeking do not need to be conjured out of nothing to respond to a new situation. The best that humanity is capable of becoming and the structures that express and support that are to be found in Jesus, in the gospel embodied in the Church. At the heart of Europe's past and necessary for its success in the present and future is 'the dignity of the person as a subject of inalienable rights.' (25)

Within this perspective faith is more than arid statements of dogmas formulated for the sake of an irrelevant past. Faith is life engendering hope. The Church is the body of Christ, display case and curator of the gospel's heritage, (though not a lifeless museum) preserving its values intact and displaying their lasting attraction to men and women who have been created to be enthralled by their charms. Fundamentally, the Church is the image of the risen Christ (27). As unity among Christians grows she will display a more beautiful and credible face that reflects more truly the face of the Lord. This metaphor enables Pope John Paul II to emphasise the pastoral nature of the Church. One thing that attracts people to Christ is his care for the outcast and people on the margins. A Church that bears this resemblance to Jesus will offer the world hope and comfort. She will also evoke in those who respond to this affection a desire to seek the Church and a sense of their need for her. This is one way in which the Church emulates Christ as the sign of hope. There is a fulfillment in divine reality for people's natural needs (29).

The Church offers real hope because hope is bestowed by Jesus of Nazareth. It is clear throughout the document that when the pope preaches the person of Christ he believes he is proposing an inescapable, concrete reality. Faith comes first in the order of things, hope is aroused in the acceptance of it. Both are gifts of Jesus Christ. Faith and hope are traditionally linked with love so it is not surprising, particularly given the centrality of the commandment of love in Christianity, that John Paul II devotes space in his Exhortation to charity.

The Church's vocation is to proclaim the gospel through a generous and enduring service of others (83). The exchange of charity is another source of hope (84.) Charity is not simply for the enhancement of physical human well being; it is a way in which people today can experience the love of the persons of the Trinity. Charity preaches the gospel. Charity too is concrete. It is a commitment to a way of life which "makes visible the love of God who abandons no one" (84). Like God's, the charity women and men exercise is for everyone. Charity accompanied by faith and hope is social cohesion, achieved not by the implementation of a social policy but by the calling forth of the full nature of humanity in its quest for God.

There is no doubt about the pope's confidence in the Church, at least in its reality as conceived and made known by God. As we shall see the pope does admit to failures within the members of the Church but in God's mind, as one might say, the Church, according to the pope is "fit for purpose". This conviction seems to be one without which faith, or perhaps the faith, will not be communicated. In technical terms, the Church is the means by which the being of God is transmitted. God is holy. Alongside that goes the three-in-one reality of the Trinity to whose life believers are being called, not only as the consummation of their lives but in the practice of their lives as members of humanity destined for likeness with Christ.

In this perspective everything is grace and all that is human is called to respond. This is the context in which the Church may be seen to have an authoritative voice in political and economic affairs. Faith comes from the gospel. It is the acceptance that what Jesus reveals about human beings with respect to their perfection in hope and charity is the true account of what human nature is. In the organisation of human affairs, economic, political, legal, moral, this template is the source of inspiration for and the measure of all that economists, lawyers, politicians, theologians and moral philosophers seek to put in place in the human city. The pope probably claims far more for the Church and for the teachings of the gospel than many feel admissible. To communicate faith effectively one thing that may need to be examined is the source and extent of our own scepticism.

## PART II WILL HE FIND FAITH IN OUR COUNTRIES?

Part I of this chapter has reviewed with some comment Pope John Paul II's evaluation of the gospel as the blueprint made known by God of human nature and human destiny. Belief in the gospel draws Christians into the life of the Trinity, promotes the virtues of faith hope and charity, and bestows holiness of life. The gospel is also a pattern for Europe's political, social, economic and legal institutions. These are also means by which the future of humanity as made in the image of God can be achieved. *Ecclesia in Europa* also contains an analysis of European culture which has lost its Christian heritage. This is the topic of Part II.

Throughout his treatment of the present state of Europe, both with respect to society and the Church, John Paul II has been guided by reflection on passages from the book of Revelation. There is an echo of scripture in the heading to this part of the article. "But when the Son of Man comes, will he find any faith on earth?" (Luke 18:8) The hope is that that cry from the heart of Jesus will be answered in the affirmative. At the time of writing the Exhortation the cry was a stimulus for the pope's own ministry. It is the Church's responsibility to preach the gospel but it is the particular respon-sibility of the successor of St Peter to strengthen the faith of his brothers. (Luke 22:32) It may not be fanciful then to hear a tone of anguish in the pope's writing as he reviews the cultural state of Europe. His declarations are more poignant against the background of the resolute note of hope which has been the characteristic of the summary of his words till now.

The pope had described the purpose of the 1999 Synod in the opening paragraphs of *Ecclesia in Europa* as the analysis of the Church's situation in Europe (2). This project was to be put at the service of the gospel (2). The first element of the description of contemporary Europe is that it has lost sight of the gospel (2). It is recorded that on many occasions during the Synod the bishops mentioned the *"loss of Europe's Christian memory and heritage."* (7) The emphasis, in the original quotation, is a sign of the pope's agreement that this is where the crisis of evangelisation lies and what it is for which evangelisation is a remedy, though it has already been shown that the restoration of that heritage is not intended to be a return to the status quo.

2 This provides another strong contrast between the pope's positive description of the purpose of the Church. Part One of this chapter stresses the view that the Church transmits life with the gifts of faith, hope and love. The more recent phrases hint at poverty and death as well as the parable of the prodigal son (Luke 15:11-32). These themes alert us to the remedy of the resurrection as well as to the Church's vocation of reconciliation. At the same time, the pope is suggesting that even in indifference and agnosticism

there are fissures in which the life of God may find a fingerhold through the Church's proclamation of the gospel. Thus he speaks of the *"widespread desire for spiritual nourishment"* to which the Church needs to be alert, urging her to see in this sentiment, however confused, a sense that human beings do not live on bread alone (Mt 4:4) (68).

Religious apathy is not without consequences. According to John Paul II it is accompanied by the creation of a vision that rejects Europe's soul. It asserts human rights but without attaching them to the roots that will bring them to true life (7). Here the pope uses the image of a tree and its sap reminiscent of the image of the vine and its branches (John 15:5).This may be a way of engaging his Christian reader but raises the question of whether the full import of what the pope is saying will be apparent to those promoting the vision he questions. However, it is to be noted that the pope does not wholly reject that vision. He is pointing out a defect.

Agnosticism does not hinder secularisation, whose advance continues, leaving the symbols of Christianity relics of the past (7). The fading memory of these symbols means that the reality they disclose is also being lost. In a way that validates the penultimate remark of the last paragraph, the pope acknowledges that declining consciousness of religious symbols makes it difficult for people to "integrate the Gospel message into their daily experience" (7). For Europe to be fertile soil for the word of God the spirit of Christianity must find an echo in an inherited outlook on life that is the atmosphere its inhabitants breathe.

The religious perspective encounters an aggressive response in contemporary Europe. This adds to the difficulties of living one's faith. In many areas it is easier to be identified as a non-believer than as one committed to a religious way of life. Unbelief is taken to be self explanatory, while belief needs to argue for its status in society, since it is neither an obvious position to take nor one that is simply accepted (7). This thought is expressed by the author in general terms and it may be that the pope accepts that adherents of faiths other than Christianity may face the same difficulties.

The loss of religious belief, either through apathy or through loss of collective memory or through its becoming the victim of persistent criticism does not lead to a society at ease with itself nor to happy people. The future is shadowed by dread. People are seized by an inner emptiness and a loss of the meaning of life. Anguish becomes prevalent and may be discerned in a declining birth rate, fewer vocations to the priesthood and the religious life as well as in a refusal to make life-long commitments (8). These alleged consequences combine a curious mixture of the philosophical and the day to day. Anguish is associated with existentialist thinking as exemplified by the nineteenth century philosopher, Kierkegaard and the twentieth century German and French philosophers Heidegger and Sartre. There is sufficient statistical evidence to support observations of decline in the social areas the pope identifies. Seeing the abstract and the empirical side by side indicates the challenges the Church faces in its task of communicating faith. Perhaps the first of these may be to convince secular society that the pope has provided an accurate account of its present emotional state as well as having provided us with a convincing rationale for fewer married couples and fewer children.

The pope describes Europe's situation as "a widespread existential fragmentation" (8) and backs this up by mentioning the prevalence of loneliness, division and conflict. It is this as much as the more concrete symptoms already described that lead to his calling this mood a loss of hope (9). Nevertheless this is the result of something more fundamental. There is an attempt to instill into Europe's general culture a vision of humanity cut off from God and bereft of Christ (9). Though he has taken a little while to reach this point it may be true to say that this expresses the heart of the pope's complaint about the contemporary state of Europe. The continent is in cultural, social and religious decline because there has been a deliberate movement to deprive its people and its institutions of the mystery of the Trinity, hitherto the source of all that made Europe what it was.

In the forefront of this movement are the mass media (9). Pope John Paul makes this assertion without any analysis. If he is right then means of communication are at the centre of the conflict between the Church's proclamation of the gospel and the secular world's determination to see its own outlook prevail. There has been some talk recently about 'the clash of cultures', meaning the violence that may erupt when a particular interpretation of Islam meets what are spoken of as western values. The appreciation of *Ecclesia in Europa* is that the clash of cultures is taking place between Europe's Christian heritage and the now well established culture of secularism. The pope makes this plain when he speaks of a new culture that is in conflict with the gospel and with the dignity of the human person (9). That final assertion is the more surprising, since in indicating its difference from the Christian past secular society is most likely to appeal to its own support for human rights and to the spread of liberty that has accompanied it.

Religious agnosticism has already been mentioned as a feature of this new culture. Additional elements are moral and legal relativism. These arise in the pope's view from confusion about human nature as the foundation of universal inalienable rights (9). He is even more forthright when he depicts present day culture as a culture of death (9). Here the pope will be perceived to be carrying the battle unapologetically into the enemy's camp. The two cultures that he has evoked, that of the Church manifest in Europe's Christian era and that of the secular world deliberately cut off from the gospel, are not simply superficially distinct. There is an essential gulf between them that makes reconciliation a supremely difficult task for the Church to tackle.

This is the context in which the pope poses his question about whether Christ will find faith in Europe on his return (47). It is a way of highlighting the seriousness of the European situation and of the attractiveness that secular culture has for humanity. In a different sort of document that attractiveness could have been the subject of a penetrating investigation; as it is, it remains a question to be answered for those who might accept the pope's portrayal of current culture and the need for the Church to address her message to a hostile environment. This point of view has had its effect to such an extent that Europe can be described as being not only in need of a new evangelisation but of a first evangelisation too (46.)

The conflict is an external one between the champions of God and those who are plotting his defeat; but it is an internal one as well. The struggle has had its effect upon members of the Church. The Synod, whose mouthpiece the pope is, recognised that the challenge facing it was not just to make new converts but to call to conversion those who have already been baptised (47). What is said of society at large must also be said of many of the baptised, that is, that they live as though Christ did not exist (47). Their allegiance is skin deep. They repeat the gestures and signs of faith but there is nothing in their lives which testifies to true adherence to the faith or to the person of Christ. The Synod bishops clearly felt that this was a fact too obvious for them to overlook even though it apparently diminishes the picture of the Church which their document persistently presents (47).

The material presented in the second part of this chapter provides a vivid contrast with that outlined in the first part. It would be too strong to say that *Ecclesia in Europa* sees contemporary culture as a culture of despair though it might be characterised as culture without hope. Even that needs qualification. What Europe apparently lacks is the Christian virtue of hope, that is, the confidence in God that opens human life to its fulfillment in a glorious future. The attempts to create a united Europe, to banish war, guard human dignity, extend liberty and guarantee human happiness are sure signs of Europe's confidence in its own ability to bring about a secular paradise, once the legal and juridical institutions and moral vision are in place. The pope's riposte is that what Europe hopes to achieve, noble as it may be, will not fully satisfy human longings unless the reality its leaders have in mind reflects the being and presence of God. This is what the Church has been called to communicate and as long as there are human beings her work will need to be done.

## PART III CONCLUSION

So far this chapter has outlined and commented on Pope John Paul II's appreciation of the gospel and his evaluation of contemporary European culture. The effect of this discussion has been to display the Church and that culture as opposed. At the same time, the pope presents the two realities as complex. The Church, according to him, has been founded by Jesus of Nazareth to communicate faith, both as the truths about God and his kingdom and as about the true nature of humanity. In addition, faith is acceptance of these realities on the part of men and women and their commitment to a way of life that attracts faith in others, inspires hope in them and nourishes them through love. Christian life has also inspired the high culture of the past. By contrast, the complexity of European secular culture is evident in the claims that it has forgotten this heritage, is indifferent to it, or hostile to it, and finds no place for it in its institutions. As a result the political and economic project of Europe may be admirable in its aspirations and achievements but will not satisfactorily establish human rights nor put in place the structures that will promote the perfection of women and men whose true vocation is to be remade in the image and likeness of God.

What seems to be missing from this polarised and schematised account is a developed sense of how the two realities may make contact. Nevertheless, there is the germ of an idea which has human dignity and human rights at its centre. This is also the place where the pope's credibility may be most lacking. It is Pope John Paul's contention that the Church has always promoted human rights and dignity. This may seem a hollow claim when it is made on behalf of a Church the common perception of which is that she promoted the Crusades and the Inquisition and condemned Galileo. Equally the Roman Catholic teaching on contraception and abortion is interpreted as a general lack of respect for women on the Church's part, a perception reinforced by the pope's refusal to allow the question of women's ordination to be discussed.

A first step to dialogue between faith and European culture needs to be the admission on both sides that each has something to contribute to the answer to the question as to what it means to be human. This acknowledgement may begin on the neutral ground of Europe's artistic heritage. One problem with drawing attention to the grandeur of Europe's Christian past, as the pope does, is that it may leave the impression that the Church has not noticed the artistic and musical achievements of post-war Europe. Contributions in both areas have been made by religious and secular artists. It would seem to run counter to the spirit of *Ecclesia in Europa* if one were to maintain that only religious art displayed high quality and that only religious art displayed the whole nature of humanity. This may be the point at which the pope's thinking about the transcendence of God and of the Church may be introduced as an important contribution to the dialogue. This train of thought indicates that aspects of the reality of God as well as of the nature of humanity, as revealed by the gospel, may be found in obvious and unsuspected places. Both sides in the debate would need to agree to approach it with open minds.

However, reservations about the Church's claims on the subject of human rights and the pope's thoughts on high culture do not mean that the pope is wrong to point to the Church's social teaching as a means by which we might build a civilization worthy of the people who are contriving it (97).

From this point of view, paragraphs 97-99 of *Ecclesia in Europa* might be its most significant. These are primarily addressed to the Church and contain the assurance that the whole of humanity should be involved in the perfection of life on earth. This may serve to dispel the suspicion, itself induced by an earlier attitude of the Church to the modern world, that the Church is concerned only to promote the kingdom of heaven as a reality entirely separate from this one and open only to those willing to separate themselves from the rest of humanity by a way of life that seems deliberately inhuman. Even so, that opinion has taken hold to such an extent that the expression of its opposite in words may not be enough to detach it from the outlook of those who hold it.

That is why it is helpful that, as has been shown, the pope is willing to acknowledge that the realm of the gospel has sometimes lost its hold on people who have been baptised. Rites and gestures may be empty of significance because those who use them lack the conviction that they promote or display the reality that God has created as primary. This may also explain why the major part of *Ecclesia in Europa*, which this article has not had time to explore, is devoted to a description of the Christian life in all its elements and an exhortation to the Christians of Europe to carry it through in the way that is appropriate to them. Christians should see themselves as bearers of hope with the responsibility of arousing in others the hope their own faith brings with it. One aspect of hope that needs emphasis is that it is a source of happiness. Hope and joy are united by the pope's own words. Joy is also the emotion of those who have been redeemed by the blood of Christ as the Book of Revelation testifies.

For all its conviction and forceful enthusiasm for the gospel, *Ecclesia in Europa* remains an abstract document. It does not provide a detailed scheme for those who are hoping to communicate faith. It does recognise, though, that theologians (52) and catechists (51) have a distinctive role to play in spreading the gospel. With humanity as a central strand in the pope's exposition of the gospel, with men and women as bearers of hope and open to be wooed by hope, a significant tactic of Christian proclamation must be through the meeting of human beings convinced that humanity is a core component in reality. The pope shows himself to be a realist in the sense that he believes that things that exist do so independently of the people who perceive them, think about them, or interact with them. This position is evident in the pope's account of the gospel, so that, as well as being recognisably the gospel of Christ, his outline of the content of faith is philosophically intriguing for those who are ready to entertain a new metaphysics with transcendence as one of its central tenets.

To speak of transcendence may risk a return to abstraction except that transcendence is associated with the reality of Jesus Christ as mentioned above. This is why the pope insists that it is the full reality of Christ, human and divine that must be proclaimed (48). The challenge of John Paul II's Exhortation is for Europeans to face a deeper reality than they are usually prepared to live with. This reality includes European history and culture in all its variety and richness, a full understanding of human nature and human rights, the true reality of Jesus Christ as the opening for humanity to the nature and realm of God as proclaimed by the Church, a philosophical outlook that takes the independent being of what exists seriously and an accompanying acceptance of transcendence. Transcendence is not nothing but the key to everything, the hallmark of the presence of God to which the Church points as she endeavours to communicate faith in Jesus, source and guarantor of the gospel of hope.

## NOTES

1   Pope John Paul II, *Ecclesia in Europa: On Jesus Christ alive in his Church, the Source of Hope for Europe* (London: Catholic Truth Society, 2003).

# *Chapter 15*

## STORIES OF AN AUSTRALIAN JOURNEYING COMMUNITY

### G.P. (JOE) FLEMING

### INTRODUCTION: FAITH AND STORY TELLING

Modern people are searching, travelling, not quite sure what is at the end of the journey, but, at least intermittently, on the way. We must be with them, helping people to discover the freedom of the road and glimpse the goal of our journeying. The Church must offer a pedagogy of freedom which is about more than making the right choices, It is becoming a moral agent whose life is discovered to have a shape and meaning. We will only be able to do this if we are people where they are, not telling them where they ought to be...Wherever we are, in whatever confusions or messes we find ourselves, this is the starting point of the journey home. It is no good telling people that they should not be divorced or remarried or living with a partner or being gay. We begin where we are now...In whatever mess we may be living, a story can be told that will make some sense of it, and a story that leads to the Kingdom.[1]

I have taken this extract from Radcliffe's challenging work *What is the point of being Christian* as the starting point of this chapter on learning and communicating faith in Australia. There are many possible starting points but it has become increasingly clear to me in the work I do, and the life I live, that a most appropriate place to start is story: stories of ordinary people who go about life and faith in ordinary but blessed ways. People's stories give us insights into joys, sorrows, challenges, victories, moments of light and moments of grey. Stories have the capacity to describe and explore where people are in the here and now. They contain the realities of living a life of faith in the 21st century. My story is that for the last thirty years my professional work has been in Catholic education and the stories that I pass on in this chapter are from that context.

Stories contain elements of setting, plot, characters and themes. The plot and the themes of the stories capture Christian identity and practice, they help us understand who we are, they help us give expression to our deep inner selves. The setting of the story is also important. Chauvet argues that

> ...the primary locus of the church is the celebrating community. This of course does not mean that Christians belong less to the church when they are scattered during the week but that the 'one, holy, catholic, and apostolic' church manifest its identity best as a concrete liturgical assembly.[2]

The particular characters in the stories come from students in schools, people in parishes, families, teachers, research groups, Catholic hierarchy. They are drawn from the all the corners of society, each bringing a particular nuisance to the larger story, the larger mosaic of faith life in Australia. As Radcliffe said in the introductory quotation, we gather with all the messiness of our own story which becomes transformed in the story of the kingdom, the reign of God. The Kingdom is here and now. God's presence is with us now, disturbing the waters of life in which we live and move and have our being.

From this point onwards there are two sections to this chapter. The first section will focus on changing trends that emerge predominantly from the analyses of researchers, academics and church authorities. In one sense they provide a mapping of the 'ground' in which the stories of faith take root and grow. The second section recounts four particular stories of faith where setting, plot and theme are seen to be interacting in real life.

## SECTION A:
## THE GROUND IN WHICH THE STORY OF FAITH IS GROWING

### 1. GENERAL CONTEXT OF FAITH IN OUR CULTURE.

Certainly the setting in which Christian faith finds itself in the world today is not what it was 50 years ago. The current story of faith has a new setting, with new characters and new plots. Overseas researchers such as Lieven Boeve have described this new setting in Europe:

> In many traditionally Christian western societies, Christian faith no longer enjoys the monopoly it once had in giving meaning to human existence. The process of secularisation has seriously restricted the all-inclusive important of the Christian horizon of meaning.[3]

In Australia this is also the case. In recent days in our news media there have been reports that a major football body is planning for the first time to hold a major sporting event on Good Friday afternoon. This is anecdotal, I know, but it does indicate that the long standing Christian practices and what they mean are no longer the dominant cultural determinants that they once were.

However, while the expression of faith within a religious tradition may be on the wane, or being reshaped, the importance of faith as central to human life and meaning is nevertheless important. Bellous argues:

> The primary assumption, then, is that every human being exercises faith. Faith cuts across secular and religious worldviews. If human beings want to be well, they are compelled to make sense of life. Faith fills in gaps in our experiences between what we are able to touch, taste, see, hear or smell and realities that we cannot perceive or empirically test. Faith attends to depths that cannot be plumbed with a measuring stick. Faith organises connections between what can be and what cannot be seen. This feature of faith is as true for scientists who study the atom as it is for those who trust an invisible God.[4]

Bellous points to the experience of necessity of faith in everyday life and the stories that follow are testimony to that argument.

In Australia, Hughes, who is a dynamic and thorough researcher, has analyzed trends of belief, faith and church across faith traditions and cultures. He reminds us of the changing faith story across time. Reflecting on what he has termed the commodification of religion in our modern culture he argues that:

> From the earliest times, people have come to faith and to religious organisations and experts because they needed assistance. They have come because they wanted rain to fall on their crops or they needed assurance that a battle would be won. They have come in times of sickness and when they have been anxious about life. As people have explored religious faith more deeply they have discovered the challenges to their way of life, the demand for social justice and moral integrity, for example. They have discovered that faith is meaningfully expressed within the context of communities gathered around worship. Religious commodities will be the starting point for most young people in contemporary society if they take an interest in religion at all. The challenge for religious education is to meet the challenges in a

way young people find engaging, and to provide ways in which encourage young people to move beyond these to something that is more holistic and communally oriented[5].

Hughes' work resonates strongly with Radcliffe. For religious and faith educators the starting point is the young people: in their setting, with their plot and their themes and their characters.

## 2. THE STORY OF FAITH AS SEEN IN RESEARCH DATA

Every five years the Australia Federal Government conducts a census and, as part of that census, data is collected on religious affiliation. When the compiled data from the 2006 census was published the Australian Catholic Bishops Conference (ACBC) released issued a Press Release In it they pointed out that since the 2001 the Catholic population had increased by 2.5 per cent but as a percentage of the population the Catholic proportion had dropped from 26.6 per cent to 25.8 per cent. Even more significant was the data about the general population. The media release stated that

> There were substantial falls between 2001 and 2006 in the number of people identifying themselves as belonging to the Anglican, Presbyterian and Reformed, Salvation Army, Churches of Christ and Uniting Church traditions. On the other hand, there were large increases in the number of Buddhists, Hindus and Muslims. The Brethren, the Mormons and the Pentecostals also recorded strong growth.[6]

This combined data gives an indication of the subtle, but nevertheless significant, movements in Australian society related to religious affiliation. The trends are clear: slow decline in percentage of Catholics; sharper decline in Christian religious affiliation; rise of non-Christian affiliation. These all add up to the fact that Australia's religious landscape is changing and that the story of faith in the community is increasingly more diverse.

More specific Catholic data was gathered by the Pastoral Projects Office of the ACBC in what was called National Catholic Life Survey. The survey conducted in 500 parishes established the profiles of those regularly attending Mass. The data found that, those aged 15-34 constituted 16% of the Mass attendees, 35-64 year olds constituted 54% and those over 65 constituted 29%. The survey also found that 61% of the congregation were female. The story of the Catholic Church (and others) is one of an ageing and feminine community.

As a follow up to this survey the Pastoral Projects Office undertook another major projected called: Research Project on Catholics who have stopped attending Mass (2007). Their project explored the major reasons why some Catholics, aged from about 25 upwards, who were once regular Mass attendees, have stopped going regularly to Mass. The major reasons found were collated under two headings:

Church-centred reasons

    1. The irrelevance of the Church to life today

    2. The misuse of power and authority in the Church

    3. Problems with the priest in the parish

    4. Lack of intellectual stimulation

    5. Concerns related to the parish as a community

    6. A sense of being excluded by Church rules

    7. Structural factors

Participant-centred reasons

    1. Family or household-related issues

    2. Crisis of faith

    3. Going to Mass simply not a priority

A deeper analysis of the data led the Pastoral Projects Office to conclude that:

> ...it was important for virtually all participants that they nurture the spiritual dimension of their lives. For some, that spiritual dimension had a strong connection to the Catholic community, while a few participants' spiritual lives had little or no connection with the Christian faith or any organised form of religion. Participants insisted that they wanted to take responsibility for the quality of their own spiritual lives, leading to an eclectic approach to spirituality and a readiness to leave aside beliefs and practices that were not seen as helpful, life-giving or leading to personal fulfillment.[7]

## 3. THE CATHOLIC BISHOPS' CONCERNS ABOUT FAITH IN SCHOOLS

Because of the sort of data outlined in the above research the Catholic Education Commission of New South Wales produced a discussion and directions report for all its schools. The report was authorised and launched by the Bishops. The title of the report is more than a title, but also a call to listen: *Catholic Schools at the Crossroads*.[8] The report states that changing cultural circumstances have radically affected Catholic schools in recent years and called on schools to embrace new evangelisation. Schools were also called to dedicate themselves to ensuring that they were truly Catholic. The report then went on to raise the following points in relation to the current situation regarding Catholic schools:

- school-aged population has grown considerably over the past two decades
- demand for Catholic education keeps rising
- most of the additional students in our Catholic schools are not Catholics.
- there has been a fall in the number of Catholic students attending our schools during this period of growth.
- half the students of Catholic families are enrolled in State schools
- other-than-Catholic enrolments have more than doubled from 9% to 20%, and may continue to rise.
- poorer Catholic children are increasingly attending State schools, while wealthier Catholic children go to non-Catholic non-government schools.
- schools have significantly increased their enrolments of Aboriginal students.
- the numbers of students with disabilities keep rising.
- within the Catholic community fewer people attend Mass;
- fewer priests and religious are in service than was previously the case.
- fewer young people now identify themselves with churches or religions.
- Society-wide trends such as secularisation, consumerism,

family dysfunction and values disorientation also impact upon young people.(p8)

## 4. SPIRIT OF GENERATION Y

In another research project from Australian Catholic University undertook a 4 year study into the spirituality of young people. The website of the project, called the Spirit of Generation Y contains a press release[9] which summarised their findings. The release stated that project "explored Generation Y's range of worldviews and values, their sense of meaning and purpose in life, the ways in which they find peace and happiness, their involvement in traditional religions and alternative spiritualities, how they relate to the society around them, and the influences which shape their outlook and lifestyle." The key findings related to belief and spirituality. Under the section on belief the following was mentioned: 51% of Generation Y (Gen Y) believe in a God, 17% do not, and 32% are unsure, Two-thirds of those who do not believe in God, or are uncertain, do believe in a 'higher being or life-force'. The section on spirituality grouped spirituality under three headings: Christian, Eclectic, Humanist. In the Christian category only 19% of Gen Y are actively involved in a church. Religion is seen by this group as a private matter, and there is a strong tide of movement among Gen Y Christians away from previous involvement or identification with a church, and even from religious belief.

The major conclusion of the study is that:

> Many young people in Australia are what we have called Humanists—following an avowedly secular path in life, rejecting belief in God and declaring that there is little truth in any religion, affirming instead human experience, human reason and scientific explanations. Some are angry at or disenchanted with organised religion, but most simply do not care or are not interested.[10]

## BRIEF CONCLUSION

What can be drawn from these four stories? The stories pointed to in this section can be read in many ways. What is clearly in evidence in the general context, research data and the concerns of Catholic education authorities is that the story of the communication of faith is facing new and demanding realities. Chief among these are the decline of the Christian hegemony, the decline in the role that institutional church plays in peoples lives and the changing context of Catholic schools. In the next section stories are presented that offer a different point of view. These stories give an insight into a Catholic faith that is alive and rich.

## SECTION 2: FAITH STORIES

### STORY ONE: COMMUNICATING FAITH AT A SACRAMENTAL NIGHT IN THE PARISH

The first story occurred one Saturday night in my local Catholic parish. As is our custom my wife and I headed to our 6.30pm Eucharist and when we arrived at the car park in the Church grounds there was the unusual scene before us, that of the car park being filled to over flowing and there was still another fifteen minutes to starting time! We said in harmony that "it must be a sacramental night". Indeed it was, and on this occasion it was twenty young people (8-10 year olds mainly) who were going to receive their first Eucharist. I will come back to this part of the story shortly.

During the homily the parish priest (in his 70s) directed most of what he had to say to the parents. He spoke about their responsibility as the prime nurturers of faith. In doing so he made some clear and interesting distinctions. He stated that the role of the Catholic primary school (from whom the children making first Eucharist had come) was to *teach* the young people about their faith. It was there that they *learnt* about the faith tradition, about God, about scripture. But it was in the family that the young people both *experienced* faith and were *nurtured* in their faith. The role of the parish was to assist the families by bring them together to engage in the *ritual* of faith. The children, said the Parish Priest, needed all three components in their journey of faith. He concluded by saying that when children came to Sunday Eucharist and that it was imperative for their spiritual growth that they received Eucharist.

This is not really an 'unusual' story at all for 2008. Had this story been set in 1960s Australia, particularly in the rural community in which I lived, it would appear out of place. Church attendance was part of life then, and there was little thought that our faith life was lived out in family, parish and Catholic school. The living of faith in Australian society today is vastly different to what it was two generations ago.

Back to the car park. Yes it is unusual to see the Church yards full – unless it is for the significant times in the Churches year (Easter and Christmas); the sacramental programs; the key moments in the life of people (weddings, funerals). Belonging to the Church for many Catholics in the 21st century (and indeed for the past 30 years) is exercised in different ways from the previous generations of Catholics for who regular Sunday Eucharist was the norm. Treston states that most Catholics do not have any regular contact with the Eucharistic assembly. He further adds that:

> Much religious education happens through events of ordinary parish life. Creative celebrations for baptism, weddings, funerals are powerful communicators of God's revelation to us. Many people who attend such liturgies and rituals have little contact with the liturgical church and their presence at such services can lead them to reconnect with the local Christian community or be moved religiously.[11]

Now people choose when, where and how they belong to the Catholic Church and when where and how they will practice their faith.

A number of elements were very clear to the community gathered and gathering on that evening. Firstly, there was a powerful sense of welcome, of belonging, of acceptance. Secondly there was a challenge given to parents and parish alike to examine the three aspects of faith life – school, family, church. Finally, it shows the importance of beginning and being 'where we are now'. This was graced filled moment that provided a space for the intersection of personal and communal stories, within the context of a traditional sacrament ritual. In this ritual they found the Spirit of God breaking out of and into their human lives in an extraordinary manner.

## STORY 2: COMMUNICATING FAITH AT A PRIMARY SCHOOL CELEBRATION OF THE FEAST OF SAINT JOACHIM AND ST ANNE.

In the liturgical calendar the feast day of Joachim and Anne (July 26th) is the only one that celebrates the life of a married couple (grandparents no less). In a small but vibrant Catholic primary school this day was set aside for both the celebration of the feast day and a celebration of and for grand parents. It was a bringing together of many elements of the school community within the context of a liturgy. All the usual things happened, the preparation, the invitations the setting up and the celebration itself, which took the form of a Eucharist. Afterwards people gathered to continue to celebrate with more words and more rituals. It was a time when stories were told and celebrated.

I came across this celebration after it was over (unfortunately). I had been asked by the school to conduct a staff meeting on the development of a vision and mission statement a few days after the celebration. Vision and mission statements encapsulate the key drivers of the school and by which the school undergoes self and external review. They are the statements that articulate the identity and practice of the school. Before I began my part of the meeting the Principal and staff had a discussion about the Eucharist celebrated on the feat day... and the discussion and the reflections were remarkable. As part of the liturgy a couple of Grandparents were asked to speak about the theme of journey, and new beginnings, and new life and reflect on their feelings on having left their own land and came to settle in Australia. They told their life story, the story of life, their life within the story of a larger faith story of Joachim and Anne. Among the many things said by the staff these few stayed in my mind:

- The school was overwhelmed by the number of parents and grandparents that attended the afternoon, weekday Eucharist.
- There was an extraordinary sense of community in those who gathered.
- The stories and reflections on the Word as told by Grandparents to the children were moving and compassionate.
- People choose to be and wanted to be involved.
- It was a joy filled liturgy.
- An experience for all to remember.

One of the most obvious points is that if people find a sense of welcome and joy in a faith celebration then they will opt to be involved in such celebrations when it is meaningful. Here I am talking not of the intrinsic and undeniable meaning that Eucharist has in itself but rather the meaning that people see in the Eucharist, a meaning that makes them want to become involved. Grace proposes that there is often a gap between the experience of faith in the parish and the experience of faith in the parish school. In his study of he found that the

    ... powerful criticism of the institutional Catholic Church and of the liturgical culture of many of its parishes in the three cities of this enquiry cannot lightly be set aside, They were voiced by a group of Catholic school leaders, all of who were practicing their faith and some of whom were members of religious orders. If there analysis has any validity then any perceive crisis in the Catholicity of the young people involved arises not primarily because of weaknesses in the schools but because of weaknesses in the liturgical articulation of secondary schools and the feeder parishes.[12]

Moreover at this time in our history in Australia only 15-20% of the Christian population are regular members of worshipping communities in parishes. It is not usual therefore that large numbers attend such liturgies. Welbourne reminds us that

> Traditionally the majority of children enrolled in Catholic schools were from church-attending families where cultural values were broadly in line with those of the school – a situation that no longer exists. The emerging disparity of values and practices between home and school presents schools with an identity crisis…This means that Catholic schools must provide an education that is socially, culturally and religiously appropriate for a diverse group of students, To do this they must recognise the need to avoid both the cultural hegemony of the dominant group and an assimilationist mentality: this reshaping calls for existing policies and structures to be more inclusive of the reality of an evolving culture in their student population.[13]

However, it needs to be noted that schools can be a special place for prayer, ritual, liturgy and Eucharist – and this story is an excellent illustration of that. With the decline of numbers of the school community attending parish the school has become not a replacement necessarily, but an alternative place for the gathering of the community. The school can be locus of faith for families who want a Catholic education for their children. But in making this choice about education they are not automatically making a choice for Church in the broader parish sense. Many families are saying, Catholic schooling yes. Catholic parish, no. There are a number of reasons why schools are successful in the provision of faith experiences and enrichment for families. Staff are highly trained with more and more of them possessing post-graduate degrees in theology and religious education. Teachers have advanced skills that enable them to structure meaningful celebrations. And finally, and perhaps most powerfully, schools are a defined community, where people know each other. The community interacts on a daily basis in an atmosphere of welcome and compassion.

## STORY 3: COMMUNICATING FAITH ON A SCHOOL FEAST DAY - THE CAPTAIN'S ADDRESS

The feast of Saint Ignatius of Loyola on July 31 provided the occasion for the school to gather and celebrate its name sake. The co-educational school is new to the Jesuit network of schools and is growing its new identity. As part of the liturgy the school captains were asked to address the school community. The female captain proclaimed that during her years at Catholic schools there were three things that she had grown to understand and to embrace.

The first thing that she had come to know was that God is present in the world and that as Christians we are called to see that we can find God in the world. God was not limited to those who were Christians, God was there for all and available for all regardless of one's religious perspective.

Secondly she said that she had been encouraged to excel in all that she did, whether this was in the academic field, sport, the arts, relationships, social commitment. She saw the pursuit of excellence as part of living life to the full, of becoming fully and genuinely human.

The third element was most poignant for those who were listening. She argued that the purpose of schooling was not personal gratification, or finishing on top of the table of examination results. While the pursuit of excellence of important what is attained is not limited to the personal, the individual. Such an emphasis in education she claimed would be tantamount to ethical bankruptcy. The point of achieving excellence is so that individuals take that to the world and transform it and assist in the elimination of disease, poverty and marginalisation. The goal of education is not to keep what one has gained for oneself, but to use what one has gained for others.

The Captain did not use words such as faith, church and religion. I was not able to judge whether this was because she deliberately avoided them, or that she did not possess that theological vocabulary. What I was able to hear in this story is that her experience in a very normal, common Catholic school was that God, self and others were the key to her meaning making, her search for a meaningful life. It was a search that was deeply spiritual and faithful. As Radcliffe reminds us

> There is an immense spiritual hunger among the young. ... They are searching for a meaning to their lives. They are often more interested in 'spirituality' rather than doctrine and they are nervous of belonging to any institutional form of religion which might limit their autonomy.[14]

This Captain certainly possesses that hunger and was an inspiration to her community of students. Here is a person fully alive with the Spirit of God, living out a view of life that is strongly grounded in the Christian tradition.

## STORY 4: COMMUNICATING FAITH AT A STAFF PROFESSIONAL DEVELOPMENT DAY

The final story focuses on the staff of a Catholic primary school and their experience of the celebration of the Eucharist. I was asked by the school to guide them through two days of reflection on the theology of the Catholic Church. In essence this was an introduction to the some of the fundamentals of the tradition: scripture, sacraments, morality, church etc. The first day was not particularly remarkable but there was nevertheless, a genuine interest in the professional development activities. But there was something remarkable that was to occur.

The twenty five staff working in the Catholic school reflected the normal demographic of Catholic school staff. Unlike 30 years ago, Catholic schools now are virtually fully staffed by lay people. There are only a handful of religious women and men who are still working in schools. Leadership positions (Principal, Religious Education Coordinator etc) are in the hands of highly qualified and committed lay women and men. The majority of staff in schools are Catholic, but not all of them. Secondly, some of the Catholic staff are not weekly Eucharistic Catholics. Finally it can be said that some in the school system do not place a high store on institutional religion and church. In this sense they are broadly representative of the level of religious commitment in general society.

After my final session on day one the staff gathered to prepare for the celebration of the Eucharist. Some of the staff gathered to set the room for the celebration, others selected readings based upon the materials that had been used during the day, others prepared music. The celebrant, a priest of many years, had been part of the day with staff – as a participant, not the presenter. He encouraged the staff to join in the preparations. The Eucharist that followed is difficult to describe, except to say, that to this day some many month after it actually happened I can still remember it clearly. The Eucharist was intimate and inclusive. It drew on the world of the staff that were there. It was intensely communal and personal at the same time.

When you have such experiences there is often the possibility that this is how you as an individual interpreted it, and it may not be the experience of all of those who gathered around the Eucharistic table. But two quite powerful things happened that made me certain that this was not just my interpretation of the experience. Many of the younger staff, who openly 'confessed' to not being switched on by church, and who only went to Mass at weddings and funerals were staggered by the power of the community ritual, the welcome, the inclusion, the meaningfulness of that Eucharist. But it didn't end there. During the evening while sitting around and reflecting on the day, a number of these same young ones came to me and asked: "Do you think we could ask Father to have another Eucharist tomorrow?" And we did. Forget all the theoretical, theological and ecclesial input I was attempting to provide. These people had a profound experience of God, of Church, of a community of faith.

## BRIEF CONCLUSION

The stories contained in this chapter are aimed at providing a description and analysis of the ways in which faith is learned, communicated and experienced in Australia by some pockets of the Catholic community. . There are two things which I believe are beyond doubt. The first is, that the setting, theme and characters in the story of faith in this country are in a phase of radical change. What people understand by faith, where they find faith, how and when they express it, are all very different from our immediate past generations. Secondly, there is a need to hold onto and to nurture the very positive signs of the Kingdom in the world. If we believe that God is present in our world, and alive in the community then we need to keep telling the stories of good news whenever we can. As the extraordinary poet, R. S. Thomas, put it:

> The Moon in Lleyn
> ...In cities that

have outgrown their promise people
are becoming pilgrims
again, if not to this place
then to the recreation of it
in their own spirits. You must remain
kneeling. Even as this moon
making its way through the earth's
cumbersome shadow, prayer, too,
has its phases.[15]

## NOTES

1  Timothy Radcliffe, *What is the point of being a Christian?* (London: Burns and Oates, 2005), p.42.

2  Louis-Marie Chauvet, *The Sacraments* (Minnesota: The Liturgical Press, 2001), 34.

3  Lieven Boeve, "Beyond Correlation Strategies: Teaching Religion in a Detraditionalised and Pluralised Context" in *Hermeneutics and Religious Education,* ed. H. Lombaerts and D. Pollefeyt, 233 (Leuven: Leuven University Press, 2004).

4  Joyce Bellous, "The Educational Significances of Spirituality in the Formation of Faith" in *International Handbook of the Religious, Moral and Spiritual Dimensions in Education. Part One,* edited by Marian de Souza, Kath Engebretson, Gloria Durka, Robert Jackson, & Andrew McGrady, 174 (Dordrecht: Springer, 2006).

5  Philip Hughes, "The commodification of religion in Thailand, USA and Australia." *Journal of Religious Education.* 55, no1 (2007):58.

6  Australian Catholic Bishops Conference Media release. Retrieved September 12, 2007 from: *http://www.acbc.catholic.org.au/org/ppo/20070627633.htm.*

7  National Catholic Life Survey Selected Results. Retrieved on September 12, 2007 from: *http://www.ppo.catholic.org.au/researcharts/ncls. shtml#selectedResults.*

8  Catholic Education Commission of New South Wales. Catholic Schools at the Crossroads. Retrieved September 12, 2007 from: *http://www.cecnsw.catholic. edu.au/.*

9  Spirit of Generation Y Media Release. Retrieved on September 12, 2007 from: http://dlibrary.acu.edu.au/research/ccls/spir/sppub/SGY.

10  Spirit of Generation Y Media Release. Retrieved on September 12, 2007 from: http://dlibrary.acu.edu.au/research/ccls/spir/sppub/SGY.

11  Kevin Treston, "Journey of faith" in *Echo and Silence. Contemporary Issues for Australian Religious Education,* ed.by M. Ryan, 167 (Australia: Social

Science Press, 2001).

12 Gerald Grace, *Catholic Schools. Mission, Markets and Morality* (London: Routledge Falmer, 2002), 221.

13 Louise Welbourne, "Responding to Multiculturalism" in *Echo and Silence. Contemporary Issues for Australian Religious Education,* ed. by Maurice Ryan, 55 (Australia: Social Science Press. 2001).

14 Timothy Radcliffe, *What is the point of being a Christian?* (London: Burns and Oates, 2005), 3.

15 R. S. Thomas, *Laboratories of the Spirit* (London: Macmillan, 1975).

# QUESTIONS FOR PERSONAL REFLECTION
## AND GROUP DISCUSSION

1. Which qualities and skills and what kinds of knowledge are needed most if we are to be effective disciples of Jesus Christ today?

2. Is education more about becoming a certain kind of person rather than gaining certain kinds of knowledge?

3. What does it mean to call the home 'the domestic church'? What kind of foundations for faith can be laid in the family?

4. What aspect of parenting and family life seems most challenging to you and challenging to faith in particular? What aspects of Christian faith have been most helpful to you in parenting and your family role? How do we, in the family, teach our children to be persons of faith?

5. What aspects of the liturgy have meant the most to you? Which aspects of the liturgy are most baffling or difficult in your experience? How can liturgy help us to be ready to share God's life?

6. What place should the Bible have in the life of faith? How are we to appreciate what it has to offer? How should we approach it?

7. What changes in the life of the Church came from Vatican II (1962-65)? Which change of emphasis, brought about by Vatican II, is most important for you? How do we assess its significance for us today? If there is to be, at some point in time, a Vatican III, what should it deal with?

8. If the implicit curriculum is what is taught 'beneath the surface' by the way things are done, by the kinds of relationships between people, the layout of rooms and buildings, the kinds of behaviour that get rewarded or penalised, recognised or ignored, how would you describe the implicit curriculum of your church?

9.  Reflect on your own experiences of attempts to educate people in matters of faith, either when you have been 'on the receiving end,' (for example, as a pupil, student, parishioner, member of a religious community or group,) or when you have been 'on the delivery side,' (for example, as a parent, teacher, volunteer, catechist, evangelist, preacher, etc,). What has helped the exercise and what has hindered it? Whether or not the activity was 'successful', what do you think was influencing how people responded?

10. In the task of Christian education – beyond the family – what factors help and hinder learning about faith?

11. What is the difference between nurturing faith and indoctrination?

12. Do we use our God-given reason to inform and develop our faith and to share it with and explain it for others?

13. How does our faith influence the way we think, not just about religious matters, but about other decisions we have to make – about relationships, money, jobs, politics, the environment?

14. What are the advantages and disadvantages of referring to our religious beliefs in discussions and debates that form part of civic and political life?

15. How do changes in our world and in our culture affect the way we hold our faith? How is the task of understanding changes in our world related to the way we appreciate, express and explain our faith?

16. Are there lessons you think we can learn from the way other Christians conduct their worship, engage with Scripture, organize and make decisions about church life?

17. What helps ecumenical and inter-faith learning?

18. What have you found helpful – in reading, in church practice, in other people, in life experience - for supporting your own spiritual development?

19. Are there ways we can 'tap into' the experience, skills and wisdom of the people in our church, thereby enriching the 'repertoire' available to the church for her mission, work and life?

20. Which voices and experiences among the people of God should we be paying more attention to than we have done so far?

21. How does age and gender affect the way we learn in the church?

22. Is the Internet relevant for learning about faith? Is it helpful, neutral, or dangerous?

23. If you could put one question each to (a) your parish priest, (b) your bishop, (c) the archbishop of Westminster, (d) the archbishop of Canterbury, (e) the Pope, what would these questions be?